I0804658

Italy: *Contemporary Domestic Landscapes 1945–2000*

Italy

Contemporary Domestic Landscapes

1945–2000

Edited by
Giampiero Bosoni

SKIRA

Cover
In the centre, drawing by Enzo Mari, *Un ambiente per "Interni": Ecco (16 × 32 × 6)*, December 1996; surrounding the drawing, some important products of the Italian design

Design
Marcello Francone

Editorial Coordination
Marzia Branca

Editing
Doriana Comerlati

Translations
Language Consulting, Milan

Iconographical Research
Anna Dacci

We thank
Gabriele Basilico, Valeria Bonafè, Anna Bonometto, Nicoletta Branzi, Cesare Colombo, Gabriele De Vecchi, Paolo Fantoni, Toni Nicolini, Matteo Piazza, Paolo Rosselli, Manuela Scisci, Viviana Vigano

First published in Italy in 2001
by Skira editore S.p.A.
Palazzo Casati Stampa
via Torino 61
20123 Milano
Italy

© 2001 Skira editore, Milan
© 2001 ICE, Istituto Nazionale per il Commercio Estero

All rights reserved under international copyright conventions. No part of this book may be reproduced or utilized in any form or by any means, electronic or mechanical, including photocopying, recording, or any information storage and retrieval system, without permission in writing from the publisher.

Printed and bound in Italy.
First edition
ISBN 88-8118-958-5

Distributed in North America and Latin America by Rizzoli International Publications, Inc. through St. Martin's Press, 175 Fifth Avenue, New York, NY 10010. Distributed elsewhere in the world by Thames and Hudson Ltd., 181a High Holborn, London WC1V 7QX, United Kingdom.

Photograph credits
Archivio Fotografico della Triennale, Milan: p. 150 above, p. 162 top, p. 162 centre
Assopiastrelle Archives, Modena: p. 118 below right, p. 119, p. 122 below, p. 123 centre, p. 123 below
Gabriele Basilico, Milan: p. 13, p. 25 top right, p. 55, p. 56, p. 57
B&B Archives, Novedrate (Como): p. 124
Campeggi Archives, Anzano del Parco (Como): p. 33 below
Cesare Colombo, Milan: p. 47, p. 66 above, pp. 67, p. 70, p. 71 below
Joe Colombo Archives, Milan: p. 30 left, p. 87
Donegani & Lauda Archives, Milan: p. 125 above, p. 162 below, p. 163 below
Edra Archives, Perignano (Pisa): p. 32 above, p. 33 above
Fondo Carlo Mollino, Turin: p. 165
Moreno Gentili, Milan: p. 179 below left, p. 181
Mimmo Jodice, Naples: p. 41, p. 51
Luceplan Archives, Milan: p. 112
Moroso Archives, Cavalicco (Udine): p. 32 below
Eredi Ugo Mulas, Milan: p. 88 bottom
Toni Nicolini, Milan: p. 29 below, p. 40 top, p. 45, p. 49, p. 50
Matteo Piazza, Milan: pp. 94–95
Gio Ponti Archives, Milan: p. 172 above
Francesco Radino, Milan: p. 141 above, p. 178 above
Robots Archives, Binasco (Milano): p. 144
Alberto Rosselli Archives, Milan: p. 31 right, 158
Paolo Rosselli, Milan: p. 58
Studio Castiglioni, Milan: p. 118 centre, p. 152
Studio Andrea Branzi, Milan: p. 163 above
Studio D'Urbino, Lomazzi, Milan: p. 160
Studio Gaetano Pesce, New York: p. 31 left
Carlo Valsecchi, Milan: p. 141 below
Andreas von Lintel, New York: pp. 34, 35, 36, 37

The publisher is at the disposal of the entitled parties as regards all unidentified iconographic sources

This book has been published in occasion of the project "Italy: Life in I style"

Italia
Life in I style

The first edition of this book has been printed thanks to ICE

Contents

Giampiero Bosoni

Type and Counter-Type in Italian "Style"

Tradition and innovation in industrial design for domestic spaces

Achille Castiglioni, Lampadina table or wall lamp, produced by Flos, 1972. Castiglioni frosts a part of the spherical surface of a globulux lamp so that it resembles a skullcap. The base is a spool for winding in the cable.

Gabriele De Vecchi, Equilpiemonte silver coffee-maker, Storia collection, produced by Argenteria De Vecchi, 1983.

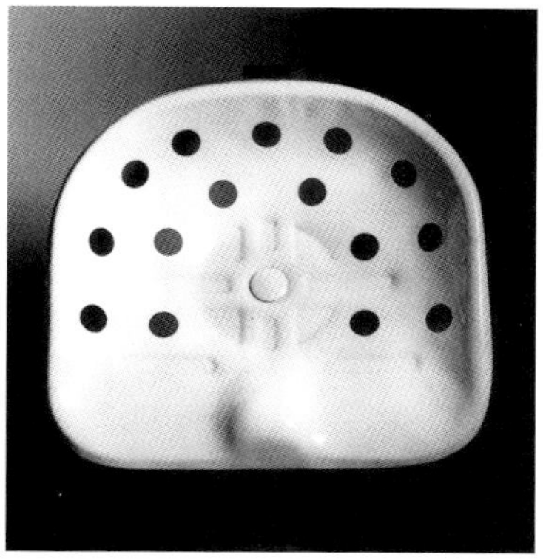

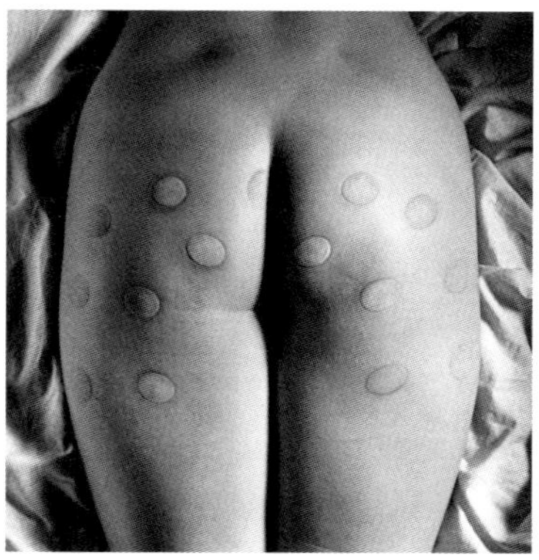

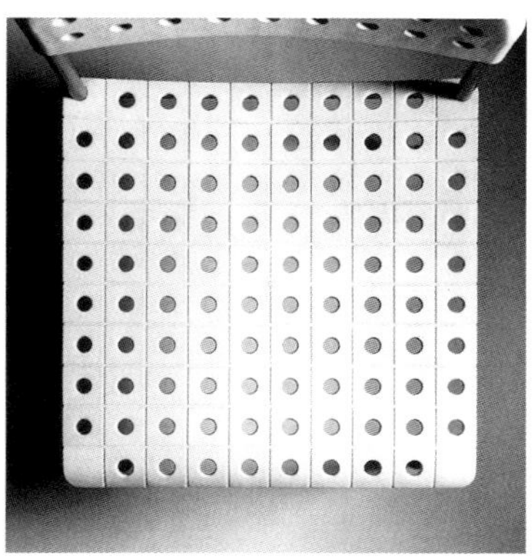

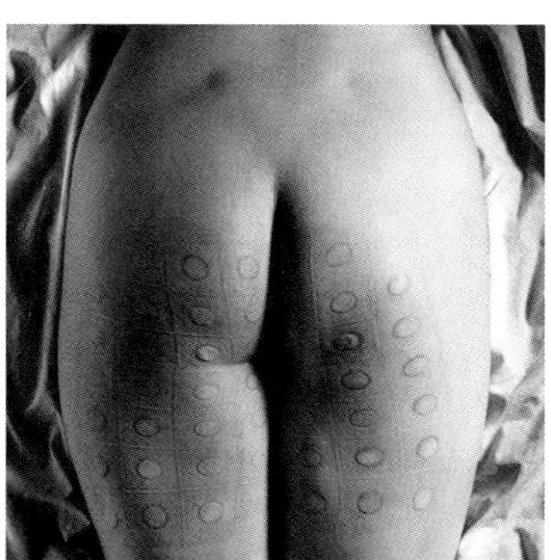

At a time like this, when Italian design has without doubt reached the highest end of the market and is regarded everywhere as a mark of quality, particular interest is beginning to be felt in many international settings as regards its origins and history. One might almost think that this curiosity aims in some way to grasp the secret of this success, as though through its history one could arrive at a magic formula or scientific strategic and planning system to be reproduced *in vitro*. In order to dispel any expectations in this regard, we must say that the vital sap that powered this rapid growth, and which continues to bear fruit, cannot be synthesized into anything more than a formula for an elementary hybrid model, which in our opinion offers very little significance.

A throwaway remark one is tempted to make is that if we must speak of a secret of Italian design, it would be best to look in the right manner not so much at "its" history – that of Italian design – as more widely upon the "great" cultural history of the entire country: a rich, complex, at times contradictory culture, used knowledgeably by the most famous proponents of Italian design as part of their tool-kit. Then, if we examine the specific case of the home, we must take the plunge into an articulated, sometimes chaotic culture, which has ancient roots and is reflected in many aspects of the Italian way of life that range beyond strictly defined notions of the home. In this sense, history teaches us to follow an itinerary that is at times tortuous and at times clear and straight, founded upon non-method, non-strategy, one might almost say non-project. An itinerary that is rather sustained by a passion, by a pleasure of seeking "for its own sake", by a sense of quality that only appears in the highest craftsmanship, by a taste for "beautiful" things in a deep, almost religious sense, that have become the characteristics constituting the DNA of

Gabriele Basilico, some images from the *Contact* photographic project, 1979. The models and associated "imprints" of the chairs can be recognized: Mezzadro, designed by Achille and Piergiacomo Castiglioni; Box, designed by Enzo Mari; Celestina, designed by Marco Zanuso; and a rattan core chair.

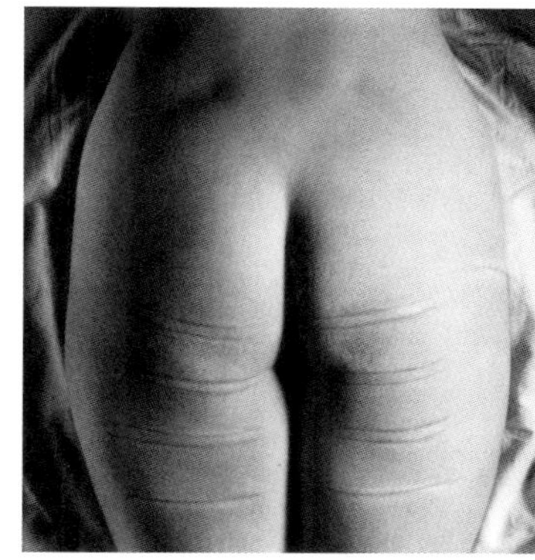

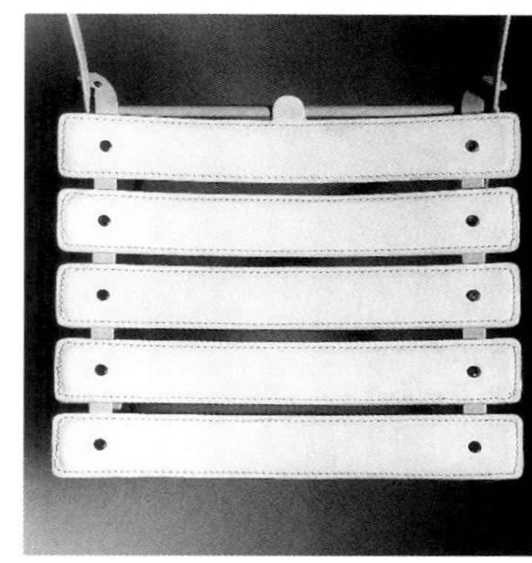

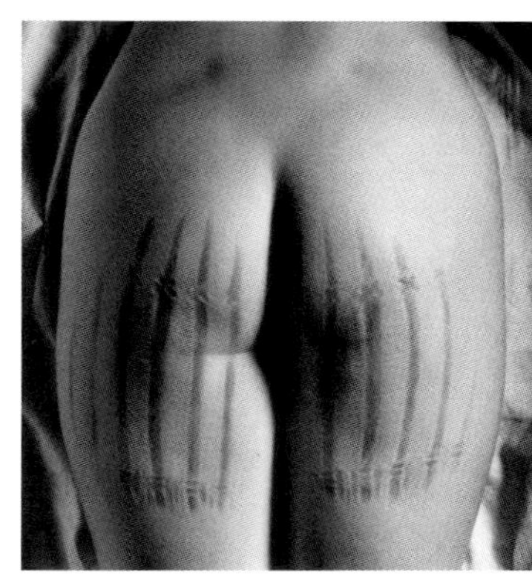

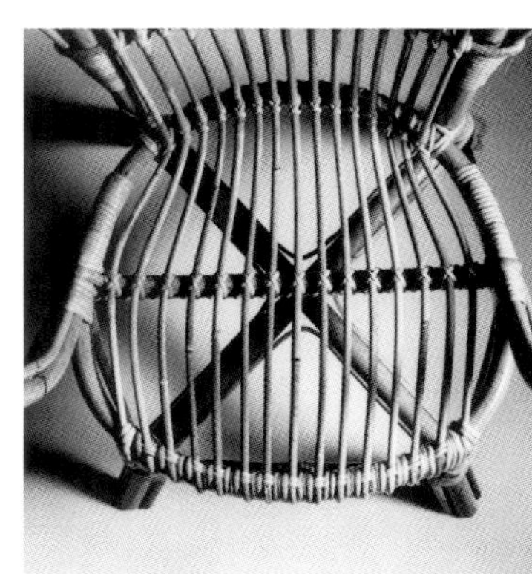

Vico Magistretti, Marocca chair, produced by De Padova, 1987. Redesign of a popular Veneto chair with the seat in plywood shaped with the folds of a rush-bottomed chair.

Enzo Mari, design of the Tappeto Volante bed, produced by Interflex, now Flou, 1988.

Achille Castiglioni, Polet armchair-bed, produced by Interflex, now Flou, 1992.

the project (paradoxically an industrial one above all), which has matured in the original way of life that took shape in Italy. In this sense, we are interested in particular in highlighting one of the most profound and typical aspects of Italian design: the fertile matching between a side which has always been dedicated to research and the reworking of historic models, of those we might call "archetypes", and another side which we can paradoxically say represents its negation, and which is almost always dedicated to research into new "object-types", or indicators of new ways of living. In order to focus better upon this crucial point, we need perhaps to take a few steps backwards and broaden our view. The design of elements that define domestic space and integrate between themselves to form the home system fully deserve to belong to the great tradition of art and craftsmanship in Italy. It forms a rich, complex culture that for the most part has seen the industrial model as a process demanded by dictates of time, and certainly not as a natural progression of a theory. Indeed, the humanist roots of Italian design have always played an important role: not only in the creative process of an aesthetic type, but also in terms of creative and technical aspects of production and the industrial process. Some have already observed that making contradiction a tool of a project is often a distinguishing feature of Italian design. The Italian designer is a difficult figure to pin down, so many are the types of research and the expressive forms. However, there is a characteristic common to designers and "producers", as opposed to the engineer, the pure technician who looks only at function and production. This feature in a project is one we find not only in creative research, but it is also very much a part of a certain industrial culture, which for some time has proven to be a winning one. The result of the complex regeneration of a rich heritage of

Gaetano Pesce, I Feltri armchair, produced by Cassina, 1987.

Enzo Mari, Daynight sofa-bed, produced by Driade, 1971.

Antonio Citterio, Sity sofas, produced by B&B Italia, 1986.

Achille Castiglioni, Hilly sofa, produced by Cassina, 1992.

Archizoom Associati, "The Mickey House". From the "Arredare è facile" section, in *Facendo mobili con…*, edited by Pier Carlo Santini, Poltronova Edizioni, Pistoia, 1977.

Ettore Sottsass, "Arredare è facile - Arredare è difficile". From the "Arredare è facile" section, in *Facendo mobili con…*, edited by Pier Carlo Santini, Poltronova Edizioni, Pistoia, 1977.

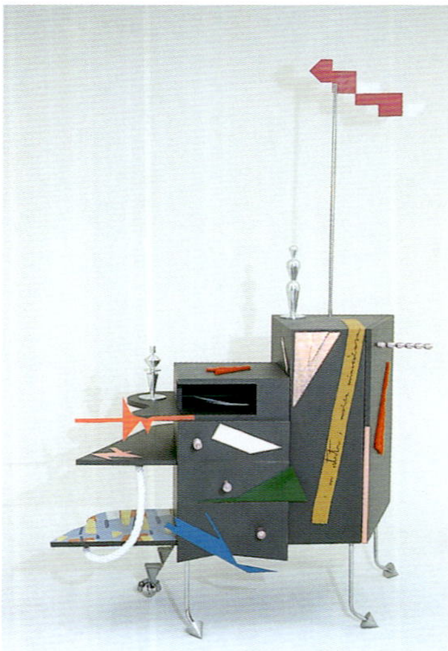

Alessandro Mendini, Mobile Infinito, produced by Studio Alchymia, 1981. The applied decorations are by different artists and designers.

Alessandro Mendini, "Wunderkammer", some aesthetic reinterpretations of domestic rooms in old-fashioned style, in *Abitare*, no. 313, 1992.

craftsmanship, it has received important international recognition for creativity, originality, innovation, and ability to adapt rapidly and meet market demands.
Thus, we speak of the "Italian design" model as a continuous play of affirmations and negations, as the mature development of the design process should always be. Italian design research has seen the appearance on the one hand of the idealization of the "type", that is the striving for an archetype in each category: the chair that is more chair, the fabric that is more fabric, the tile that is more tile, silver that is more silver, marble that is more marble. In this sense, much has been done by some designers who focus in their work on innovative research into the so-called "re-design" of mainly anonymous objects in a tradition that is mainly popular or middle-class. However, on the other hand, we see the same designers together with others more disposed to choices that run counter to the current or are in some way rebellious, enjoying themselves in destroying the "arrogance" of a single, standard type that is always the same. They seek new types, many, enjoyable types for many, different habits and emotions. Their world is often contradictory, but just because of this, it is rich in ideas and avenues of research that are open to transformations; a world accustomed for centuries to the ephemeral and hence disposed through a natural sense for survival to find the most practical solution without, however, ever losing view of the pleasure of the form, even in the smallest details.

Ross Lovegrove, Pod Lens lamp, produced by Luceplan, 1998.

This condition has not always brought about positive results for the country as a whole, but in this field it has undoubtedly laid a fertile base of strong contrasts which today are for the most part well matched: craftsmanship and industry, art and technology, design and utopia, and in this case we can also add "types" and "counter-types" of the home system as expressed in Italy. From the union of these fertile layers made of different cultures – science and theory, humanism and aesthetics – the most interesting industrial categories in the varied Italian panorama have emerged: models that still today are beacons for the rest of the world in terms of creativity, innovation and style.

Some protagonists of Italian design have repeatedly declared their authoritative consideration for those deep roots of design, using different forms that highlight the undoubted archetypal value of some models, whether they are masterpieces of the past, or the equally loved world of anonymous and popular design. But beyond this sensibility in observing and reviewing the historical origins of a project, whether cultured or not, the masters of Italian design have often been capable of giving form to alternative, unforeseeable models of the "counter-types", able to satisfy or even solicit the appearance of new ways of living, of living together.

The aim of this book is thus to offer a vast, international public that is increasingly attracted to and curious about Italian style, an instrument providing different approaches, enabling a broader viewpoint to be gained whilst at the same time exploring in greater detail that rich, complex system that has been and continues to be the culture of living in Italy.

Speaking of culture in this case means first of all bearing in mind the rites, customs and habits that express themselves in different forms which, let us recall, manifest themselves through sensorial, perceptive, symbolic and gestural values before taking on the features of objects.

Such primary expressive values may be found both in the craftsman's rich experience and skilful handling of his materials, and, we may say, through a logical extension in the concept of living and the home, in the typical and original creative preparation of Italian cooking. Similarly, it may be found, still in a particular extension of the concept of home (in this case, "nomadic" as clothing is), in Italian fashion, which is celebrated throughout the world for its originality in interpreting the model of "clothing as living".[1]

However, all of this today is also an economic and industrial system that, from the middle of the '50s onwards, developed through a singular and original process of modernization of both the craftsman's culture, transferred into a small and medium-sized industrial setting, and the design and artistic culture of the humanist tradition, re-elaborated in that cultural phenomenon known by everyone as Italian design, or rather, Italian style, for the home.

This development and its numerous facets are described in this book in a way that is open to different disciplines: from anthropology and sociology to economics and technology, from the history of design of objects for the house to the complex historical itinerary of Italian architectural theory regarding the home, without forgetting the relationship between artistic research interwoven with the different phases of the domestic landscape in Italy.

[1] In the Italian, there is a play on words *abito* = clothing and *abitare* = living (*editor's note*).

Paola Antonelli

Italian Design between Globalism and Affectivity

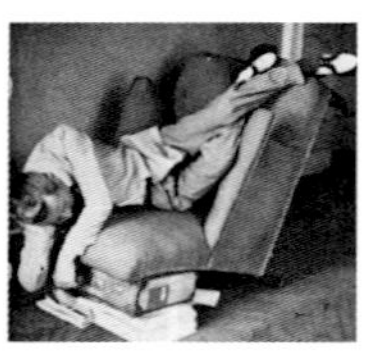

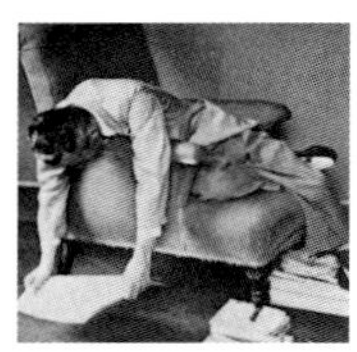

Bruno Munari, sequence of images ironically illustrating the search for comfort in an uncomfortable armchair, '40s.

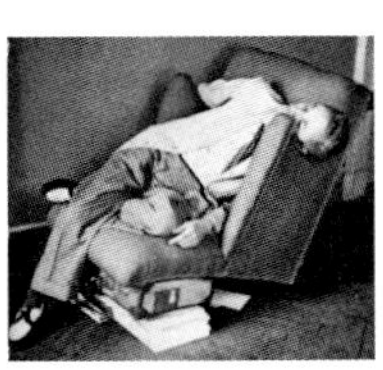

In the early '50s, a new store opened on Fifth Avenue in New York. The Olivetti showroom, designed by the Milanese architectural studio BBPR (Belgiojoso, Banfi, Peressutti, and Rogers), was a showcase not only of typewriters, but also of Italian creativity and craftsmanship. Its large glass windows framed a lofted space decorated, among other things, with ample mural bas-reliefs by artist Costantino Nivola.
The whole store was almost completely prefabricated in Italy and sent across the Atlantic for final assembly. The floor was covered in large stone tiles, some of which bulged like hills from the floor in an upward lava-lamp-like movement. At their peak, a small iron ledger carried a typewriter. The floor continued outside, beyond the angled entrance door, and one of the typewriters stood there in the open air on its pedestal, in order to subtly attract the passerby's curiosity. There was joy in the invention and in breaking the traditional boundaries, pleasure and humour in the alliance of creativity and pride in the display of an all-Italian treasure. The image of the BBPR masterpiece, which was dismantled a few years later, is engrained in the memory of many a New Yorker as an example of interiors architecture sublime.
In the United States, such architecture would normally be called "commercial", as opposed to "residential". This classification has nonetheless never given much pause to Italian architects, whose attachment to the context – urban, historical, cultural – and to their own vision is always stronger than their commitment to the legitimate destination of the space. Italian architects are not specialized and many of the great makers of interior architecture have also raised buildings and laid out cities. What brings together some of the celebrated Italian interiors of this century from Carlo Mollino's, Gio Ponti's, and Carlo Scarpa's to Gae Aulenti's, Ettore Sottsass's, and Mongiardino's, is rather a surprising interpretation of the space achieved by means of architecture, design, and art.
It is a skill that has been learned throughout the centuries. Shying away from the introversion of a *Gesamtkunstwerk*, the great Italian architect is an imperious director who is able to extract the best from all his many characters and thus compose a memorable film from heterogeneous sources.
Synthesis, composition, and operatic marvel are what the world has come to expect of Italian architecture and what Italy has often delivered. It is a lucky stereotype and a sweet responsibility.
To this day, the field is male-dominated and the flag is vigorously held high by several young architects. One of them, Fabio Novembre, who has designed the exuberant Café l'Atlantique in Milan and Tardini store in New York, does not mince words when it comes to celebrating his architecture's ideal inspiration:
"Architecture is like a beautiful woman, one would like to see it naked, sculptural in its most intimate and structural form, perfectly real and as brash as shouted sex", are his words. It would be hard to come up with a more fitting version of the American stereotype about a creative Italian heterosexual male.
The grand master of carnal architecture of this century, Carlo Mollino, perpetrated the same deed, his actions louder than his words. Mollino, architect, designer, erotic photographer, and airplane pilot among other incarnations, is the paradigm of Italian masculine sensuality in architecture. His works, from family residences to dance clubs, all had the warmly decadent and sexy quality of boudoirs and brothels. Entering them was like entering a space of wonder and license, where the rules of the outside world could become irrelevant.
Italian minimalism, rich and luscious with details and intolerant of Germanic ideology, was equally, if differently, sensuous. Terragni's, Persico's, and

BBPR (Belgiojoso, Banfi, Peressutti, and Rogers), Olivetti store in New York, 1954.

Ettore Sottsass, small table made of lacquered green iron tubing and laminar natural beech wood, Fede Cheti furniture show, Milan, 1949.

Carlo Mollino, Orengo house, Turin, 1949, in a photograph by Gabriele Basilico.

Marcello Nizzoli and Edoardo Persico, Parker shop in Largo Santa Margherita, Milan, 1934.

Luigi Figini and Gino Pollini, interior views of the Villa-studio for an artist, 5th Triennial, Milan, 1933.

Below: advertisement for the Moka Express domestic coffee-maker, Bialetti, showing a typical domestic setting of the period, mid-'50s.
Right: the famous Bialetti trademark, known as "the little man with the mustache", which is a caricature of Signor Bialetti.

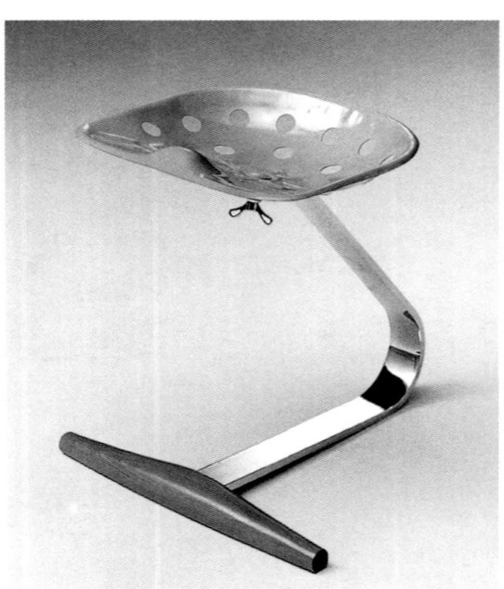

Achille and Piergiacomo Castiglioni, Mezzadro stool (1957), since 1970 produced by Zanotta.

Pagano's interiors were made of fire and ice. Above and beyond any romantic declaration about Italians, their virility, and their secret recipe to success, stands the exceptional effectiveness of Italy as a 20th-century design case study. Nowhere in the world can one find so many varied examples, in terms of both conception and formal outcome; so many applications of diverse technologies; such a complete representation of all applied design forms, from fashion and graphics, to product and set design; such an extensive and multifaceted documentation recorded in literature; and such an international resonance as in Italy. By engaging the best industrial and cultural forces of the country in a single-minded and spontaneous operation of national image building, Italian Design has become an icon in itself, almost independently from its products.

Every country has its own manual of style, a listing of positive stereotypes built to reinforce and expand its own international market, and the transformation of national identities into merchandise in a homogenized world is often boosted and supported by the national governments themselves. In design in particular, "Made in Italy" is a label that contains a whole set of cultural references for the use and consumption of buyers all over the world. Design is another clever way Italians have devised to export their footloose and fancy-free winning image. As a matter of fact, Italians produce beautiful objects that look great, most of the time work well, are manufactured impeccably, and yet express vulnerability. Just like romantic novels, they take the shortcut to the heart of the international public. A Vespa, the Valentine typewriter, a Ferrari, a Bialetti coffee-maker, Joe Colombo's Visiona and the postmodern folly furniture of the '80s, all exude the romance and passion that many other countries desire so much. Italian design is successful for matters of global balance.

According to stereotype, Italians can inject anything with sentiment, even a typewriter, not to mention a car. Italians historically set the grounds for appreciation by being slightly amoral, politically and economically insecure and therefore not threatening, and then fun-loving, and, after all, enviable. As a matter of fact, many of the Italian design icons that are unanimously loved around the world belong to the '50s, when Italy was at its most vulnerable to outside political, economic, and cultural influence.

Italian designers have created icons by setting objects in time and endowing them with personality. Each design evokes an Italian spectacle that makes it even more desirable: Sofia Loren sits sideways on a Vespa, spike heels and scarf to keep her hair in place – the '50s; in the '60s, Ettore Sottsass, everybody's beloved, types love letters with two fingers on the passion-red Valentine by the light of a candle; leftish intellectuals, elegantly negligent, rest their revolutionary brains on Sacco chairs – the '70s. A foreigner who buys an object made in Italy, be it a chair, a suit, or a coffee-maker, is buying into a whole image that makes one's statement not only stylistic, but also visual and evocative.

Outstanding Italian design's first romantic construct is the story of how it was born. In the early '50s, ingenious architects without jobs fortuitously met enlightened industrial manufacturers in search of products. It was a coup-de-foudre. In the background, the mechanical and chemical industries were bubbling with innovations waiting to be applied. Together, they established the collaborative formula based on sharing technical knowledge, dreams, and goals, that became a model worldwide. The best examples of Italian design reflect this tight collaboration, a personal relationship that to this day provides designers from all over the world with exceptional support for experimentation. Meanwhile, to add to the interdisciplinary effervescence of the

Joe Colombo, Tube Chair, produced by Flexform, 1970.

Joe Colombo, Visiona 69 habitat, produced by Bayer, installation at the Museo della Scienza e della Tecnica, Milan, 23–28 September 1969.

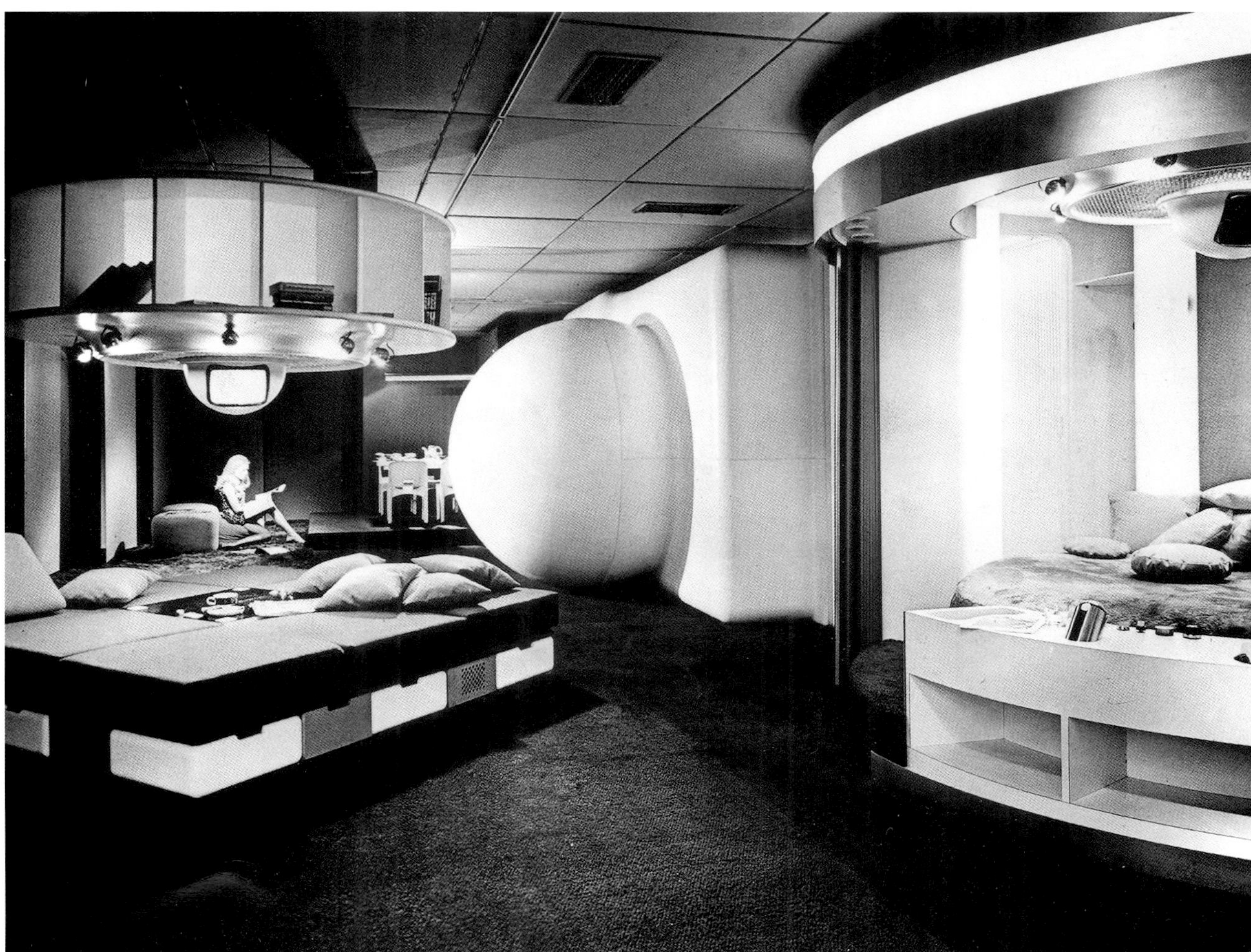

Ettore Sottsass, Valentine typewriter, produced by Olivetti, 1969.

national scene, the architecture and design community sparked a lively dialogue with the rest of the world and fostered the spectacular edge of Italian design through publications like *Domus*, *Abitare*, and *Casabella*, and international events, like the Furniture Fair of Milan, established in 1961, and the Triennials. Italy became the epicenter of the design world.

The golden moment of Italian design culminated in the 1972 *Italy: the New Domestic Landscape* show at The Museum of Modern Art in New York, an exhibition of new models of living spaces and lifestyles organized by Emilio Ambasz. The title was brilliant and meaningful, as the architects called upon to design the new domestic modules – Gae Aulenti, Marco Zanuso and Richard Sapper, Mario Bellini and Alberto Rosselli, Ettore Sottsass and Joe Colombo – really envisioned a new way of living that foretold many upcoming lifestyle revolutions. From the futuristic and technological unification of facilities suggested by Joe Colombo, to the fragmentary and mysterious fiberglass landscape ventured by Ettore Sottsass, it was clear from the show that there was not just an encounter but a clash of new directions in Italian design. Some consider the show its swan song.

The oil crisis and the "Leaden Years" of terrorism took a toll on Italian design's optimistic attitude, yet could not defeat its visionary soul. The Memphis phenomenon and the postmodern activity of companies like Alessi exemplified a new Italian approach to design, more attuned to the fashion industry – that is when companies started using the word "collection" in their production catalogues – and focused on the designers' signatures, supported by the company's well-studied image. Italian design companies have been able to maintain to this day their status, their exceptional manufacturing standards and expertise, as well as their traditional experimental verve. They are attracting the best talent from all over the world.

And Italian interiors remain a paradigm of refinement for the middle class, all over the world.

That is where another secret of the success of Italian style in domestic interiors lies: rather than shocking the bourgeoisie, most Italian architects and designers of this century have sought the highest common denominator and attempted to make elegance and style available to a wider public. Gio Ponti is the most luminous example: he was able to standardize certain steps in the design of domestic interiors, especially the decorative elements – tiles, cutlery, knobs – and nonetheless maintain the handcrafted exclusivity of composition that was in the '40s and '50s the first requirement of an upper class domestic interior. Neoclassic with several twists, his homes are elegant, inventive, reassuring in their undeniable style, and non-threatening, as their cultural references fly at general height. They are subtly luxurious and stylistically durable, much like an Armani jacket or today's homes by Antonio Citterio. They cannot possibly go out of fashion.

I have devised a theory, called *Existenzmaximum*, about the spaces that we will inhabit in the future. It finds Italian design culture at the forefront and it could even further ensure the permanence of its residential interiors as paradigms of domestic landscapes. The Germanic neologism is prompted by an earlier idea that is both its opposite and its polemic generator, the *Existenzminimum*. In the late '20s, when Le Corbusier preached the need to design the ideal home as a machine, his German contemporaries formulated their own proprietary version of this vision and called it *Existenzminimum*. They had a positivistic approach to the design of human life and their priority was to accommodate the working class in livable, organized dwellings. With similar mathematical precision, the German

Ettore Sottsass, "Una stanza nella stanza", in *Domus*, no. 457, December 1967. Photo Toni Nicolini.

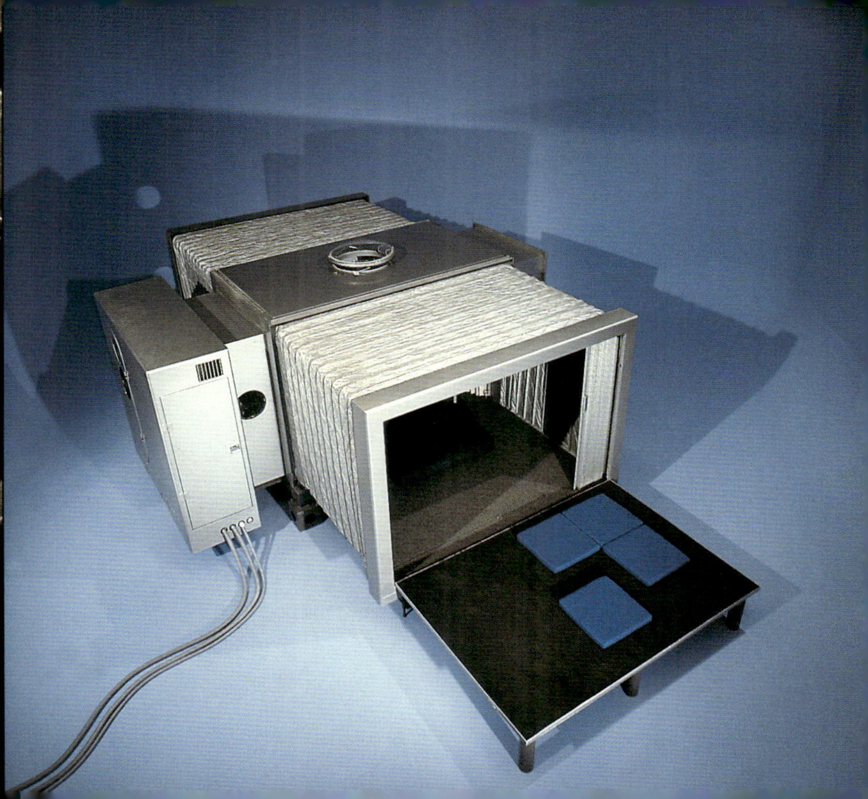

Francesco Binfaré, Flap sofa, with back, arms and reclinable front supports, produced by Edra, 2000.

architects organized many dwellings in giant ingot-shaped buildings, and disposed those buildings according to sun exposure and other variables in housing estates, the *Siedlungen*, powered by traffic and service vessels and akin to equation systems.
In a varied range of degrees of rigidity and climates, this metric approach to life became a worldwide standard in the design of private spaces for the lower class. It survived even longer in the design of offices and other technical spaces, to this day calculated ergonomically.
However, the '60s made this concept, like many others, burst at its seams.
The introduction of objects such as the radio, the telephone, and the television set had already pierced holes in the domestic walls. The small domestic shell had become more flexible and permeable by the outside. All over the world, the visionary architects, artists, and designers of the '60s were learning to use the tools of their trade to design spaces that were apparently functional and small, yet made expandable by mental and physical activity. The *Existenzmaximum* begins as a small, yet extraordinarily comfortable spatial device where the physical boundaries are protective, rather than oppressive, thus letting the senses and the spirit roam free. *Existenzmaximum* can be found, for example, in nature, in Baroque and Mannerist architecture, in mirrors, in armchairs, as well as in many customizable minimal units of our times, such as the interface of a computer or the Walkman. Italians, after centuries of metaphysical experimentation in architecture, are in this fatal juncture somewhat advantaged. Through the mandatory study of the works of Borromini, to mention just one among many historical masters, they have already learned how to provide the environment with hidden doors and windows into lateral dimensions. They have learned to maximize our physical space by enabling our metaphysical activities.
In the '60s, some, like Joe Colombo, took the task literally and designed portable and foldable multifunctional structures that were made possible by the most recent developments in the technology of materials, such as plastics and fiberglass. Others, like Sottsass, disclosed the space through its articulation and the exotic

Achille Castiglioni and Ferruccio Laviani, 40/80 chair, produced by Moroso, 1999.

Giovanni Lauda and Dante Donegani, Passepartout chaise longue, produced by Edra, 1998.

Giovanni Levanti, Xito deckchair, produced by Campeggi, 1999.

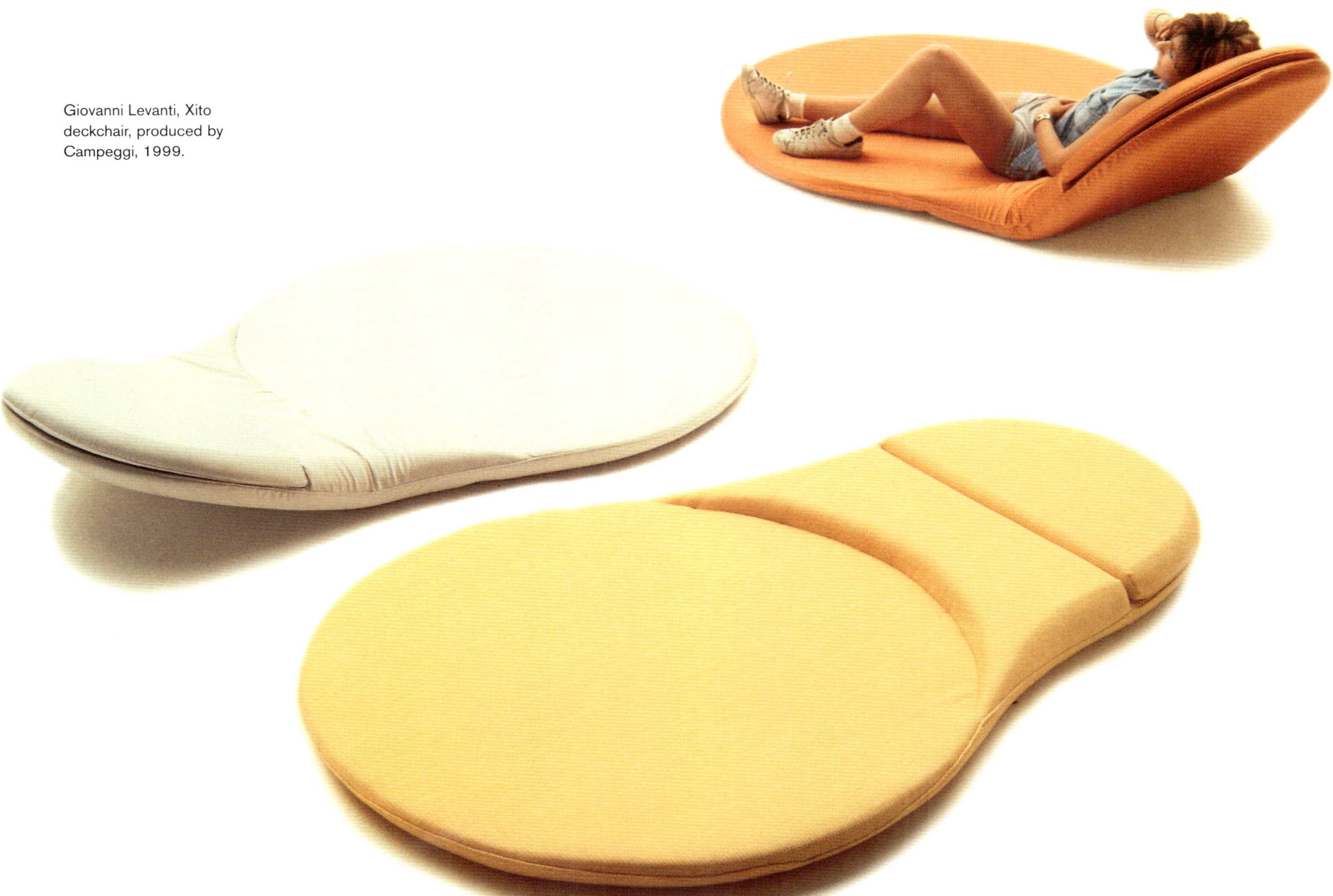

Paolo Deganello, installation at the exhibition *Exercises in Style*, Abitare Italia 2000, New York.

Studio Cerri & Associati, Limiti, installation at the exhibition *Exercises in Style*, Abitare Italia 2000, New York.

Claudio Silvestrin, Seamlessness, installation at the exhibition *Exercises in Style*, Abitare Italia 2000, New York.

Antonio Citterio & Partners, installation at the exhibition *Exercises in Style*, Abitare Italia 2000, New York.

playfulness of the finishes. The most revealing designs, though, were the ones devoted to single objects able to create fields of space around them. The Sacco chair, for instance, designed by Gatti, Paolini, and Teodoro in 1968, which became known and copied around the world as the Beanbag chair, had unexpected qualities that were set in action by its use. Womb-like, amorphous, embracing, and tribal, the Beanbag is a subtle example of *Existenzmaximum*. Its unusual seating height, its rolling quality, its massaging flexibility made it suitable for communal political discussions and lonesome meditations alike. In that way, the Beanbag was the minimal space to doze off and meditate, an isolation chamber *ante litteram*.

Today, the era of *Existenzmaximum* is upon us. The boundaries between the various design fields – graphic, industrial, and multimedia – between art and furniture, are vanishing. Space is not what it used to be. Out of a necessity to give structure to the immense immaterial world of the Internet and other networks and to expand metaphysically the restricted physical space allowed to the individual, architecture is becoming the universal paradigm. It is a new kind of architecture, one which needs to be very flexible, pragmatic, and versatile, while it also needs to have a strong intellectual background. Italy, in accordance with the stereotype, remains endearing, scandalous, and chaotic. Behind the stereotype's curtain, though, is a culture of immediate response to changed circumstances, fuelled by inexhaustible curiosity and intelligence and strong on its industrial feet. I cannot think of a better attitude for the future of architecture.

Franco La Cecla

A Matter of Taste

*The home "made in Italy"
in the popular imagination*

Armchair transformable into a bed, deck-chair and sofa, produced by Guizzardi Athos. Ornamental patent deposited on 21 May 1960.

"Here arises the question of the destiny of architecture is posed, just at the moment when it aspires to some truth. "When it is a question of the relationship between the project and some truth, that is, the determination to carry out a plan, to meet social and political needs, to be a transformer of social data, with a cultural, pedagogical mission, etc.

"In short, everything that nourishes the official discourse and touches the conscious will of the architect himself.

"Well, fortunately or unfortunately we realize that these programmed goals are always hijacked, diverted by those very people for whom they are intended, by the users, by this mass whose original or perverse response can never be registered in the project. There is no automatic registration of the social relationship, of the needs of the masses, whether in politics or in architecture. There is always a duel and an unexpected reaction. It is the reaction of an actor that is often included as a passive element, but does not necessarily obey the rules of the game and the laws of the dialogue. The masses appropriate the architectural object in their own way and, if the architect himself is not distracted from his programme, the object will be conducted along other paths in all ways, and the users will take responsibility for giving it the destination and the unexpected destiny it is lacking. Here there is still an involuntary form of radicality" (J. Baudrillard, "Verité ou radicalité de l'architecture", in *Truth, Radicality and Beyond in Contemporary Architecture*, A. Papadakis Publisher, Buenos Aires Biennial Exhibition of Architecture, July 2000).

These words by Jean Baudrillard describe the situation of architecture at the dawn of the new millennium with great clarity. Baudrillard talks of radicality, with this term intending to embrace the set of architectural practices of the last decade of the 20th century. In the great works, in the exploits of Frank Gehry, in the monumentalism of Norman Foster, or in the "événementiel-ism" of Rem Koolhaas, he sees the signs of a discourse "in excess".

Radicality is that of the sign as an end in itself, of the monument that is consumed in a few years, of giantism that is self-justified: an architecture that has abandoned any external motivation and that in order to affirm itself must be the virtual spectacle of itself.

In the slang of contemporary architectural criticism, this kind of work is nicknamed a "Rolex", using a word that on one hand defines its self-celebratory and status value, and on the other the absolute redundancy, the almost gross desire to impose itself.

These architectures are not "habitable" in the complete sense of the term. The exemplary case is the Hong Kong Bank building, designed by Norman Foster, whose megalithic hall is occupied on Sundays by thousands of Filipino women working as domestic helpers, who meet there to eat, to put curlers in their hair, to party, and who are promptly dispatched by the police. The building did not envisage any social use of its great spaces. These had not been conceived to be inhabited, just as the hall of a large hotel or the grandiloquent steps of a war memorial are not. If users occupy these spaces, it is as squatters.

Baudrillard means to tell us that never so much as today has the distance between architecture and living been so structural, marked by the tendencies of the leading architects and by the intelligence of the masses, going in very different directions.

The situation he describes is also applicable – with a few slight touch-ups – to Italy. If in this country architects find it harder to realize their "Rolexes", nonetheless, buildings and planning are increasingly distant from the real processes of housing development.

Toni Nicolini, view of an inhabited town road, Salaparuta, Sicily, 1967.

Opposite: Mimmo Jodice, internal courtyard of a *palazzo* transformed into a living-room space, Naples, 1994.

House in Venice with façade decorated by mechanical games, early '80s.

The despot and the rebels: "Without the consent of the architect furnisher they dared expose that statuette." From Giuseppe Novello, *Dunque dicevamo... 100 disegni di Novello*, Mondadori, Milan 1950.

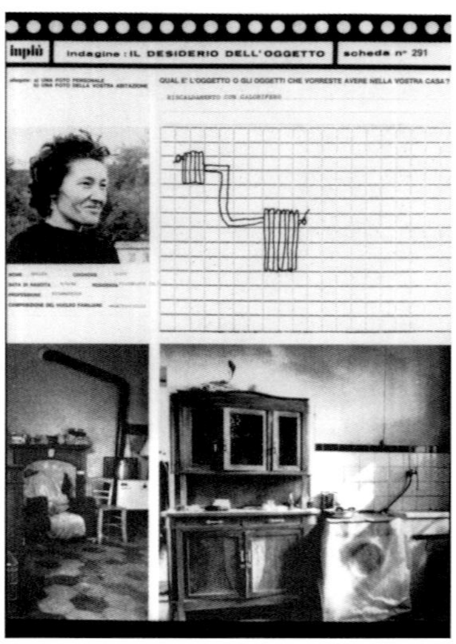

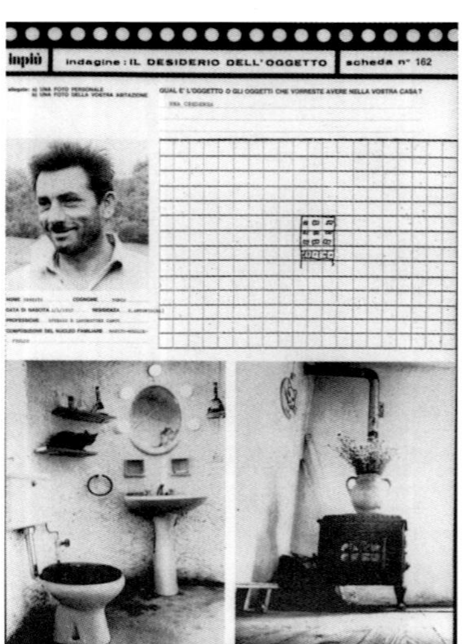

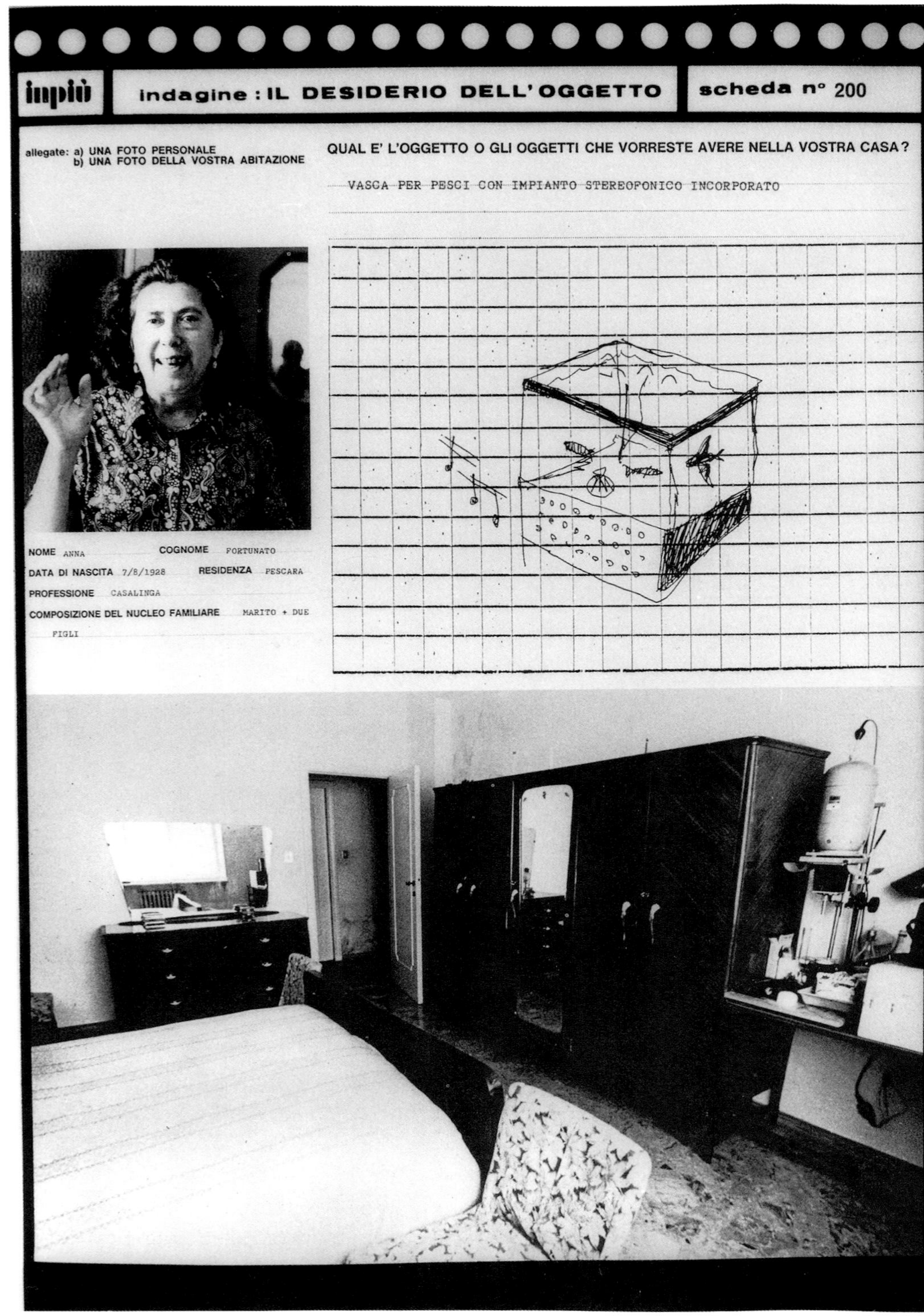

In this page and opposite: Investigation "The desire of the object": "What is/are the object/s that you would like to have in your house?" From *Inpiù*, no. 1, October-November 1973.

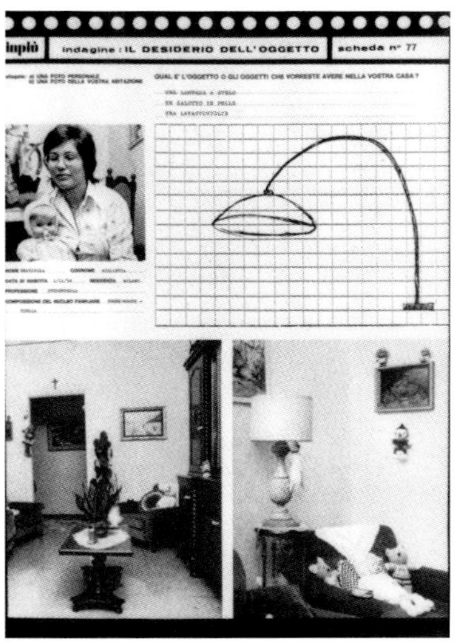

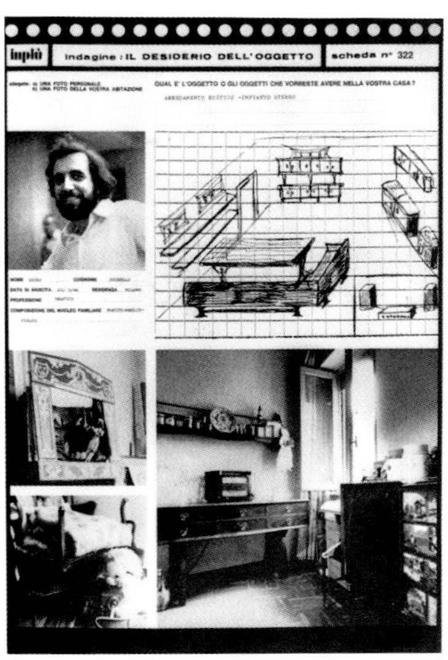

To reconstruct a history of the latest, most recent habitation practices in Italy means having to observe this gap, to enter the fracture, with its advantages and disadvantages.
When we think of the history of homes in Italy in the last fifty years, what immediately spring to mind are the major urbanizations, the devastation of the landscape and the enormous development of illegal constructions, whether in the form of building clusters, as in Gela or Irpinia, or houses spread around the city-non-city fringes of Treviso or Brianza.
What does the Italian desire for a home resemble in this constellation? A dream of privacy that is on one hand bordering on tribal patriarchalism, and on the other on the family firm, where people mind their own business.
In Italy the "big brother" model, that is, privacy conceived as boundary walls around something "in the home and away from the gaze", is a gossipy and intrusive declination of Anglo-Saxon privacy. The little single family houses in Luino or Dolo do not allow for images of perfection with private lawns and white letterboxes. More than anything, it is a conception in which the home has become a place with annexed garage, to store, conserve, stock – mostly piled up and in disorder – the wealth accumulated by Italian families since the war. There is no status to be shown off, no bourgeois symbology, no decoration reminding those passing by that here there is wealth and money in the bank.
In the South the situation is slightly different. There remain situations of traditional housebuilding, in disrepair, often devastated by interventions for the purposes of "modernization".
The image of the home here is perhaps more intrusive, it goes beyond the threshold of the house, it overflows onto the balconies and plants that invade the outside. Yet there remains the strong system of the family, the image of an attention to the private and an absolute disregard for the public, but with an ostentation that may be expressed in dwarves and columns. This is more closely related to the American vulgarity to which Southern Italy, by history and emigration, is most closely tied.
A recent investigation linked to national censuses, intended to delineate the character of the interiors of Italian homes from the Alps to the Channel of Sicily, has in fact revealed an extraordinary homogeneity: bedrooms, dining rooms, children's rooms are strikingly similar to each other everywhere. Ruling the roost is the image of "respectability", of the family that fills the home with furniture all "cotton wool and pillows", a doll's house that must express the childishness of relationships, the non-living of tensions.
Shiny quilts, mirror furniture, heavy glass tables, "Swedish" bedrooms for the children, where decoration and furnishings are aligned with the taste of the Smurfs and a form of gadgetization of decoration is all-conquering.
In the country of design and fashion, the interiors reveal a preference for the gross and the sugary that would be surprising were it not to correspond to a strange Italian version of Anglo-Saxon privacy.
It is in the absolute falsehood of these environments that their sincerity lies.
In reality Italians live elsewhere: the Venetians and Lombards in their garages and the Sicilians and Campanians outdoors, in the street, in the car.
On the other hand – and here the issue gets tricky – the apparent vulgarity of the Italian home conceals certain permanent elements, which turn out to be the differences that distinguish us from the rest of Europe: above all the taste for a little bit more life as neighbours, next door and opposite, the presence of odd figures such as the "doorman", the neighbourhood effect that

in the '80s not only held out, but was even reinforced.
Italy can still offer the foreign gaze a taste of life in society, an urbanity that is in our great tradition. A taste that administrators, architects and urban planners have rarely grasped, assailed, as ever, by the abstract frenzies of speculation or reformism from right or left.
It was foreigners who grasped the presence in our cities of a civic taste, of an urbanity that we have carried with us ever since then. The terrible leap of the '60s and '70s was the negation of this taste, the pretence at modernization in concrete and shopping malls that has made it difficult to walk, to live in the open air, to enjoy life in society. Above all the great victim has been external space, in cities such as Milan, which have almost completely lost it, and its replacement by a foolish conception of pedestrian space for the purposes of shopping lanes, roads flatly transformed into supermarkets and emptied of residence, losing the sense of "stopping and sitting" and meeting up.
The historic centres of Italian cities have been interpreted as though to "fit" more modern rhythms. Having abandoned the engineering utopia of automobile disembowelment, we have moved on to the economist's utopia: what better destination than a shopping mall! It is surprising that, despite this havoc, some life remains, even if in certain historic cities the life that disappears completely at a certain hour shows us that we have transformed the historic centres into flat commercial enterprises.
The winner is the utopia of Italy the

Above: Advertisement for the Bialetti Moka Express domestic coffee-maker. From a magazine from the early '50s.

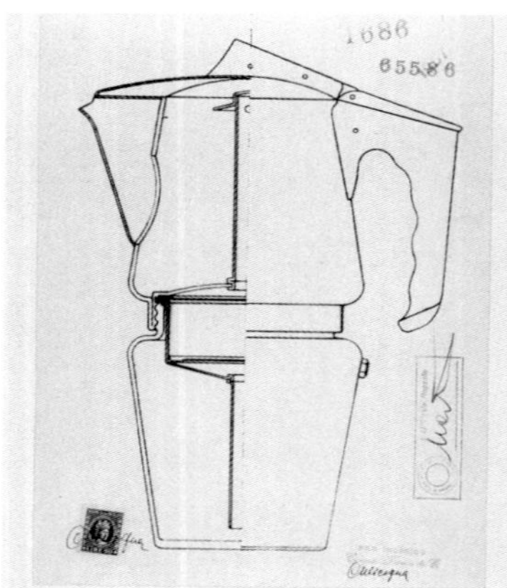

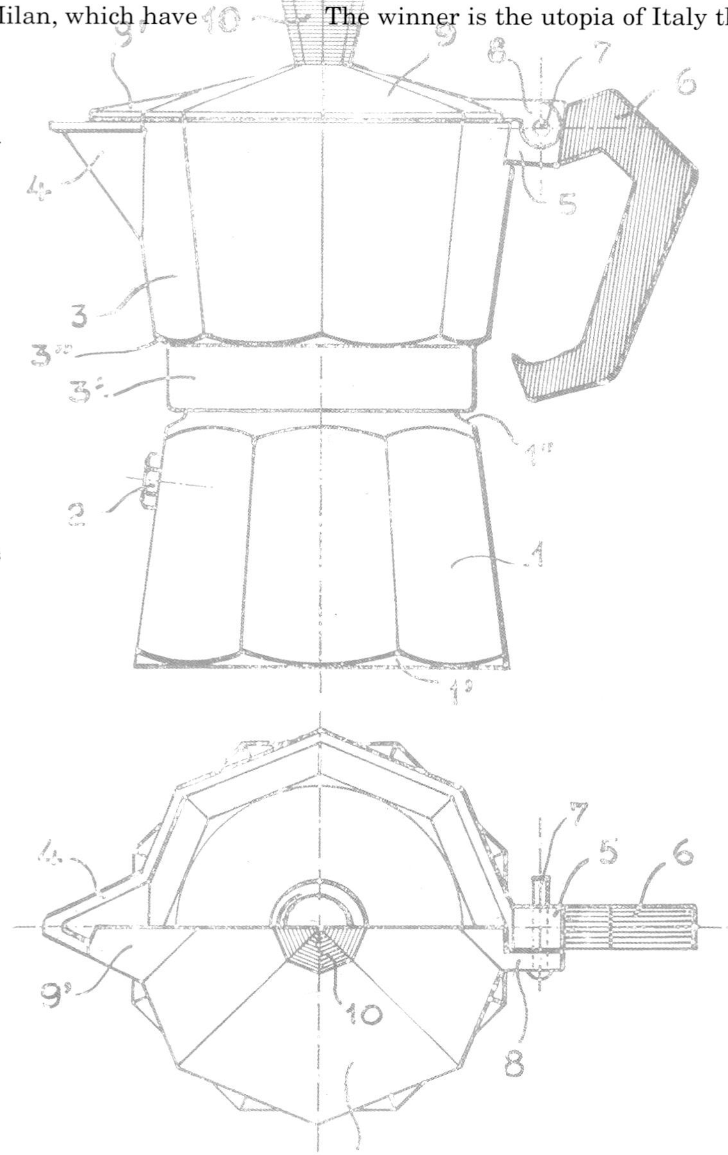

Left and right: Some ornamental and utility patents for coffee-makers for domestic use, from 1951 to 1957.

Toni Nicolini, view
of gallery building, Turin,
1969.

View of a street market in Palermo.

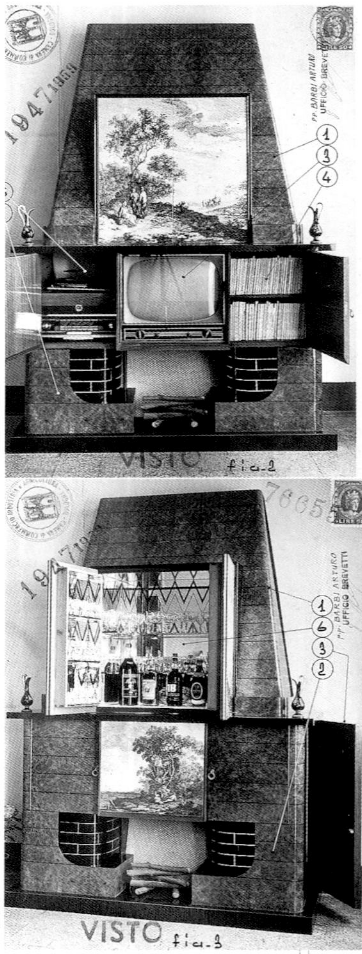

Fireplace furniture item functioning as bar, bookcase, radio-phono-television-holder, produced by Arturo Barbi. Ornamental patent deposited on 8 February 1960.

Hair-dryer incorporated into a volume representing a bird, produced by Elettroplastica Super Elettrodomestici. Ornamental patent deposited on 23 August 1963.

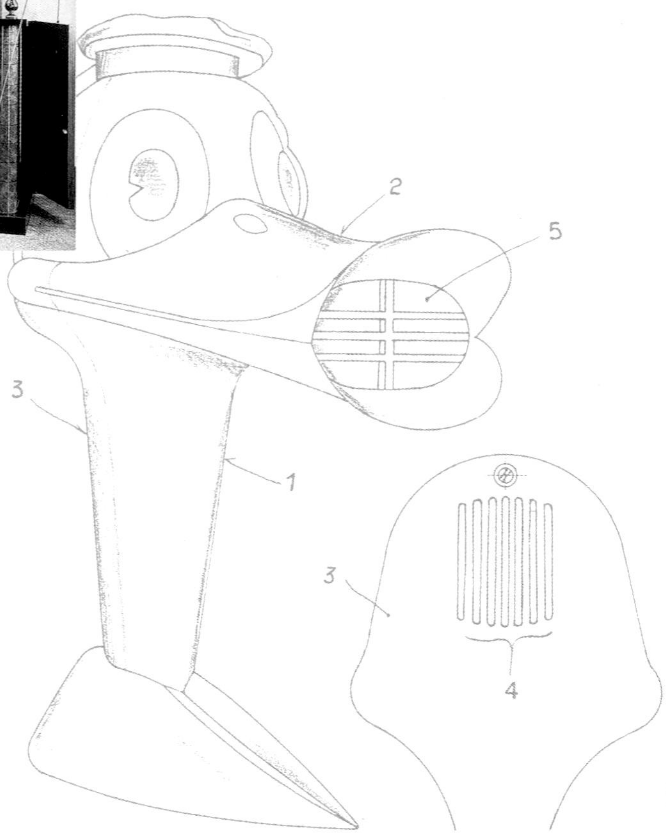

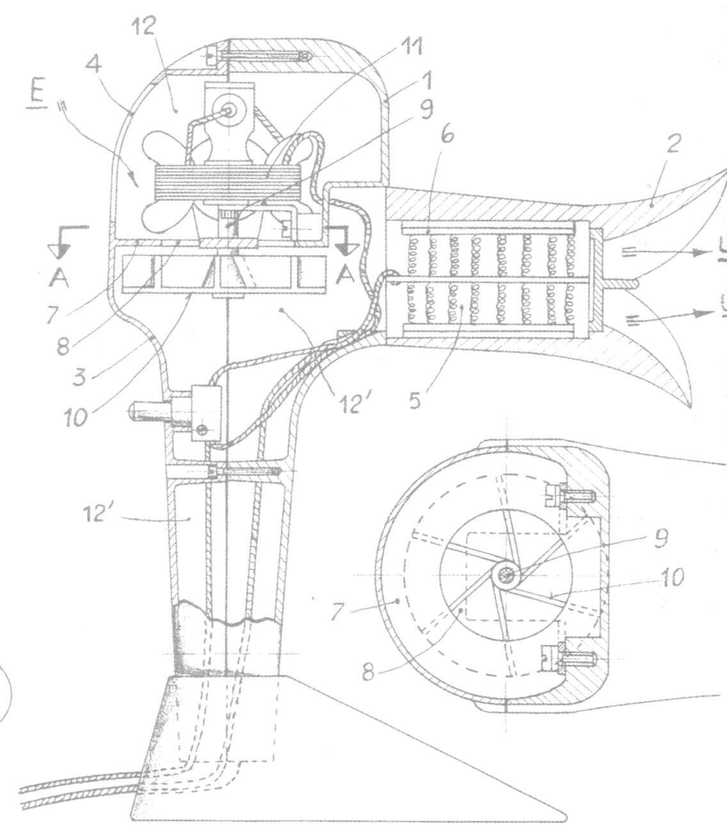

Cesare Colombo,
domestic interior in the
Gallaratese district, Milan,
1981.

shopkeeper and the loser is Italian *dolce far niente*, the city to be enjoyed with all its complexity. Here too on the part of the planners, other utopias have triumphed, to a large extent bankrupt ones, borrowed from the north of Europe when there they were already bankrupt. Here, there has never been an autochthonous elaboration: open-air markets, pedlars, the joy and chaos of Italianness have been sold off to municipal regulations, mercantile and trade-union bodies. Fortunately and unfortunately, as Baudrillard would say.

The urban planners and architects have created manufactured articles and orders that have never worked, the people have created others that for their sheer grossness have competed with the blunders of the former.

It must be said, to echo Baudrillard, that there is an interesting radicality in the process of creating grossness: at times it is the most direct and homely way of affirming the contrary of grandiloquence. The gross has a rhetoric without frills; it is there, so false that it does not need to be justified. It laughs at the hypotheses of reforming society that, whether honestly or not, politicians and urban planners try to promote.

The picture is not complete, as the most painful note needs to be added – housebuilding and the landscape. But before doing so we need to ask ourselves whether we should stop here: is it all discouraging, is it the victory of the ugly, of egotism and Italian parochialism? Perhaps not. But it is the "foreigners" who tell us that; those people who, when visiting this country, realize that it is still more habitable than their own countries, that life is more pleasant, sweetly and casually drifting. The fact is – and this concerns that strange thing that is the local mind of a people, the odd faculty to live in a certain way and not in another – that despite all the building of these last fifty years, Italy has maintained some of the qualities that tourists find there. Because some structures of habitation are invisible, they have to do with visions, postures, relations between bodies and spaces; in short, they are meat and stone. Just as in Japan, despite all the devastations following the war, on the disfigured face of the cities has been imposed the ancient way of living in villages, *roji*, private roads behind big buildings, and the old areolar conception of the city of villages has prevailed over the external image of the merciless metropolis; and likewise in Italy, despite all the devastation of the territory, the way of feeling space and our local mind to fill it have sometimes been left unsaid, sometimes expressed.

Let us move on, however, to the painful: the greatest opprobrium has been perpetrated in the field of residence. Detaching the habitation from the road, using the dreadful IACP council house districts of the '70s and '80s as the place of experimentation on the guinea-pigs of a dormitory model that never existed before in Italy. In a country in which residence was inextricable from all the other activities, these monsters have been created, within which such a large bubonic growth has appeared as to then devastate the historic centres themselves through contagion.

Today they are beginning to demolish – much less than abroad; but demolitions, or the desire for demolition, are a very important and new symptom for this country. It is understood that some fabrics are not rebuildable, that some spaces are not redefinable, unless the theoretical and practical offence committed is not eliminated.

The demolitions of the *case popolari* (public housing) of the dormitory districts, of the "low cost" districts, are part of that radicality that habitation requires. They tell something that architects and administrators find it hard to hear.

Toni Nicolini, close-up view of a "modern" council house where the public ritual of leaning out of the window is perpetuated, Turin, 1969.

Toni Nicolini, interior of rural house near Menfi, Sicily, 1967.

The idea that architectures, most of them, are not made to last, is an idea that people have always had. The monuments themselves, whether the Teatro di Marcello in Rome or the Beaubourg by Renzo Piano in Paris, are made to be transformed by use and sometimes eliminated by it, if the use proves to be suffocated by the construction.
On people's minds and their way of life, a significant part of the residences built in Italy are already old, outmoded. Is it still not clear today how much older a '70s building appears than a '50s building? In their grandiloquent pretension, in their heavy materials (reinforced concrete, steel), these buildings are already dead and stand as dead in the daily life of a city. The demolitions remind us that people live in living places.
Finally the landscape. Alas for us, devastations, negligence, the collapse of countryside and seaside culture, everything plots to make Italy lose its unique beauty; here too, habitation, absent habitation, is only replaceable by the external gaze.
We must accept it, Italy must be reinhabited by the tourists, the foreigners, the millions of them who still

know how to inhabit its landscapes. The territory must be safeguarded for them, they who are one of the greatest resources of this country.
Italians will understand, later, perhaps; coasts, beaches, mountains, castles and forests will return to being lived in. Habitation can be replaced by an external gaze that would like to understand how people lived here in these regions.
Habitation is the only hope of life and radicality for the territory: it preserves it from the dreams of those who want to infrastructure Italy, to build all the bridges, motorways, harbours; the dream of those who do not understand that this too is already old, irreparably destined to be demolished.
When will we start to demolish our useless motorways? When will we start to demolish the canalizations of the rivers, those immense horrendous useless power stations, large and small, today, when we can infrastructure a territory in a light, almost invisible way?
Let us close with Baudrillard, smiling at the idea that in sniffing out the tendencies, the drifts, and in feeling the pulse of the century, some great architects sometimes understand what the inhabitants of a place understood, disrupting everything, ten years ago.

Mimmo Jodice, domestic interior of a *trullo*, Alberobello, Puglia, 2000.

Guido Martinotti

The Virtual Desktop within the Writing Desk

New rites and new myths of the Italian lifestyle

Enzo Mari, *Un ambiente per "Interni": Ecco (16x32x6)*, December 1996.

Some time ago, an architecture and design magazine asked me to review an interesting photographic study of Italian homes. The first reaction I had on seeing the images was a sense of liberation: all books have been rigorously banned from Italian homes. In my 90 sq m home in Milan, not only do I have books laid flat (those who know will understand me) which cover all usable surfaces, but also about 12,000 volumes properly ordered. In physical terms, they occupy 190 m of shelving; plus those I have in the cellar, plus those in my mother's country home, where I keep my collections of weeklies, plus those I keep in another cellar which I rent at exorbitant cost. At last: hundreds of homes free of this curse! And I do not say this ironically; I really do wish for a big house with not much in it, and, in the middle of a large empty space, a big table on whose top I can have the things I need arrive: texts, sounds and images. In short, to succeed in placing all the windows I need with ease on the desktop, rather than have to squeeze a writing desk into a small box as is the case now. All of which without a single wretched cable and above all without a single sheet of paper in the house: paper as a medium would be completely banned. I am convinced that the excess of paper that plagues me and other Italian colleagues is not a sign of intellectual distinction, as a certain mythology continues to have one believe, but the perverse effect of something we lack. For example, excellent libraries that work. For example, a decent and cheap broad band enabling us to navigate the web quickly and efficiently.

But while I was comparing this aspiration (which will certainly make furniture-makers apprehensive) with the reassuring images of the photographic collection I was speaking of, in which I saw beautiful houses full of things, but clean and tidy, I asked myself in what sort of houses we have chosen to live. Because there was something other than books (occasionally spotted here and there) missing in these houses. The urbanist and anthropologist Franco La Cecla proposes the hypothesis that these houses lack the personality of their inhabitants: "spaces that do not reflect the people living in them" is the fine definition he gives. A sort of idea of "non-place" as per Melvin Webber, applied to places *par excellence*. In reality, as per the idea of non-place, which reveals its weakness when we try to grasp it firmly, this indication also helps us to understand only a little more than what it states.

It is not true that Italian homes lack personality. More simply, they reflect the personality of those living in them: disorientated individuals who have willingly or unwillingly abandoned the rural or small-town habits which they only knew they were supposed to be ashamed of, without, however, finding a compass to guide them other than that offered by the immense, but shapeless world of advertising and the media. It is a little like when one goes visiting in hospitals: you see all those elderly people who clearly have stripy pyjama faces, like those in De Filippo's films, but who wear shapeless garments in those vaguely vomit-inducing colours of the "backpack generation". Luckily, nobody feels it incumbent upon them to go after the houses of the old élite: candelabras, brocades, *boiseries* and crystal. Not to mention the "white telephone" homes,[1] which are once again exerting a certain fascination, and which take on inevitably perverse connotations as in Benigni's film, *La vita è bella*, although they have not been reinvented for mass consumption. However, the new élites have not been able to impose a different model: where is the beautiful modern Italian house? But above all, they seek in vain the traces of these things, of those entities which have truly formed the contemporary home, that is, the "machines for living".

We are used to considering mechanization as something typical of factories, but

[1] A reference to the typical interiors of Italian films from the '30s (*editor's note*).

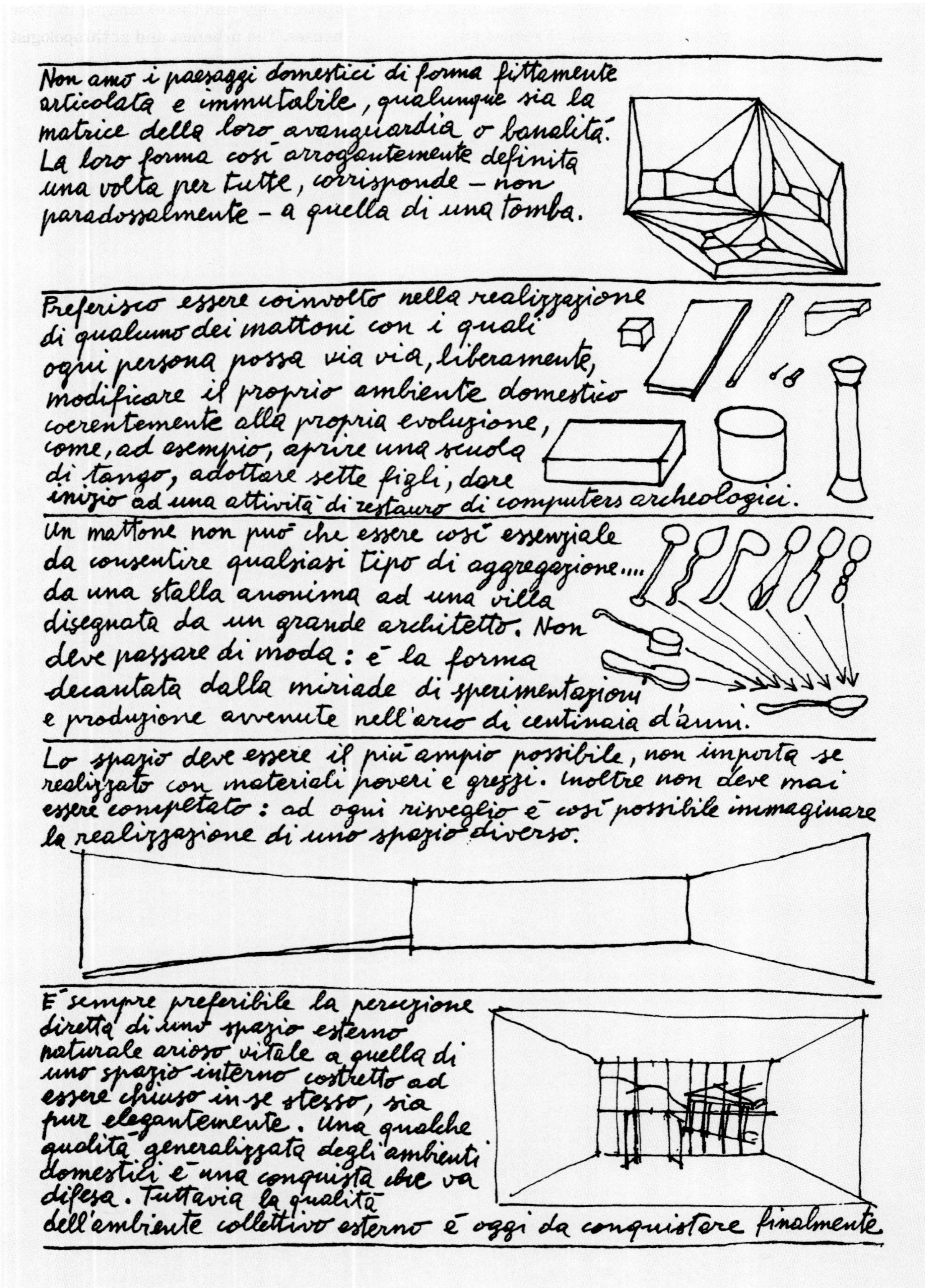

Non amo i paesaggi domestici di forma fittamente articolata e immutabile, qualunque sia la matrice della loro avanguardia o banalità. La loro forma così arrogantemente definita una volta per tutte, corrisponde – non paradossalmente – a quella di una tomba.

Preferisco essere coinvolto nella realizzazione di qualcuno dei mattoni con i quali ogni persona possa via via, liberamente, modificare il proprio ambiente domestico coerentemente alla propria evoluzione, come, ad esempio, aprire una scuola di tango, adottare sette figli, dare inizio ad una attività di restauro di computers archeologici.

Un mattone non può che essere così essenziale da consentire qualsiasi tipo di aggregazione.... da una stalla anonima ad una villa disegnata da un grande architetto. Non deve passare di moda: è la forma decantata dalla miriade di sperimentazioni e produzione avvenute nell'arco di centinaia d'anni.

Lo spazio deve essere il più ampio possibile, non importa se realizzato con materiali poveri e grezzi. Inoltre non deve mai essere completato: ad ogni risveglio è così possibile immaginare la realizzazione di uno spazio diverso.

È sempre preferibile la percezione diretta di uno spazio esterno naturale arioso vitale a quella di uno spazio interno costretto ad essere chiuso in se stesso, sia pur elegantemente. Una qualche qualità generalizzata degli ambienti domestici è una conquista che va difesa. Tuttavia la qualità dell'ambiente collettivo esterno è oggi da conquistare finalmente.

Some reflections by Enzo Mari on domestic interior design, in *Ottagono*, no. 122, March-May 1997.

I do not like domestic landscapes of a highly subdivided and immutable form, whatever strain of the avant-garde or ordinariness they represent. Their form, so arrogantly defined once and for all, corresponds – not paradoxically – to that of a tomb.

I prefer to be involved in the realization of some of the bricks with which each person can, in his own way, freely modify his/her own domestic environment according to his/her own evolution, for example, in opening a school for tango, adopting seven children, beginning a restoration activity for archaeological computers.

A brick cannot be anything but so basic as to allow any type of aggregation… from an anonymous stable to a villa designed by a famous architect. It must not go out of fashion: it is the exalted form of the myriad of experiments and production over the course of hundreds of years.

The space must be the largest possible; it does not matter if it is created with humble and rough materials. Furthermore, it must never be completed so that every time you wake up it is possible to imagine the realization of a different space.

The direct perception of a natural, airy, vital external space is always preferable to that of an internal space forced to be closed in on itself, no matter how elegantly. An overall quality of domestic environments is an achievement to be protected. Nevertheless, the quality of the outside collective environment is today still to be conquered, finally.

Rosanna Monzini, library space in a Milanese apartment, early '90s, in a photograph by Gabriele Basilico.

Following pages

Interior of the apartment of an architect and contemporary art collector in Rome, mid-'80s, in a photograph by Gabriele Basilico.

Interior of the '30s-style apartment of the collector Boschi, Milan, 1982, in a photograph by Gabriele Basilico.

machines have to do with work, and if it is true that for a certain period much of this work is done in factories, it is also true that a good deal of this work has always taken place in the home, and, in parallel to what was going on in factories, the first generations of machines for living were labour- and time-saving. What does this mean? The industrial revolution is based upon the replacement of human labour with natural energy in the form of heat or electricity. This conversion is effected with tools we call "machines", which have the advantage of being stronger, more precise and faster than man. The machines were originally constructed for the factories, but subsequently many "machines for the home" were also made. In the last century, cast-iron stoves enabled coal (which provides more concentrated energy than wood) to be used efficiently; these were followed by gas, methane and electricity. The time needed to cook was greatly reduced, leaving several free hours available to those who were responsible for these tasks. In particular, this benefited housewives, who began no longer to be totally taken up with household chores. This greater availability of time was linked to changes in the family which, from units virtually totally subordinated to a patriarchal figure, evolved towards a social nucleus based more upon affections and reciprocal collaboration. There are even those who have linked the extra time provided by the cast-iron stove with the expansion of the suffragette movement. I do no know if this is true, but for sure the cast-iron stove started the great transformation of the rooms in the homes in industrial cities. No more smoky, dirty kitchens. A day area and a night area, where the fire can be contained in small cavities and used solely to provide warmth.

Until a few decades ago, energy for the home (wood and coal, and often also water, as well as grease, wax and oil to provide lighting) needed to be stocked directly by the residents. Today, a home is supplied by a complex grid system for water, natural gas and electricity. One needs only open the gas tap or press a switch to have unlimited quantities of energy, although it must be paid for, of course. The great availability of domestic energy has made it possible to build those machines for the home that have one by one saved a great deal of time and labour: the washing machine, the vacuum cleaner and the refrigerator. Only habit makes us forget the savings in time and effort provided by the refrigerator; these are, above all, savings in time for women. The washing machine completes the triad of basic machines without which a contemporary home is uninhabitable. The others, from the vacuum cleaner to the dishwasher, have a less universal distribution.

However, the time that can be saved in a day is a finite quantity and so the market for the first generation of machines for living was saturated fairly quickly. Today, as is known, it is above all a market for replacement machines: heaters, washing machines and refrigerators that are increasingly efficient and aesthetically pleasing, which are less and less machines and more and more items of interior design. But even when hidden, they are still machines and for the moment are not being developed. The next jump in this chain of events will be the entirely

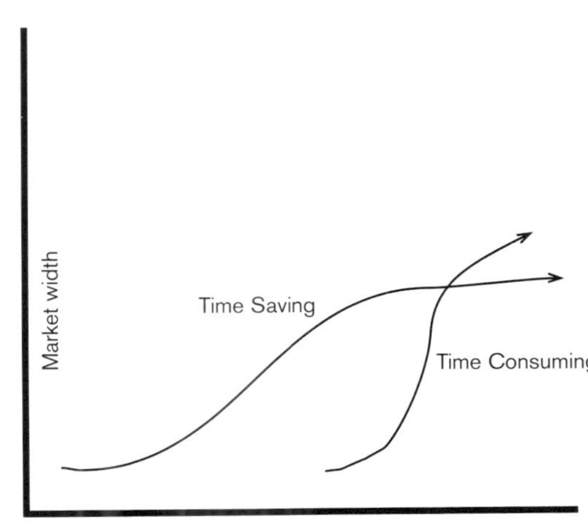

Penetration of Entertainment Equipment and Services1995–2000. In the period between June 1999 and February 2000, the penetration of satellite reception equipment, pay-tv, videogame consoles and DVD video players saw a rapid acceleration (data Niche, *Il reeingineering della casa*, 2000).

	June 1995 %	June 1998 %	June 1999 %	February 2000 %
2nd Television	38.8	50.1	56.8	59.1
3rd Television	9.8	13.8	17.4	17.6
Televideo	48.0	62.0	64.7	66.4
VCR	57.0	65.9	74.8	76.9
DVD Video Player	-----	-----	3.3	6.2
HI-FI System	45.3	49.6	56.7	55.5
Videocamera	14.6	18.6	23.9	24.4
Console for Videogames	14.7	12.9	17.7	23.1
Satellite Receiver	2.1	5.9	8.8	12.0
Pay-TV Subscription	4.0	5.4	6.6	9.5

automated house, but numerous technological advances are still required for this to occur.
However, a second generation of machines for living is spreading. These consume the time saved and are thus dubbed "time consuming". They include radio, television, hi-fi and the latest arrival, the computer. These machines have also influenced the structure of the home, especially television, which has introduced a new point of socialization. The place in which television is watched is not only the centre of intimate family life (what the Americans call the "den"), but also a place in which an eventual guest is welcomed without excessive formality, unlike elsewhere in the house, perhaps including the kitchen. These other areas are still divided into public (sacred) and private (profane) spaces. In few Italian houses does one enter straight into the kitchen, as one used to in rural homes and as occurs in many American homes in which neighbours and friends appear through those flimsy back doors that have such an important role in American films.

Everyday domestic scene, Milan, 1993, in a photograph by Paolo Rosselli.

Systems supplying energy to the home have now been joined by others carrying information. The information is used by the telephone, the radio and the television or, in the form of disks or tapes – of transportable media – for video-recording, hi-fi, cameras and PCs. These new machines for the home, the television above all, have one important feature in common: they do not serve to save time, but to fill it.
The home becomes a pleasant place, increasingly warm and comfortable, in which it is also possible to be entertained and to learn. The television is an open window on the world enabling one to stay comfortably in an armchair or in bed and participate in important events, often at the very moment in which they take place and with no limits of distance. But television is also a breach through which the world blunders into our private life, influencing our ideas, life-styles and behaviour. Very often, this "televisual window" does not allow the real world to enter but instead a fictitious or virtual one which replaces facts with suggestions and opinions that are unknowingly or deliberately misleading, and against which we must learn to defend ourselves using a critical sense that must be kept alert.
All these transformations affect our way of life and above all our habits regarding mobility. One of the reasons the metropolitan area is important and

Dante Donegani and Giovanni Lauda, Serie Compact closable desks that hold all the things necessary for working at home on the computer, produced by Radice, 1999.

largely unexplored is the matter of "social morphology". For the lifelong retired town-dweller, the suburbs represent little more than an unspeakable horror. A part of the town to be leaped over by air or in a car, hoping you do not take the wrong exit from the freeway as tragically occurred to Sherman McCoy or to the protagonists in *Last Stop in Brooklyn*. Thus, there has been no attempt as yet to distinguish between the real objects that are located in a town's outer shell on the part of the most important centres, as Sudjic stated (1993), discharging flashes of strength in the specific locations, taking into account the link with the hollow centre, but without depending closely on it. It is obvious that some places, such as Segrate, Fiumicino and Roissy live independently of their nearby cities of Milan, Rome or Paris, but it is also true that no-one would go to live in an Alessandria-San Felice. At least, not until the metropolitan field extended as far as that. The coral reef that emerges from this (Bocca, 1993) is part of the fragmentation of the urban phenomenon of which Vittorio Gregotti speaks (Gregotti, 1998) but it cannot be explained solely by this.

The urban society that is emerging cannot be understood critically unless we enter the logic of the strategies of time and space of the population that lives, works and consumes in the new city. New phenomena occur, amongst which one which tells us that the time spent commuting daily is proportional in a symmetrically inverse manner to that of the old industrial or first-generation metropolis. Navigating in the city's outer shell is the activity that requires an increasing part of the talents for daily living needed by the new metropolitan inhabitant.

It is true that "many of the institutions that used to bring people together – a main street, a union hall, a town meeting – no longer work as before. Many people spend most of their day alone at the screen of a television or a computer. Meanwhile, social beings that we are, we are trying (as Marshall McLuhan said) to retribalize. And the computer is playing a central role" (Turkle, 1995, p. 178). This is

Massimo Morozzi, Cubista Soft modular sofa, produced by Edra, 1999.

Philippe Starck, Lazy Working Sofa (LWS), produced by Cassina, 1998.

certainly taking place, but let us not fall into the error of believing that transport has vanished or is in the process of disappearing, nor that in general the so highly extolled "immaterial society" is eliminating the material nature of the city of things and people. It is now noted that the power of communications to replace transport as a reliable means – at least in the mid-term – to reduce energy waste and pollution is far less than expected because of a complex series of factors, some of which are inertial, but some structural and therefore impossible to eliminate even in the long term.

Finally, from an ecological standpoint, seen as a combination of the physical and human aspects summed up by the level of energy waste and pollution (Bettini, 1996), the existence of the city's outer shell can be associated with many of the problems of the contemporary city. The mobility inherent to the metropolitan system of the "100 mile city" is the greatest factor of energy consumption (as well as investments per fixed capital) and pollution production (atmospheric, noise, mortality and relative costs) of the entire urban system. And the more the outer shell is developed, as in the large American metropolises, the greater is the energy consumption (and associated pollution). The difference can be seen by comparing the pro-capita energy consumption of fuel in a sample of large US cities, averaged at 58,541 Mj (Megajoules) with a peak of 74,510 in Houston, as against the 13,280 Mj in European cities (Newman-Kenworthy, 1987).

But mobility is a consequence of the localization of a triad of activities: the home, work, and access to public and

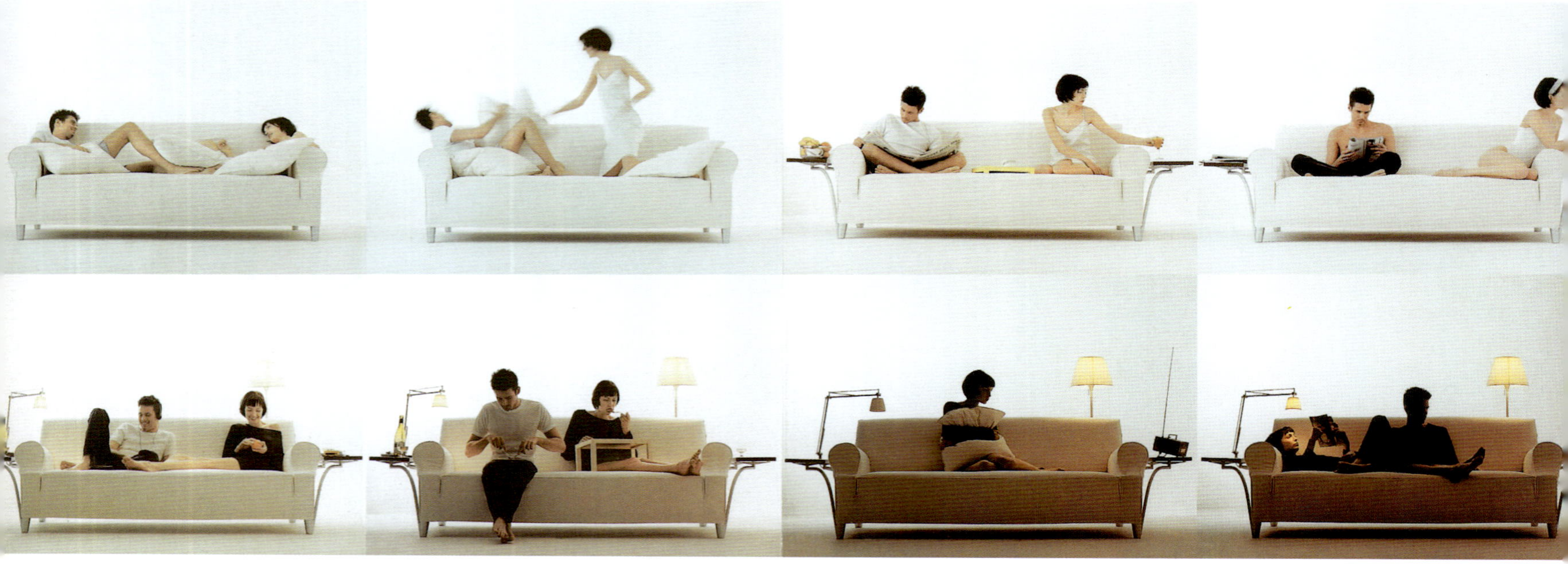

private services. The distribution of these different "generators of mobility" and their internal transformations constitute the matrix of the new city. "The keyboard is my cafe", writes Mitchell. "Each morning I turn to some nearby machine – my modest personal computer at home, a more powerful workstation in one of the offices or laboratories that I frequent, or a laptop in a hotel room – to log into electronic mail... Traditionally, you needed to go someplace to do this sort of thing. But the world-wide computer network – the electronic agora – subverts, displaces, and radically redefines our notions of gathering place, community, and urban life" (Mitchell, 1995, pp. 7–8).

Today, television is losing its centrality: in 60% of homes, there are two television sets, and in 18% a third set; televisions are dotted around the home in the different rooms and are inserted into the home decor, a trend that will be greatly accelerated by the advent of flat screens. And the PC? The PC is not yet widely distributed in Italian homes, but where it is, it has begun to be an important presence, with cables, peripherals and accessories. Perhaps it will become the central point of the home, but I hope with ever fewer cables and cubes to stare at hypnotically, and instead with increasing intelligent solutions put at our disposal to do away with dusty cables and stimulate our skills and creativity. But above all, with the hope that they reverse a trend, that they provide more time and enable us to go out; if television has made the world come into our homes, let us hope that the net will enable us to go out of our homes into the world.

Claudio Dematté

The Secrets of the Italian Supply System

Innovation in small and medium-sized companies in the house sectors

Marc Newson, Wooden Chair, produced by Cappellini, 1992.

Enzo Mari, Serie Elementare majolica tiles, produced by Gabbianelli, 1968–72.

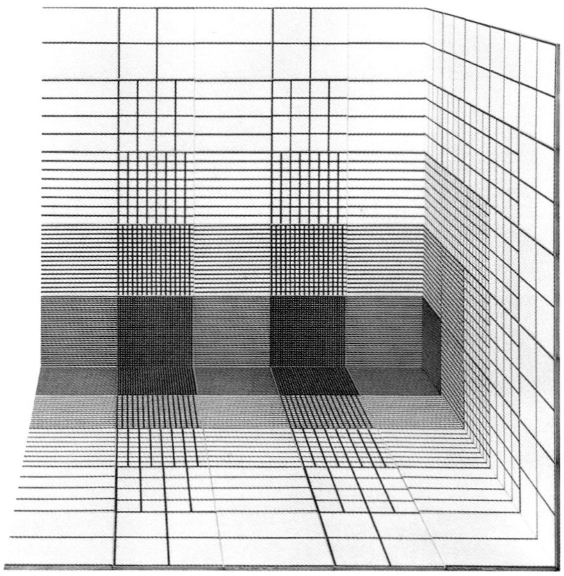

Economics is not an exact science, as physics or mathematics. Still it has developed some general laws that maintain their validity at a high level of confidence. One of these laws says that a country, as it develops and its salaries increase above a certain level, is condemned to lose a certain type of activities – those with a high labour content – in favour of the less developed countries.

This rule holds for all countries. It has been contradicted – to my knowledge – on a large scale only in the case of Italy and for a set of activities which produce goods for the housing and for personal care: furnishing, tiles, marbles, faucets, silverware, home textiles and even garments, which is not strictly within the area we will consider in this essay.

To stick to the general rule, even Italian economists since the '70s, when Italian salaries came close to those of the other European countries and became a multiple of the salaries of many less developed countries, have been predicting year after year a turning point in these growing industries, which has never materialized.

To be precise, the imports of this type of goods have been growing in the latest years. But the exports have been growing as well, so that the net result is still not only just a surplus in the balance of payment, but, more importantly, a growing surplus. This result defies the above-mentioned law and it is a mystery to many observers, foreign as well as domestic.

How can a country whose salaries have become much higher than the salaries of countries which appear to have an equivalent competence in producing this type of goods still remain competitive in the international markets?

Have the repeated warnings of the economists predicting an incoming crisis dismantled the general rule?

What kind of forces have been conspiring to defy the inevitable drift that hands over the labour intensive industries to the less developed countries?

These questions are at the heart of my essay.

Before entering into the explanation of the mystery, let me expose just a few data to document the indisputable success of the set of activities under consideration.

Table 1
Performance of the furnishing and interior design industries*

Year 2000 in millions of Euros	
Turnover	54,100
Export	21,800
Foreign trade surplus	14,000
Employees	541,341

* It comprehends: furnishings, tiles, marbles, taps and silverware

Table 1 presents the data about production; imports, exports and the net result in the balance of payment in the last years. Everybody can check the same type of data for the other industrialized countries and will discover that all of them have been experiencing a steeper increase in imports and a growing unbalance in the foreign trade. For all countries the outsourcing in less developed countries has been increasing at a high rate. For the producers it has become a question of life and for the retailers a way to bypass the domestic producers that did not adjust to the process.

Even Italian producers followed the same trend, but at a lower speed and by a parallel strong increase in the foreign demand of Italian-made products. In the meantime these products have become renowned all over the world for their distinctiveness: a symbol of design, elegance and quality, something that an increasing number of sophisticated consumers everywhere aim to have around them.

Phase in the production of the Selene chair by Vico Magistretti for Artemide, 1969.

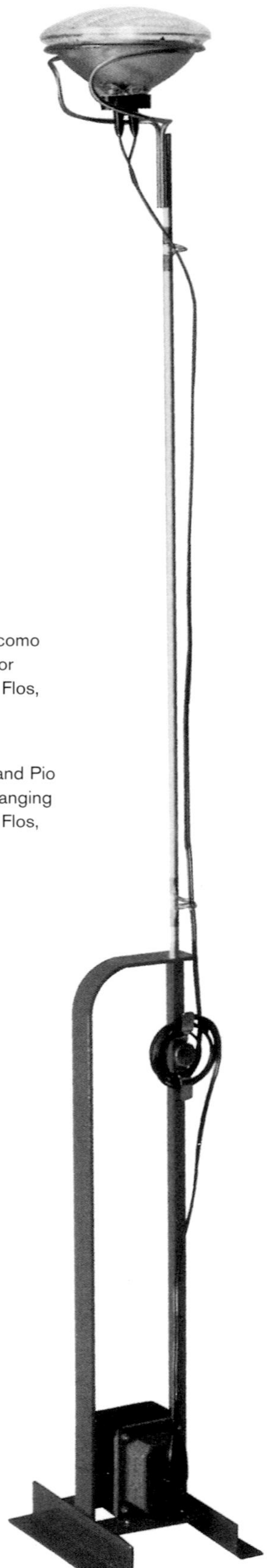

Achille and Piergiacomo Castiglioni, Toio floor lamp, produced by Flos, 1962.

Opposite:
Achille Castiglioni and Pio Manzù, Parentesi hanging lamp, produced by Flos, 1970.

A tentative explanation of the mystery

Understanding the reasons why a set of traditional and labour-intensive industries have remained under the domain of a developed country – against the general law – is an intriguing issue for a scholar. It is also important in order to make better forecasts for the future than those formulated in the past. For the practitioners the issue is not only intriguing: it is vital, both for the winners and for the losers, because it explains the real nature of the competitive game.
I will approach the mystery first by mapping the elements that characterize the Italian competitive model; then I will reinterpret the general rule regarding the international migration of industries with the lessons of the Italian experience and a subtler argumentation of the process.
The elements that characterize the Italian supply system in these industries are basically two: 1) the type of products that are offered; 2) the system by which they are produced and sold.

The type of products

Given the size of the industry, the large number of companies that make up the supply system, and the different regional cultures, the spectrum of products that are offered by the Italian producers is quite heterogeneous and diversified. This could go against a clear and well-defined typology of the Italian supply.
However, the same variety and the richness of the supply are, by itself, a distinctive and a key success factor. Few countries have the capacity to provide such a wide range of alternatives, each one fitting a specific segment of spending capacity, each one distinguished by a different style, each one using a variety of materials, different colours, different sizes and formats. In some sectors even single companies, like Natuzzi, are capable to provide an incredible and unmatchable variety. As we will see later, the capacity to produce variety is not so commonplace and it is not a normal output: it is the result of complex combinations of factors which few countries, and even less

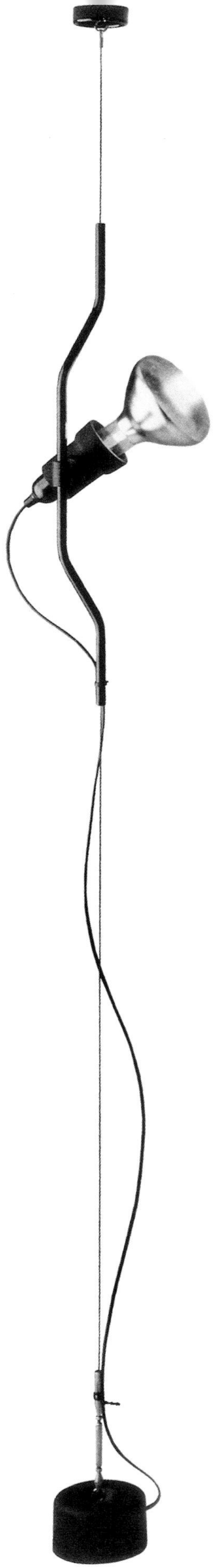

companies, are able to put together.
Despite the variety, the Italian supply is notwithstanding pretty much characterized and distinct from other countries' supply for a number of specific elements that are caught inside the highly valued brand "made in Italy".
The first type of characterization is due to the superior capacity to inject into the products an intangible quality: the aesthetic dimension and a soul so that the product becomes almost a symbol, with a lot of intangible value, rather than just a commodity. This type of differentiation is made possible by the longstanding tradition in architecture, interior design and visual arts, going back for centuries and deeply rooted into the Italian environment, as it is well documented by the impressive artistic heritage of most Italian cities. As it is well known, the capacity to produce aesthetic qualities is deeply linked to the capacity to perceive the changes in the way people think, hope, and fear. The cultural dimension goes along with the ability to visualize the feelings.
The differentiation through the addition of aesthetic qualities is a subtle one: it is difficult to replicate (although many foreign producers try to anyway); it carries with it a bundle of cultural and even existential meanings; it provides the consumers with a peg to distinguish themselves around spiritual clusters.
A second differentiating factor is represented by the capacity to provide the products with the traits of craftsmanship, even when they are produced serially with industrial methods. This gives the products a sense of uniqueness, which pleases the customers a great deal. In order to personalize the products further, some Italian products are even "signed" with the name of the designer who conceived them. Both elements provide the customers with a sense of being unique or, even better, of being part of a selected and privileged group of people sharing a common set of aesthetic and even existential values. Even this differentiating factor is difficult to imitate and replicate by the producers of other countries: high quality craftsmanship is not so widely spread. In the case of Italy it is the result of a long tradition that goes back in the Middle Ages (or even further) and witnessed a large diffusion and a high reputation in the most advanced countries already during the Renaissance period. Few countries can count on such strong and widespread capabilities that have resisted and survived even the industrialization process.
A final characterization of the Italian supply is the capability to provide a reasonable price even for differentiated products, allowing a relatively large group of customers to access to a class of products previously reserved only for the elite. This trait is due to the ability of the Italian producers to combine craftsmanship with the technology and the production systems typical of the industrial model.
The combination of the above factors has given the Italian producers a strong and defensible competitive advantage compared to the markets of both the less developed and the industrialized countries: competitiveness based on quality and distinctiveness against the former; strong differentiation together with price competitiveness against the latter. The peculiarity of the Italian case depends precisely on its ability to escape the dual grip from both sides of the competitive challenge.
Competing through differentiation does not always pay off: it works only when the consumers become annoyed by the supply of standard products and have enough spending power to look after the custom-made or cluster-made products. The Italian producers were quick to sense the change which was taking place in the market of the industrialized countries in the '70s, by exploiting the competencies

Working wood manually for the production of furniture.

Large cooling plant during the final phase of panel production, manufactured by Fantoni.

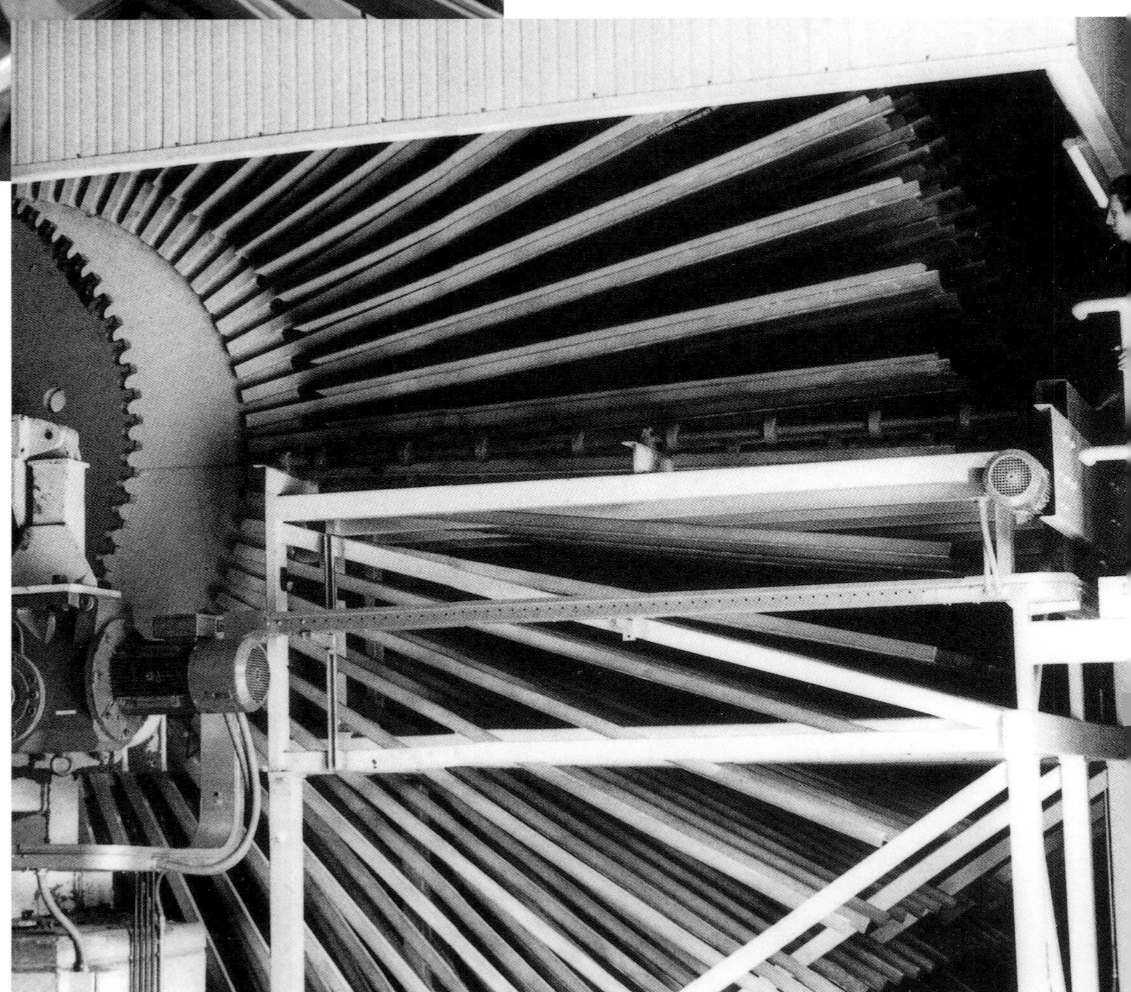

Preparation of the padded part of an armchair produced by Frau.

Sewing the leather covering for some models of armchairs and sofas produced by Frau.

Production area for the Sindbad armchair designed by Vico Magistretti and produced by Cassina.

Preparation of a frame for a bed produced by Casanova.

Ron Arad, Victoria & Albert sofa, produced by Moroso, 1999.

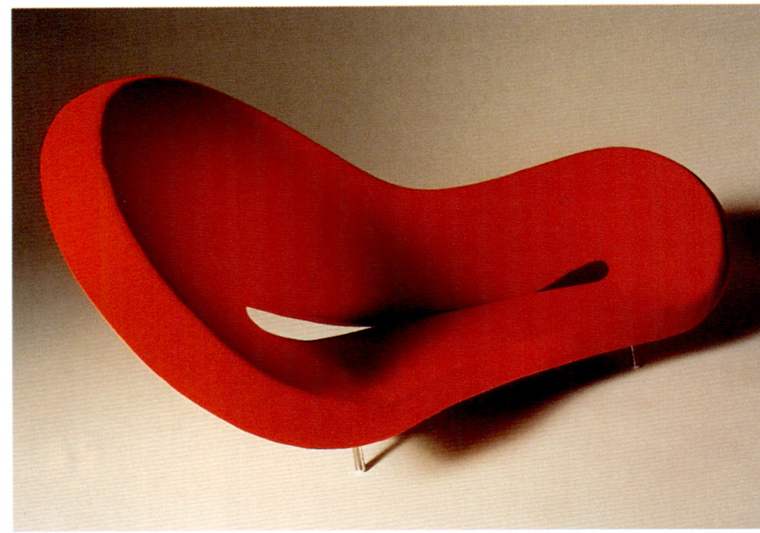

Oscar Tusquets, Tea & Coffee Piazza silver service, produced by Alessi, 1983.

Paolo Deganello, Regina chair, produced by Zanotta, 1991.

Philippe Starck, Miss Sissi table lamp, produced by Flos, 1991.

which were disseminated in the country and by riding the first experiments in industrial design which took place before, but especially after, the Second World War. Now that we have explained the factors on which the Italian companies have played the competitive game, we need to understand the second element which has made the Italian model very peculiar: the supply system.

The Italian supply system

How come the Italian companies have been able to withstand the tough attack by the less developed countries on the above-mentioned sectors and at the same time take over a relevant share of the market of the most industrialized countries? What has made the Italian companies capable of providing a strong differentiation in their product portfolio and at the same time a reasonable price? What has made them so quick to capture the changes in the market and also so flexible to provide a variety of products, fine-tuned for different market segments, for different tastes and for different geographical markets? How could they be so competitive, given the poverty of local raw materials for most of the industries under discussion and the need to import them from far away?

As M. E. Porter made clear in its famous book *The Competitive Advantage of Nations*, the international competitiveness of an industry does not depend on one single factor, but is the combination of a cluster of elements both economic and social (Porter, 1990). The Italian model for furnishing and related industries rests on a peculiar mixture of factors that could appear weaknesses, rather than strengths, if considered each in isolation from the others.

The supply system is indeed made of : 1) a large majority of small or even minuscule companies, most of them, if not all, being family companies, unlisted; 2) each company is indeed very often a co-ordinated group of smaller companies, each of them focused on a single product or a single phase of the value chain; 3) many of the companies operating in the same field are located very close to each other in industrial districts and most of them belong to virtual networks; 4) they compete aggressively against one another, but they also co-operate in order to gain economies of scale in the production of certain common components or services; 5) the local and family nature of the companies creates an entrepreneurial environment where not only the owners feel committed to the success of their companies, but also the employees, who

Marcel Wanders, Nomad Carpet, produced by Cappellini, 1998.

Opposite: Production area for Anna Castelli Ferrieri's bookcases and rotating tables, produced by Kartell.

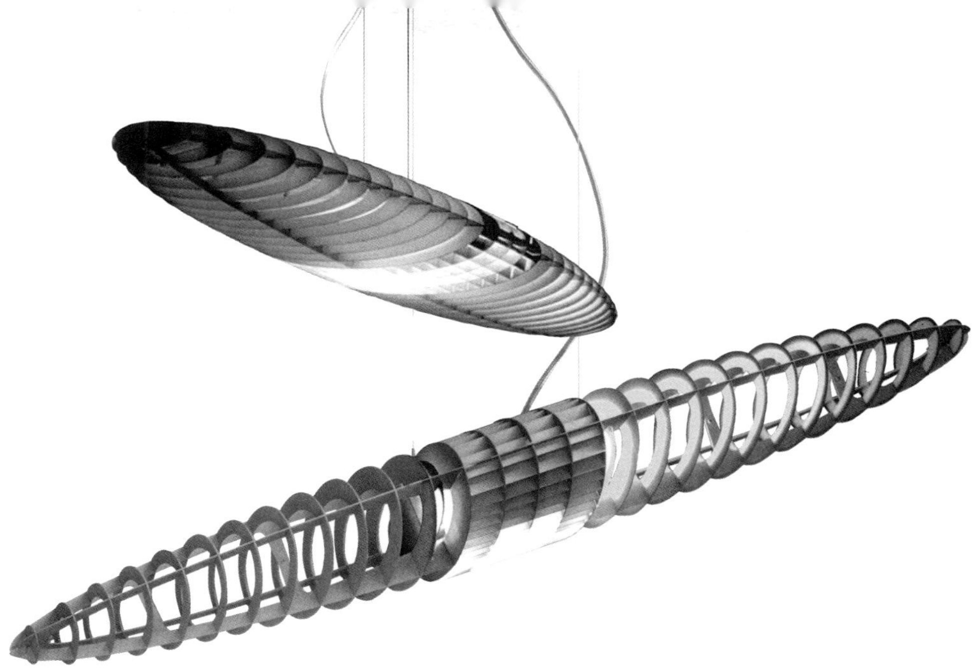

Alberto Meda and Paolo Rizzatto, Titania hanging lamp, produced by Luceplan, 1989.

Storage area of the modular panels produced by Lema.

often turn into entrepreneurs themselves through spin-offs or outsourcing; 6) the companies live in an environment where many workers are descendants of craftsmen, where everybody is exposed daily to masterpieces of arts, and where architects and designers like to engage in industrial design; 7) workers, being shaped by the culture of craftsmanship, have a strong propensity to experiment and to increment innovation, although structured and well funded R&D is usually scarce; 8) most companies are also located in communities with a well developed social tissue, a long lasting tradition of civil rights, great mobility and limited disparities, compounded also by a system of family and social solidarity.

As I have already mentioned, each of the above factors, if taken alone, could look more like a weakness rather than strength. The small size of most companies should be a terrible handicap in a market which is enlarging its borders day after day; the family nature of the companies, while it provides the commitment and the resources of the family, it often inhibits the aggregation of strong managers; the disaggregation of the companies into a group of distinct legal entities rather than in divisions creates a burden of legal and administrative obligations; the co-operation practised in order to exploit economies of a scale unattainable otherwise, given the small size, is often burdensome, slow and inefficient.

Despite all these single handicaps, the combination of the above factors have produced a supply system which is able to produce variety, is very flexible, fosters continuous innovation, provides the right environment for integrating creative designers and keeps costs and then prices under control.

The small companies, each one focused on a single product and often on a single phase of the value chain, practice the principle of "stick to your core business" and they reach a level of specialization which is unparalleled by any other company spread over a portfolio of products and vertically integrated. Of course, being small has also its disadvantages that need to be addressed. Integration in a network, proximity to a pool of companies producing components, and immersion in a rich environment, where access to finance and services is easy, provide the countermeasures for the small dimension. Being small helps a lot when markets are volatile and flexible and niche strategies are needed.

The small size would be a handicap

Paolo Rizzatto, Costanza table lamp, produced by Luceplan, 1986.

anyway in a market that is globalizing, since marketing, sales distribution and aftersales service cannot be provided efficiently far away without a minimum size.

But here another characteristic of the Italian model comes into play: the existence of a number of medium-large companies that play a pivotal role. They outsource a lot of the manufacturing activities to the small, specialized companies, while they develop those steps of the value chain that require a larger dimension. Some American scholars have named this fragmented but closely knitted production model "post-modern" (Priore-Sabel, 1984). They got convinced that such a model is particularly suited for industries where creativity and craftsmanship are key success factors and need to be integrated through flexible organizations. But they are also convinced that it is a model which will take over also the Fordist mass production system which prevailed until recently also in other industries. The new ITC (information and telecommunication) technologies and particularly the Internet will provide the means for connecting a fragmented production system into a cohesive organization potentially as powerful as a large corporation, but much more flexible.

Migration of labour-intensive industries in not inexorable

The Italian industries considered in this essay will continue to experience the pressure from the producers of the less developed countries, just because they are labour-intensive. But an increasing pool of consumers all over the world is looking for differentiated products that need, in order to be produced, not easily replicable intangible competencies, like aesthetic or quality refinements based on rare skills. In these cases countries with high labour costs can not only resist the competition of the new competitors, but they can even expand their activities at the condition that they are ready to expand in the foreign markets to capture these thin but expanding segments.

Italian companies have followed this strategy: they have abandoned or outsourced the low end of the product spectrum and have focused their attention on the high end, differentiated segment of the market and on those parts of the value chain where differentiation is created. By positioning themselves this way, they have escaped the apparently inexorable law that predicts the migration of labour intensive activities away from companies located in the developed countries.

KRD Shona Kitchen and
Ab Rogers, Monster seat,
produced by Edra, 2000.

R. Semprini and
M. Cananzi, Tatlin sofa,
produced by Edra, 1989.

Giampiero Bosoni

Architecture of Interiors 1945–2000

The Italian school and the culture of the home

Achille and Piergiacomo Castiglioni, Rampa cabinet, produced by Bernini, 1965.

A research laboratory of domestic design

To talk of an Italian school of interior architecture for the second half of the 20th century may appear to the most careful scholars of the subject to be bending classifications somewhat. In effect, we need first of all to agree on the meaning of a school brought into the highly structured dialectical context of the design of the domestic space in Italy, of which an adequate historical reconstruction has not yet been attempted, much less an organic in-depth reading.

Generally a school is understood to be an institute where an intellectual community with precise rules divulges a body of knowledge that is common, shared, that is, codified and consequently orthodox. But the school can also be understood to be a model of reference converging towards which are dialectical experiences sustained by common principles and by a similar value of the research, indeed, definable also as a research laboratory, where a space for comparison is offered to different voices, heterodox in methods and with differing languages, yet inspired by common ethical and moral claims in the pursuit of similar utopias.

Above all with respect to other international "schools", more internally "cohesive" and "orthodox", the Italian experience in the planning of interior architecture from 1945 to today (but this certainly also applies to many other spheres of design research), can be understood as a laboratory-school, where certain basic characteristics can be recognized, making it one of the most original forums of experimentation of contemporary living.

A thread made of chosen affinities, of lively debates, of experimental exposures, of personal research on common bases, interweaves this history. The fact remains that the strong personalities that have studded its evolution – many of whom are recognized today as the authentic masters of the architecture and design of the 20th century – have represented both strong theoretical positions and original poetics, giving rise to many different design directions, each of which merits a school of its own. Just as in some prestigious universities there are great thinkers representative of different schools of thought working and comparing notes, the set of contributions arising from this Italian laboratory of the domestic project can be seen in the same light.

To better understand this apparently complex and disjointed context, we also need to bear in mind that in Italian architectural culture the planning field defined as architecture of interiors has always found considerable difficulty in constituting itself as an autonomous discipline. This is because the modern culture of Italian architecture has always conceived a continuity of architectural space and design on all scales, rejecting specialist subdivisions and particularly the merely furnishing conception of the domestic space. With respect to this, although there are many examples that can form a path in their own right for the interior architecture project, this design field has in fact participated in a full sense in the history of modern Italian architectural culture.

This condition in some respects has surely dignified its general design value, but unfortunately has also consequently reorganized its contribution with respect to the architecture of the city, not making the richness and scope of the research conducted starting with the domestic interior sufficiently clear.

It is a specific innovative field in which the phenomenon of the design of Italian furniture has come to life, but also the place of experimentation of new typologies for the contemporary home, which in many cases have been able to anticipate the times, inspiring original forms for the home, even on an urban scale.

Giovanni Muzio, Muzio home in the Ca' Brutta building, Milan, 1919–22.

Giovanni Muzio, furnishing in Minetti house at Presolana, 1925.

From the "old Italian-style home" to the "new home" (1928–1940)

Architecture and design in Italy after 1945 cannot be understood unless we establish at least some fixed points in the lively and deeply-felt cultural season experienced by the country between the two world wars. Interwoven in the twenty years dominated by Fascism, between bitter disagreements and fatal attractions, is the research work into Italian Rationalism and Neo-classical forms expressed by the group of artists and architects denominated "Novecento". In the background of these design laboratories, we hear the echo, in a deep undertow that merges everything together, of the noisy mocking provocations of Futurism and the intense suspended expressions of Metaphysical painting. The list of authors and works of this historical phase would be too long to digest in this text, which is intended to look in depth at the period following the Second World War, but a couple of references to certain theoretical positions that were to remain constant in the following decades deserve to be remembered. A first milestone is the editorial entitled "La casa all'italiana" (The Italian-style Home) written by Gio Ponti in 1928 for the first issue of the magazine *Domus*, founded and edited by him, with a few interruptions, until 1977. The role performed by this publication until today in the field of architecture and design makes the reading of some passages of this declaration of love for a timeless Classical model even more meaningful. "In the old Italian-style home", wrote Ponti in 1928, "there is no great distinction in architecture between interior and exterior; elsewhere there is even a separation of forms and materials: here the architecture of outside penetrates inside, and does not neglect to use inside, as outside, either stone or plaster or the fresco... From the interior the Italian-style home comes back out into the open with its porticoes and terraces, with pergolas and porches, with loggias and balconies, covered roof-terraces and belvederes, comforting inventions for serene dwelling and both in Italian and in every other language they are called with the names from here... The old Italian-style home is outside and inside without complications, it welcomes household furnishings and beautiful works of art and wants order and space between them, not crowds and mess. It comes to be rich with the modes of grandness and simplicity, not with those of preciosity. Its design does not descend solely from the material demands of living. So-called 'comfort' in the Italian-style home is not only in things to meet needs, the conveniences of our lives and the organization of facilities. This 'comfort' lies in something superior: it lies in giving us a measure for our very thoughts with architecture" (Ponti, 1928). If on one hand such a homage to a certain Italian tradition of the home well represents the artistic culture of the "Novecento" group (of which Ponti himself was part in those years), on the other we find in this text the roots of a classic key theme of Ponti, the so-called "Italianness factor" (Ponti, 1930), which, in its long course through the debate of European modern architecture, was also to constitute a recurrent motif for his work as ambassador of the Italian model. Ponti's crafty capacity to make maintaining the "Italianness factor" – which, as he explained, guaranteed the "authenticity of origin" – appear "useful" and "winning" for the economy of the country, undoubtedly anticipated with great foresight the conditions of the success of Made in Italy products. This was a conception of the Italian model that Ponti knew how to convey with great elegance and not a little unscrupulousness throughout the whole war period with the magazine *Stile*, which he created and ran from 1941 to 1947, abandoning the editorship of *Domus* for that period (for a lucid historical reconstruction of the life of *Stile* magazine, see Martignoni, 2001).

Luciano Baldessarri, two studies for Bolchini house, 1933.

Ignazio Gardella, interior of the Gardella apartment, 1937.

Franco Albini, Albini apartment in which may be seen the famous Veliero bookcase (1938), the radio cabinet in Securit glass (1938) and the Mitraglietta armchair lamp (1938), Milan, 1940.

However, if for Ponti everything is linear and harmonious, the complexity of the cultural and aesthetic tensions that were manifested in the period between the wars, also with respect to furniture design and interior architecture, is perhaps better represented by the elegant thought of Edoardo Persico, the theorist of reference of Italian Rationalism. In an unfinished essay, written in 1935, which did not reach print, entitled *La casa nuova* (The New Home), Persico affirms that "the idea of a new home is not a 20th-century paradox, a polemical pretext; but something extremely serious in which the moral destiny of the modern European is committed" (Persico, 1935). The housing cell, according to a typical expression of the Modern Movement, is in fact the element placed at the basis of the formation of architecture, and hence of the urban whole. There are many authors (Figini and Pollini, Terragni, Baldessarri, Albini, Muzio, De Finetti, Asnago and Vender, Mollino, Cosenza, Libera, Pagano, Levi Montalcini, and so on) to whom the flowering of this theme in those years was due, and it was especially in that period, thanks to these protagonists, that the theme of interiors developed according to autonomous and parallel declinations. In this regard, from the experimental and programmatic standpoint, it was thanks to the research work on housing models proposed at the Triennials of 1930, 1933 and 1936, as Giacomo Polin has written, that the history of the home in Italy had an "exemplary" development" (Polin, 1987).

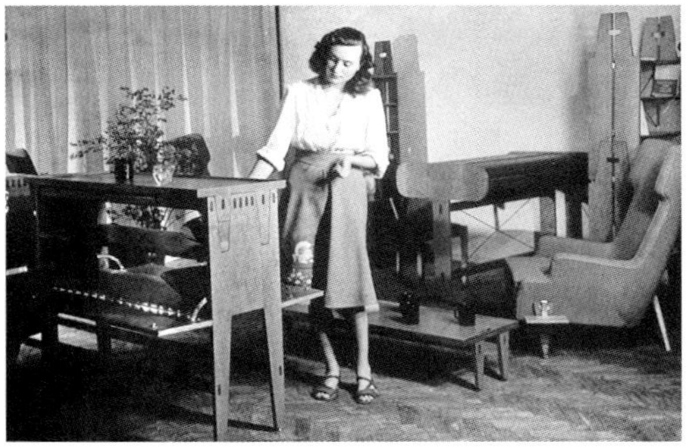

Ignazio Gardella, domestic space fitted out for the RIMA exhibition, Palazzo dell'Arte, Milan, 1946.

Vico Magistretti, corner of the domestic space with small folding cloth armchair and bookcase with movable shelves, prepared for the RIMA exhibition, Palazzo dell'Arte, Milan, 1946.

The reconstruction and Neorealism

In 1945 Italy was a country severely scarred by the destruction produced by the war. The collapse of the Fascist regime that for twenty years had governed the country's life, suffocating free and civil cultural growth and politics, sparked new and exciting democratic prospects for the reconstruction of the country. A new cultural and artistic season, defined as Neorealism, also pervaded the search for new housing models and new furnishing elements that civil society urgently needed to reconstruct houses and cities.

The Neorealist spirit set old intimist and aristocratic models in opposition to the new democratic and social values represented by the people who were building this new history: workers, farmers and partisans. The Roman school, with Mario Ridolfi and Ludovico Quaroni at its head, but also the Florentine school led by Michelucci, well represented that research into the spontaneous and vernacular architecture that is most associated with the idea of "Neorealism" in architecture. The discourse concerning the Milanese school is a different one; here this moral commitment was deeply felt, but was immediately interpreted in the Rationalist and industrial programme passed on by the masters of Modern architecture who tragically died during the war: primarily Pagano, Persico and Terragni.

In 1946 Ernesto Nathan Rogers was called upon to edit *Domus*; he was the theorist of the BBPR group, who opened his brief editorship with a new and symbolic half-title: "Domus - La casa dell'uomo" (Domus - Man's Home). In his first editorial, where he recalled the miserable conditions of the cities destroyed by the war and the extremely urgent need to design useful and practical houses and furniture, Rogers observed, among other things: "a house is not a house if it is not warm in winter, cool in summer, calm in every season to welcome the family in harmonious spaces. A house is not a house if it does not contain a corner to read poetry, an alcove, a bathtub, a kitchen. This is the home of man ... it is a matter of forming a taste, a technique and a moral, as the terms of the same function. It is a matter of building a society. There is no time to waste on illustrating trifles" (Rogers, 1946).

The magazine opened a section entitled "Pronto Soccorso" (First Aid), where five young architects (Gandolfi, Latis, De Carli, Tevarotto and Mongiardino) proposed certain solutions in the sphere of the reconstruction to meet precise housing demands for different users. These new Neorealist proposals, tending towards the formulation of a new language, translated – especially in the Milanese area – into the search for sectional, transformable furniture, into experimentation of new materials. In that period there were certain important events, such as the RIMA (Italian Meeting of Furnishing Exhibitions), the Fede Cheti exhibition, the 8th Triennial (1947), participating in which, with their projects, were architects who would leave their mark on the history of Italian architecture and design, such as Gardella, Magistretti, Castelli Ferrieri, Chessa, the Castiglioni brothers, Albini and Zanuso. Various research paths were then being developed within interior architecture, which – as well as showing interesting interpretations of Neorealist expression to meet the demands of reconstruction – also showed a need to broaden their own horizons, rebuilding interrupted dialogues both with international research work, and with the historical roots of the culture of the home in Italy. Particularly the US and Scandinavian experiences, and the reconstruction of an enlightened bourgeois world, the ideal model of a cultured and evolved society within a cultural and constructive tradition, were the focal points from which to trace these new perspectives. Ponti had long had much to

Ettore Sottsass, relaxation area for domestic space prepared on the occasion of the Fede Cheti furnishing exhibition, Milan, 1949.

Carlo Mollino, Orengo house, Turin, 1949. View of the studio area.

teach, with his idea of Italian creativity founded upon the handcrafting experience of this country. Moving on a different plane, decidedly more of a Rationalist matrix, but in some ways similar to that of Ponti, were Luigi Caccia Dominioni, Ignazio Gardella, the young Magistretti (all three also united by the experience of production for Azucena) and Franco Albini, interested in reaching, also in the field of interior architecture, a synthesis between the old and the new, the ancient and the modern. A case apart was the design line of Carlo Mollino, who was to continue his original research into domestic space, working with the materials of history interspersed with fragments of modernity, to fit out fluid, oneiric environments, the expression of a radical interiority. A similar case to Mollino's, as regards autonomy and originality, but with a totally different poetics, was to also begin to distinguish the "narrative" research of Carlo Scarpa, impregnated with the Byzantine refinement of the Venetian area, grafted onto the impassioned reinterpretation of the organic design of Frank Lloyd Wright.

Economic recovery and the birth of Italian design

In the meantime, at the Triennial in Milan the theme of industrial design was becoming increasingly clearly established, with the appearance, in the cycle from the

Carlo Scarpa, apartment in Venice, larch staircase and polished plaster wall composed with rectangular geometries, 1947.

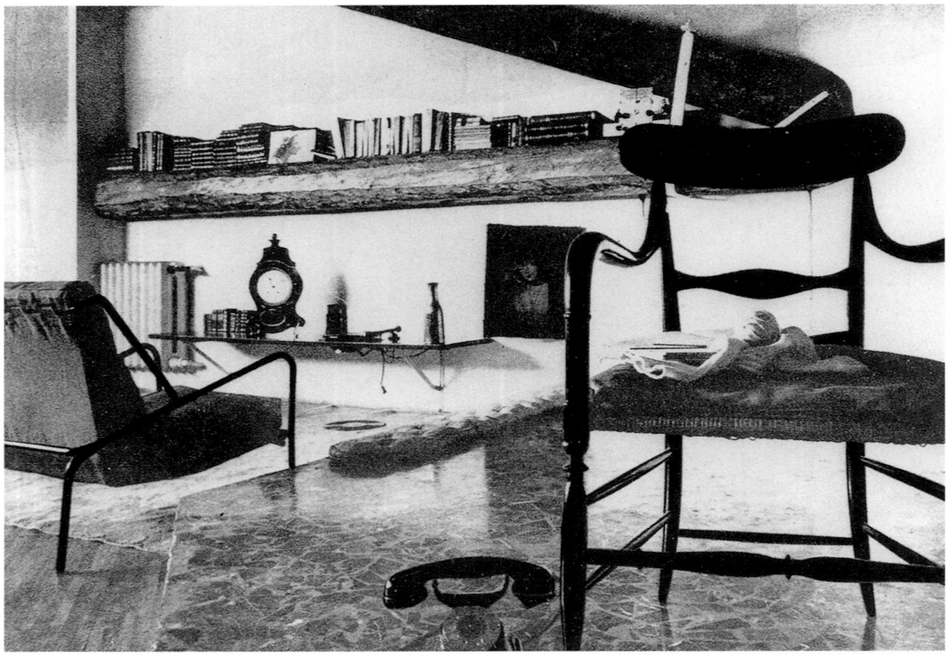

Marco Zanuso, apartment in an attic, Milan, 1949.

Ico Parisi, an architect's home-studio, 1957.

Vittoriano Viganò, Viganò home, Milan, 1956.

9th (1951) to the 11th (1957), of furniture design as the strong point of this innovative drive. Standing out in this field were the research projects into the industrial production of foam rubber padded seats by Marco Zanuso for Arflex (1951), followed by those by Borsani for Tecno (1954). But, apart from some sporadic exclusively industrial projects, long to remain a constant of Italian furniture design was the fact of arriving at mass production after initial conception as single items for specific housing spaces. In the mid-'50s a meaningful watershed was the emerging personality of Vittoriano Viganò, who, thanks precisely to certain symbolic works in interior architecture, and particularly in his house (1956), was to be recognized at an international level as one of the most interesting representatives of the tendency that in the '50s was to be nicknamed "Brutalism", of which Le Corbusier, with his new creative vein, was indicated by many to be the leader. Beyond the "Brutalist" label, which restricts too much to one period what was an architectural itinerary supported by the continuous commitment to merge design ethics and artistic research in his work, Viganò represents the attempt to bring architecture with a capital A "to the unifying vision of 'an integral architecture' in which every part, fragment or detail is included" (Muselli, 1995). The Viganò house became a model of reference particularly on account of its wise interplay of affinities and contrasts between colours and materials, in a continuous mutual pursuit of complementary elements, "positive and negative", stalactites and stalagmites, in a chiaroscuro sequence with frequent changes of scale, in the search for the maximum unity and continuity of interior spaces.

With the economic recovery, what had been the emergency planning of the post-war period became an industrial problem that saw many planners giving rise to a major process of renewal of the models and forms of consumption, particularly for the home. From the Triennials to the competitions announced by the exhibition centres of Brianza, from the initiatives of the La Rinascente department stores (see the Compasso d'Oro prize for 1956) to the Milan Fair, which in 1961 saw the creation of the Salone del Mobile (Furniture Show), arriving at the competitions announced by the trade magazines, everything moved towards the creation of a production and commercial system to target the domestic sphere.

Trolley with silver carafe designed by Cesare Lacca, made by Piero De Vecchi, circa 1955.

The economic boom and the reconstruction of a middle class universe

By now the premises of Neorealism had run aground in a crisis brought about by a series of "failures" that definitely dampened the illusions and hopes matured in the enthusiasm of action. These were years when the certainties of the Modern Movement were now placed in doubt, and were translated by most into a sterile and cold International Style. So there began that phase of coming to grips with history and the environmental "pre-existences" that was to lead to a series of very significant creations, such as the Casa alle Zattere (1958) by Gardella in Venice and the villas in Arenzano (1956) by Magistretti. The paladin of this new Italian path of the "orthodoxy of heterodoxy" (Rogers, 1957) was E. N. Rogers, who was editor-in-chief of *Casabella* from 1954 to 1963, and in turn with the BBPR group, in the forefront also as an architect with the design of the Torre Velasca in Milan. In this period, the research work by Scarpa, the BBPR group and Albini played a particularly significant part in what Tafuri defined as "the furnishing of the 'houses of art'" (Tafuri, 1982), namely museums. This first shock wave was to be added to a few years later, with a front that was even more openly "historicist", "i ragazzi di *Casabella*", that is, the editing team composed of A. Rossi, V. Gregotti, G. Aulenti, G. Canella, and with them other external collaborators, such as Umberto Riva and Roberto Gabetti, who in 1960 were to "burn their velleities", as Tafuri has written (*ibid.*), in the exhibition *Nuovi disegni per il mobile italiano* (New Designs of Italian Furniture; Canella and Gregotti, 1960). This episode, provocatively defined by some as "Neoliberty" (Zevi, 1959a and 1959b; Portoghesi, 1959), and commented on by the well-known English critic Raymond Banham as "the childish Italian retreat from the modern movement" (Banham, 1959) was to become a groove into which research of

Ernesto Nathan Rogers, Rogers apartment, Milan, 1958.

Gio Ponti, Villa Planchart, Caracas, 1955.

Ignazio Gardella, apartment inside Casa alle Zattere, Venice, 1958.

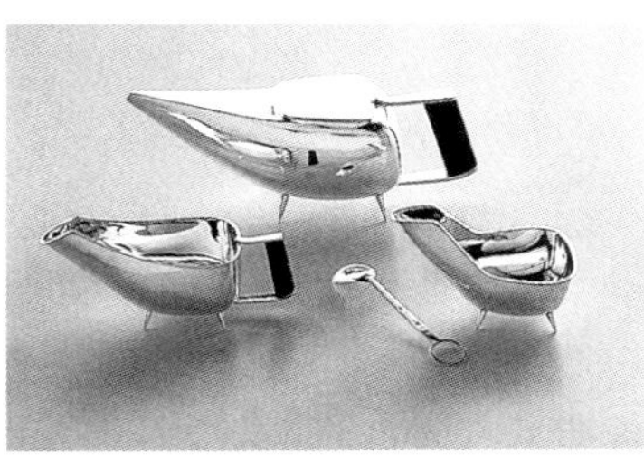

Gio Ponti, silver tea service, made by Piero De Vecchi for Calderoni Gioielli, 1956.

Gae Aulenti, Neo-liberty living room, 1960.

Ettore Sottsass, furniture unit in Tchou house, 1960.

Ettore Sottsass, detail of a living room with an element of the Kubirolo sectional system (1965) and the Asteroid lamp (1968), designed by Sottsass for Poltronova.

great interest would be channelled, but also a tortuous path in which marshy bends would be created where many epigons of the most banal "revisionism" would be concealed.

Destruction and monumentalization of the domestic space in the consumer society

With the early '60s the scene changed and some new masters came under the spotlight, masters completely free from the ideological and disciplinary antecedents that had conditioned the architectural culture of the '50s. On one hand Ettore Sottsass and on the other Joe Colombo, both architects closer to the artistic ferments of the period than to the academy of architecture, gave rise to two separate research programmes, conducted also through the design of objects for the home, especially in the design of the domestic environment, interpreting the social and technological revolutions under way. The former, with a series of creations regularly published by Ponti in the magazine *Domus*, almost as a programmatic path, drew a new domestic landscape made of "warm", collective, informal spaces, punctuated with symbolic figures and "sacred places", representative of a destructured system that uses "emotions" and "sensations" as a compositional material. The latter author, also extensively published by Ponti in *Domus*, tended to represent a society that had transcended its archaic models and entered a modernity made of plastic capsules, which included every hypertechnologizing functional component, paving the way for a high-tech idea of the home conceived as a "total furnishing unit" where the elements that compose it decrease in number, each tending to become a full-blown service machine. Inside these two alternative proposals we see the watermark on one hand of the American artistic avant-garde of Pop Art and the quasi-mystic utopias of hippie counterculture, and on the other the futuristic utopias of the radical avant-garde, especially the English Archigram group.

It was to be in this climate of great renewal, in which many fences were seen to fall, that at the University of Florence, far from the Milanese and Roman hegemonies, the avant-garde of Italian radical architecture took shape. Their research into the housing conditions and the characteristics of the city, in the age of the "continuous consumer fair", form the basis of many important transformations in the designing of increasingly informal and destructural objects for the home. Particularly the groups Archizoom (A. Branzi, G. Corretti, P. Deganello, D. Bartolini, L. Bartolini, M. Morozzi) and Superstudio (P. Frassinelli, A. Magris, R. Magris, A. Natalini, A. Poli, C. Toraldo di Francia), but also other personalities and groups that came to grips in those years with the Radical phenomenon, such as Gaetano Pesce, Ugo La Pietra, Piero De Rossi, Nanda Vigo, Alessandro Mendini, De Pas, D'Urbino and Lomazzi and the young Michele De Lucchi, were the standard-bearers of new visions of the domestic space. A turning point was marked by the exhibition *Italy: the New Domestic Landscape* staged by Emilio Ambasz at the MoMA in New York in 1972, where the creation of fourteen experimental environments designed by some of the main Italian designers of the period constitute an interesting frame of reference.

The design field of interior architecture was to meet with particular attention in the '70s, to the point of almost creating a specialization, as in the case of Gae Aulenti, Cini Boeri, Afra and Tobia Scarpa and Carla Venosta. Once again, as had happened for Gardella, Magistretti, Caccia Dominioni and Albini in the '50s, the phenomenon of the transfer of the research into the design of made-to-

Joe Colombo, apartment in Via Sismondi, Milan, 1963.

Joe Colombo, Visiona 1 habitat, produced by Bayer, 1969.

Gae Aulenti, the Collector's house, Milan, 1969. Photo Ugo Mulas.

Cini Boeri, Bobo sofa, one of the first examples of monoblock seat made exclusively using polyurethane foams without internal structures, produced by Arflex, 1967.

Archizoom, some images of the *Residential parking lot* series, 1971.

measure elements for the home into mass production was repeated. The open-plan space, often played out on a number of levels, appeared as an increasingly destructured environment in which living was done informally. The living-room, which even in Italian was to be habitually called "living", tended to encapsulate a number of functions of the home, becoming a kind of experimental condition of the "loft" space. These were the years when modularity came out of the kitchen and became the compositional standard of small and large sectional containers, reaching the point of the accessoried wall for the home. A strong complete and coordinated character nevertheless remained present, with the tendency to give a uniform and very made-to-measure design. We had not yet reached an authentic "casual" construction of the domestic space, as was seen in students' residence halls. The question of houses for all, after the urgent needs of the post-war period, returned to being a powerful social question that rekindled an interest in minimal housing models and also in original solutions, such as the reclamation of industrial spaces.

New metaphors in multicultural living

The Memphis phenomenon of the early '80s continued to see Sottsass as protagonist, this time accompanied by new young travelling companions, after the years of success of Italian design with a rationalist, industrial and technical stamp. Now it relaunched an explosive, colourful, symbolic design that alluded to new metaphors of the multicultural and multiethnic home.
The growth of the global market, sustained by the media strategies on the new horizon (advertising, magazines, television), enabled design to become a commodity in its own right, which prevailed over the product itself. People

Archizoom, Mies armchair, produced by Poltronova, 1969.

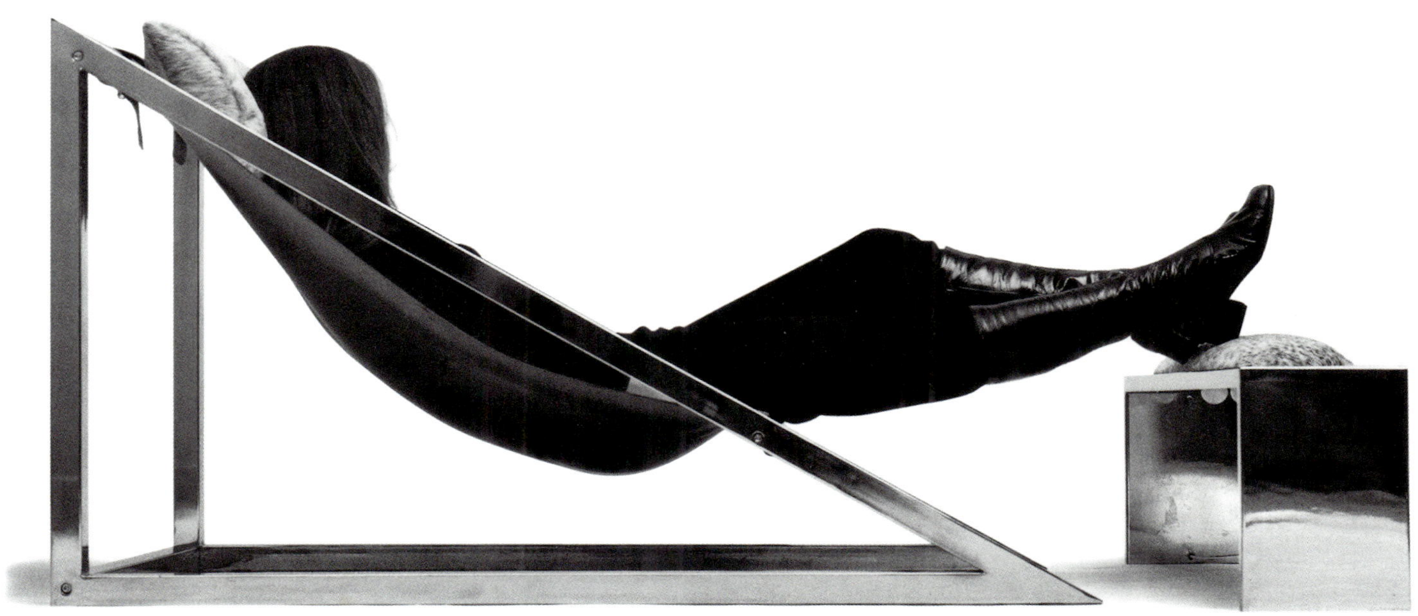

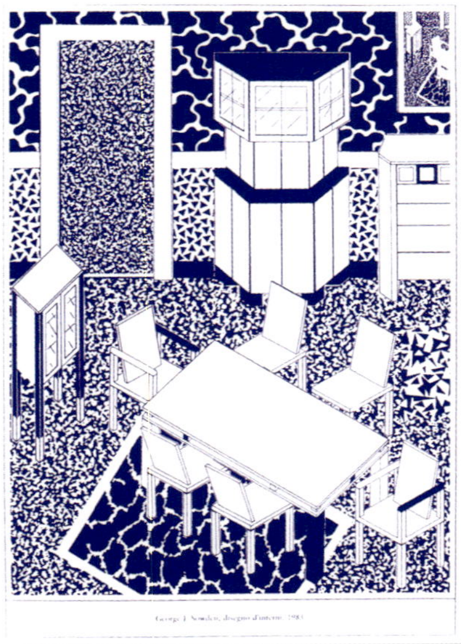

George J. Sowden, design of domestic space fitted out with furniture produced by Memphis, permeated with designs by the Memphis group for Abet Laminati, 1983.

Masanori Umeda, Ring Tawaraya bed, produced by Memphis, 1981.

sought the name, the representation, the model of reference: a phenomenon that – not by coincidence – accompanied the growth of Italian *prêt-à-porter*. The expression "Postmodern", indiscriminately used to justify all the forms pouring onto the market to satisfy, with old or new stylemes, the demand for linguistic pluralism, became the buzzword for most of the '80s. But this Postmodern condition, as it had been defined by its main scholar, the French philosopher Paul Lyotard, acted much more in depth and represented radical cultural and productive transformations that led to the definitive disappearance of the contrasting of strong and dominant thoughts. We witnessed the proliferation of forms, of styles, of fashions, a galaxy of fragments of thoughts, seen by some as the proof of a new "democracy", and by others looked at with the concern to identify in this chaotic scenario the signs of a superior and hidden power tending to homogenize consumption.

However, as we have already said, the Italian course of interior architecture, being not very dogmatic and potentially pluralistic, was vaccinated, so to speak, against this gravitational phenomenon. New authors, the bearers of new research, continued to join, but they also were the continuers in their own way of certain design schools inspired by the masters of the '30s. The projects by Umberto Riva (Milanese school) and Toni Cordero (Turinese school) were meaningful in this regard. Over the years, Riva proved one of the busiest enthusiasts of interior architecture, showing in his autonomous and patient work an original reworking of that particular Rationalist experience with elements of a certain surrealism typical of Albini, Persico, Figini, conjugated with the magic organic visions of Scarpa, inspired by Wright, or even the clear spontaneity of Ridolfi, arriving at a unity of fragments in perfect harmony with each other.

Toni Cordero, who recently passed away,

Umberto Riva, Insinga house, Milan, 1989.

Gaetano Pesce, Shuman apartment, New York, plan and views of the living area, 1991.

with his fragmentary and sometimes Baroque figures, embraced the scenographic and oneiric settings of Carlo Mollino, renewing their charm.

The "new simplicity" and the revival of mental and moral customs

Thus, we come to the late '80s and early '90s, where we note a general tendency towards a new "simplicity".
A Neorationalist seam was reaffirmed, softening over the years under the denomination of "Minimalism".
Distinguishable in this renewed continuity of Rationalist research, particularly that of the Milanese school, were the design paths of Antonio Citterio, Pierluigi Cerri and Guido Canali. In particular Citterio, who had become one of the best-known designers in the sector of furnishing elements, devoted himself to a sort of exercise of style around the rich catalogue of forms developed by the architects of Milan and Como from the '30s to the '50s.
A separate case is that of the research by Gabriella and Massimo Carmassi, which developed primarily in the tradition of masters such as Albini and Scarpa, in the increasingly light and harmonious refinement of the relationship between ancient and modern. This constant theme of the Italian experience in interior architecture found a renewed value in the widespread tendency to go back to living in the historic centres, particularly those of the small towns.
At this point, the so-called Italian school of interior architecture made another generational leap and opened up to new approaches, without forgetting the work of the masters. Let us recall the tidy signs of Claudio Silvestrin, who paid homage to the abstract spaces of the more metaphysical Rationalism and at the same time also to his direct master A G Fronzoni; let us also recall the composite and voluptuous forms of Italo Rota, who paid homage to different masters, through a particular course going from Mollino to Albini, via Ponti. We cannot fail to mention, in this case, that the most significant works of these authors are found in London, Paris and

Italo Rota, apartment in Paris, 1989.

Toni Cordero, apartment in Mantua, 1998.

Claudio Silvestrin, house in Provence, 1996.

Claudio Lazzarini and Carl Pickering, apartment in Montecarlo, 1997. *Above*: day and night views of the terrace. *Opposite*: living area.

New York, the latter city where "old" Gaetano Pesce, with unbiased mastery, has recently designed highly evocative interior architectures, authentic manifestos of his avant-garde poetics. Yet it is not a matter of seeing in this an internationalism of Italian interior architecture, as is now evident for fashion and design, but rather to confirm an international interest in that historical matrix of the Italian style for the home. Thanks also to magazines such as *Abitare*, *Domus* and *Interni*, an attention and a debate was kept alive on interior architecture, which enables us to see architects of the latest generation at work (Calvi, Merlini and Moya, Lazzarini and Pickering, Camagna, Camoletto and Marcante, Manolo De Giorgi, Marta Laudani, Marco Romanelli, Bruno Vaerini, Studio GA, Massimo Curzi, Nardi, Migliore and Servetto, Raboni and Della Giusta, Giussani, Antonio Besso and Caturegli and Formica, among others), dedicated with passion to the regeneration of this domestic space. We may conclude by attempting a list of the constants maintained by the laboratory-school of Italian architectural culture in the designing of interiors: the context, the environmental "pre-existences" as a value to come to grips with, respecting it, converting it point by point, or working it by counterpoint; the continuity between inside and outside, partly as a natural correspondence to the geographical condition and partly as a confirmation of a constant search for the organic vision of architecture; material and chromatic research, always conducted on a programmatic plane and not a purely decorative one; the absence of a certain model of reference, but rather the pursuit of a fleeting ideal model that always leads to an experimental risk tending to transcend the most orthodox schemes; the privileged relationship with artistic avant-garde research as a critical instrument of reflection to experiment with new dimensions of the domestic space; a narration by fragments recomposed in an internal equilibrium within the specific system; the solution of detail supported by age-old handcrafting experience.

A confirmation of this continuity can also be read in a quote from Gio Ponti. This time the Ponti of the '50s, who in his splendid book *Amate l'architettura - L'architettura è un cristallo* (Love Architecture - Architecture Is a Crystal), in 1957, forecasting a bright future for the domestic space, commented as follows on his 1928 text in *Domus*, with which we began our historical excursus: "This is the old Italian-style home: how will the modern one be? We will be capable of making a modern home, but like this? ... Is it the empty, abstract home? Or is the home 'with us', living? If art is the possibility of the impossible, the home must be admirable as though it were empty and intimate as though it were full. The perfect home is the one that stops us on the open threshold, intimidated by its human secret and by its architectural beauty... From this ancient home we extract some perennial laws, perennial mental and moral (philosophical) habits and not forms (although some may say that forms and customs coincide): let us continue them in our different forms. We cannot be sure that forms and customs coincide. Certain forms have died, even if we still use them, and certain moral and mental customs are alive, they are rediscovered, in new, pure forms" (Ponti, 1957, pp. 107–108). At the start of a new millennium, in an age of transition, where major epochal transformations are brewing, these words may appear to some to have been transcended by events, but in our view the future of an original Italian school of interior architecture, and of design for the home and architecture in general, is its strength and its regenerative spirit in that broad cultural scope recalled, almost fifty years ago now, by Gio Ponti.

Francesca Picchi

The Landscape of Daily Life

List of industrial forms deposited in the archives of Italian model patents

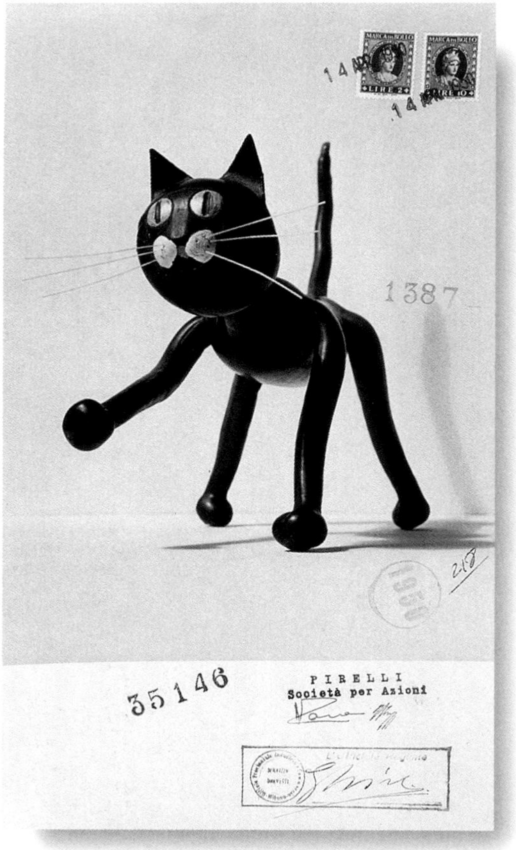

Bruno Munari, Meo Romeo toy cat, produced by Pirelli. Ornamental patent deposited on 20 September 1950.

Bruno Munari, Zi-Zi toy monkey, produced by Pi-Gomma. Ornamental patent deposited on 30 May 1953.

What makes a typewriter a typewriter? What makes a bucket a bucket? An armchair an armchair? And what do the forms of these very different objects have in common, as though they were linked by a common thread?

There is a period in the history of objects (which it is possible to frame within the first post-war years in Italy) in which artists, intellectuals, architects, poets, philosophers, but also common people, housewives, artisans, mechanics, gamblers – in short, everyone – seemed attracted by a mirage: to improve the world with the force of thought. Or to invent themselves a new world made of typewriters so smooth and sinuous as to attract to themselves the benevolent caresses of the most inveterate typists, or sewing-machines so slick and shiny as to give the sensation of intoxicating speed even for such sedentary activities (does the Mirella sewing-machine by Marcello Nizzoli perhaps not express a swift line worthy of even the most aerodynamic racing car?).

That is it. I think that the strength of the Italian design of the post-war period (when it was a matter of starting from scratch after the *tabula rasa* of the war) lay in the capacity to dream: the dream of consumers who found in their hands objects so dense with meaning as to make them believe that, along with a basin, they were taking home the tangible sign of the progress of technology and the wonders of industry, but also the dream of the designers who entrusted the secret of a possible change to their projects and used them to focus on the prospect of a new world.

Italian designers, faithful to a cultural continuity that recognizes its roots in the distant history of the Classical world or the Renaissance, did not limit themselves to seeking the correct correspondence to a specific function in everyday objects: they expressed the ambition for objects to speak of something else; that same type of illusion of which Siegfried Giedion speaks (in his admirable introduction to that sacred text of design, *Mechanization Takes Command*), when in a normal coffee spoon he perceives a mirror in which the sun is resplendent. This feeling was not the aspiration of a dreamer isolated from the world, but the conviction shared by a whole generation of intellectuals, persuaded that beauty was something to which everyone had the right (who borrowed from a foreign language the name "designer" when its meaning was not yet clearly understood). Industry appeared on the horizon as the instrument, the means that would allow them to put the dream into effect, to multiply it and disseminate it at affordable prices: any home inhabited by objects and machines so perfect could no longer be touched by evil and injustice; a little like Socrates thought, when he affirmed that only those who know good can refrain from practising evil. No intellectual could refuse to seek the arcane secrets of a beauty to share and give generously through what then must have appeared to be the most appropriate vehicle for promoting the modernization of the country and thus spreading a new doctrine of comfort and happiness: everyday objects. Objects must have seemed the most immediate means of directly communicating a model of life inspired by sun, light, air (the celebrated triad of the modern home), and not forced into houses packed with objects weighed down by memories of a past that could not have produced anything much good if it had led to the disaster of the war.

Some phrases taken here and there from the editorial that Ernesto Rogers wrote in January 1946 for his *Domus* dedicated to "man's home", faced with an Italy still stunned by the devastations of war, describe the awareness of an arduous task and at the same time the essential tension towards utopia and the dream: "Those who travel through Italy, along the Aurelia or the Via Emilia or in the Puglias or in

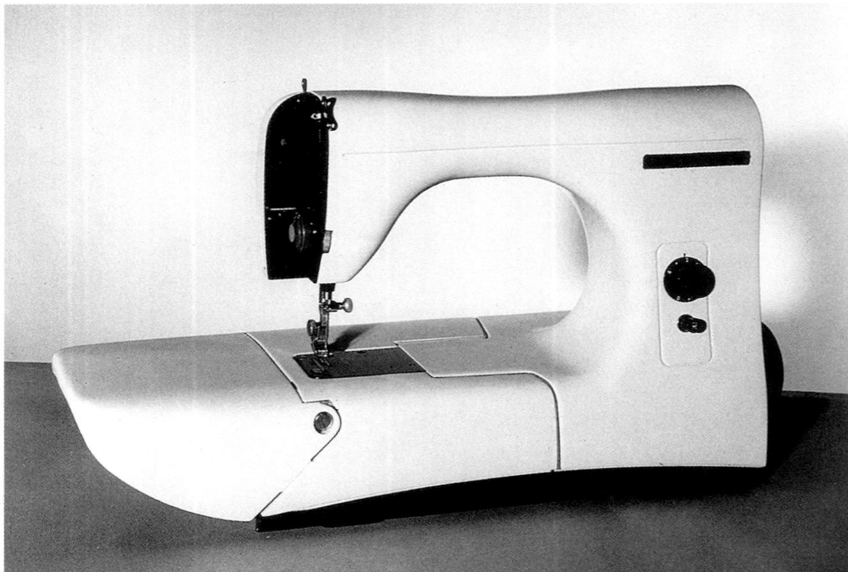

Marcello Nizzoli, Mirella automatic sewing machine, produced by Necchi, 1957. Ornamental patent deposited on 26 January 1958.

Production phase of the die-cast aluminum body of the Mirella sewing machine, 1958.

Advertisement for Mirella sewing machine, "studied and created to give every home a modern machine with minimum encumbrance", in *Selezione*, 1958.

La prima macchina per cucire
in tutto il mondo
così bella
così leggera
così pratica
così economica
mirella

la nuova
splendida NECCHI
studiata e realizzata
per dare ad ogni casa
una macchina moderna
di minimo ingombro.

elettrica
L. 66.000
+ I.G.E.

a mano
L. 49.000
+ I.G.E.

NECCHI
La macchina per cucire più bella

Inviando questo tagliando alla NECCHI S.p.A. - PAVIA - riceverete gratis un pieghevole illustrativo della nuova NECCHI "Mirella" la macchina per cucire più bella

118 *Febbraio*

albergo ricorse a una variante di questa tattica. Piú volte aveva notato una bella ragazza nell'atrio dell'albergo, ma non aveva mai avuto il coraggio di parlarle. Scrisse allora una lettera spiritosa e lusinghiera, la mise in una busta e s'avvicinò alla ragazza. « Scusate » le disse con disinvoltura, come se fosse un impiegato dell'albergo « credo che questa lettera sia per voi. Il vostro nome è... » Finse di leggere l'indirizzo, come se gli riuscisse difficile decifrarlo.

« Smith » disse pronta la ragazza. « Mary Smith. »

L'uomo tirò fuori la penna e mentre la ragazza l'osservava perplessa scrisse solennemente sulla busta: « Signorina Mary Smith. »

« Sí » disse con serietà « è per voi. » Gliela porse, fece un inchino e s'allontanò. Rimase ad aspettare, dandole tempo di leggere la lettera e di pensarci su. Quando le si avvicinò di nuovo fu accolto da un cordiale sorriso.

Ma la classica presentazione, secondo me, fu quella escogitata una sera da un mio conoscente ad Amburgo. Cenando in un buon ristorante, notò una bella ragazza sola a un tavolo. Si regolò in modo da finir di mangiare contemporaneamente alla ragazza e quando questa fu pronta ad andarsene si alzò anche lui. Mentre la giovane scendeva gli scalini che portavano in istrada, il mio conoscente le si avvicinò e le disse: « Scusatemi, potreste darmi un'informazione? » Il tono era importante... fece la sua richiesta con serietà, come un turista a un altro, come se avesse domandato che tram

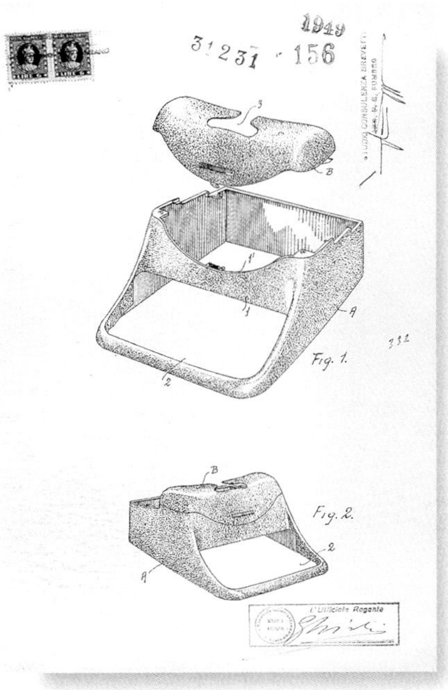

Marcello Nizzoli, Lexicon 80 typewriter, produced by Olivetti, 1958. Utility patent deposited for the die-cast aluminium body on 28 April 1949.

Sicily, see an immense decay: ruins upon ruins. Certainly, the same is true of Provence or Brittany. The same goes for every road in Europe." Faced with this essential reality, he cannot help but wonder: "What value does beauty have for this people?" Later in the editorial he states with conviction: "No problem is solved if it does not respond to utility, to ethics and aesthetics at the same time."
All this shows that the problem of form was not to be considered a secondary one.
At this point it is worth opening up a parenthesis. In Rome, conserved in an austere building designed by Giovanni Muzio (chance would have it that he was the same architect who designed the Triennial in Milan: a place intended to be the Mecca of design), are the hundreds of thousands of model patents deposited in the years of the Italian post-war period, recently restored and offered again, after years of oblivion, for the public to consult. The overflowing of the River Tiber years earlier had separated this fragment from the rest of the documents compiling Italian inventiveness from the unification of Italy to the present. The random choice of circumstance, made through the river, could not have proven more fortunate, as it allows us to isolate our study to those brilliant years in Italian design culture.
First of all it is necessary to mention why the patent document, and its relationship with the concept of design, are considered so important. With the expression "industrial model" the laws indicate summarily "a category of intellectual creations that, in a first approximation, can be identified with the *original form of an industrial product*".
Ornamental model or utility model patents represent a form of legal protection (they protect the ownership of an idea), as they attribute the right of exclusivity on the new forms of an industrial product, whether functional or aesthetic. The inventor's property right is only recognized for a certain period of time, after which the idea becomes the patrimony of the community, who can profit from it as they see fit. This is the democratic principle on which the idea of progress is founded: a common good that is nourished by the initiative and creative capacity of the individual. The words of the legislator clearly articulate that "the idea must contain a creative contribution with respect to the intellectual patrimony of the age in which it is devised; it must possess a certain something to qualify it": I believe that it is in this "certain something" that the meaning of the design can be recognized.
It can be easily understood that the issue of industry and the renewal of the everyday landscape was an open question for the men and women coming out of the war. At the time when the question of the form destined to be multiplied by the machines made available to industry touched a category of intellectuals who were "experts in form" (are we not in fact talking of intellectual creations?), the debate opened up to include discourses of a higher order, touching the meaning of form, the concept of original, the principle of industry contrasted with that of craftsmanship. In an age when, according to the statistic data, most Italian workers were employed in the agricultural sector, the challenge of industrialization could not leave insensitive a generation of intellectuals who were in the front line in the battle for formal and social renewal. The hope of every possibility of economic "recovery" was entrusted to the industry on the horizon.
There is no need to underline that the debate was extensive and wide-ranging. Industrial design was greeted like a lighthouse illuminating the road in "determining the alliance of art and production within a harmonic culture", as Marco Zanuso stated on the occasion of the 10th Triennial in 1954, one of the famous Triennials of Design, during which the first "exhibition of industrial design"

Lodovico Barbiano di Belgiojoso and Enrico Peressutti, with graphics by M. Huber, *La forma dell'utile* exhibition, 9th Triennial, Milan, 1951.

Achille and Piergiacomo Castiglioni, with graphics by M. Provinciali, *Mostra internazionale dell'industrial design*, 10th Triennial, Milan, 1954.

was held. Designers of great class, enthusiasts and activists of design (Achille and Piergiacomo Castiglioni, Roberto Menghi, Marcello Nizzoli, Alberto Rosselli, Augusto Morello, Michele Provinciali) took part in the debate, facing head on the "problem of form in the industrial production process". As a commission, they sifted through all the products of which they had become aware, to admit among the ranks of an exemplary production 150 objects considered of such indubitable quality and beauty as to become models of that fusion between art and industry that was so sought after. This selection of course included Scandinavian, German, Swiss, US and Canadian designs.

In the same year, 1954, the Compasso d'Oro competition was set up by La Rinascente department store to play the important role of aesthetic arbiter; at the same time the magazine *Stile Industria* was founded, becoming the place for theoretical discussion around these themes. It was "the first Italian magazine of industrial design" to be directed at "industries, the public, the artists, to affirm and promote the aesthetic values of the product" and to declare "the need and actuality of a new relationship between aesthetics and production technique, or rather, between art and industry". From the pages of the first issue, under the large black type of the editorial entitled "Design, a factor of quality", Alberto Rosselli, who was its editor-in-chief, expressed the need to combine "utility and beauty". In the following issue Gio Ponti seems to order the terms of the problem: "While in primitive people the 'original' form of things (weapons, amphorae, objects, etc.) is pure, true, essential, in our modern civilization, so fertile with technical creations and new usages, the initial form with which an infinity of new things is manifested is paradoxically contaminated by superimpositions of every kind, traditional or stylistic, or of fashion pure and simple; our innovations are not born pure and naked, but immediately dressed in fashion. To reconstitute the original purity of the relationship between form and function is today a fact on another level, which is on the elevated plane of a higher order of culture and sensibility, derived from a full-blown aesthetic demand for which we feel the mental need to take objects to what should have been their true, original form, to give them back their essential form. But what is this Italian line? It is not a new calligraphy; it is not a fashion; it is the result of having conceived the forms of things only concerning ourselves with that essence with which we operate in art, of having conceived them without commercial concerns." As can be noted in these few lines, the language itself moves under a constant dialectical tension: the word industry is inevitably combined with the word art; production with quality; technique with aesthetics; utility with beauty; practical values with human values. Italian designers spoke of industry and thought about art, man, a better society.

So the question on the table was: what is the true essence of industrial form? It was clear that this offered the opportunity for a great work of formal renewal and cultural updating.

Yet, while the selections of products used as examples in the exhibitions, in the competitions and on the pages of the magazines, corresponded to a certain nobility of the production and in a certain sense represented the peak of a complex and fragmentary phenomenon, as was the framework of a country in the process of industrialization, the submerged or parallel world that coexisted with that model of quality did not escape the attention of the meticulous cataloguing work on the "original forms of industrial products", implicit in the normal patent practice; indeed it sometimes ran after it, attempting to emulate it, or even went down paths that were frankly bizarre.

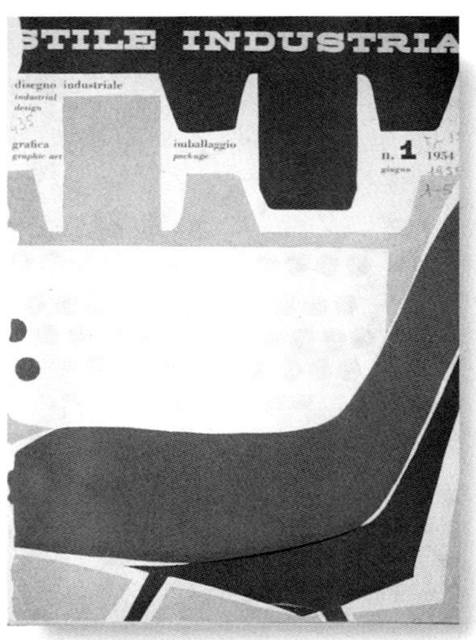

Cover of the magazine *Stile Industria*, no. 1, 1954, showing the profile of the DU30 chair, designed by Gastone Rinaldi for RIMA, 1954.

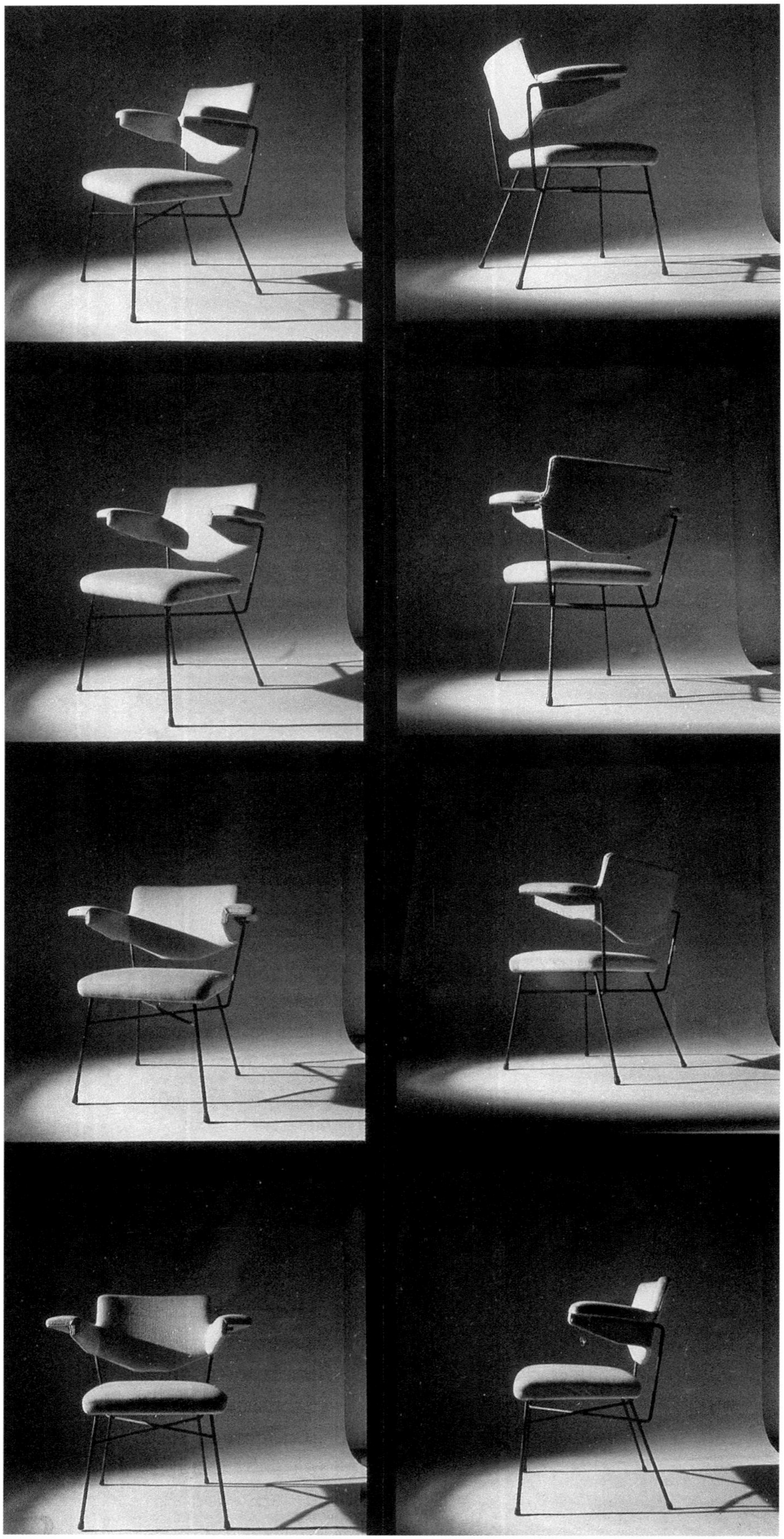

Belgiojoso, Peressutti and Rogers, Neptunia chair, produced by Arflex, 1953. Ornamental patent deposited on 6 February 1957.

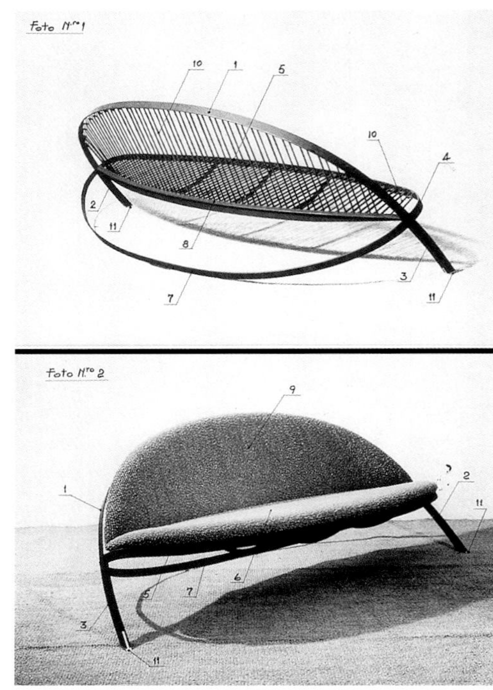

Gastone Rinaldi, Saturno sofa, produced by RIMA, 1958. Ornamental patent deposited on 12 October 1958.

Gastone Rinaldi, DU30 chair, produced by RIMA, 1954. Ornamental patent deposited on 23 February 1954.

Carlo De Carli, model 683 chair with curved plywood surfaces on heartwood structures, produced by Cassina, 1954. Ornamental patent deposited on 30 June 1954.

Gio Ponti, model 852 sofa with fabric designed by Lucio Fontana, produced by Cassina, 1954. Ornamental patent deposited on 10 July 1957.

Franco Albini, Gala cane armchair, produced by Bonacina, 1951. Ornamental patent deposited on 7 March 1958.

Marco Zanuso, Lady and Senior armchairs, produced by Arflex, 1951. Advertising image from a Pirelli-Sapsa and Arflex brochure.

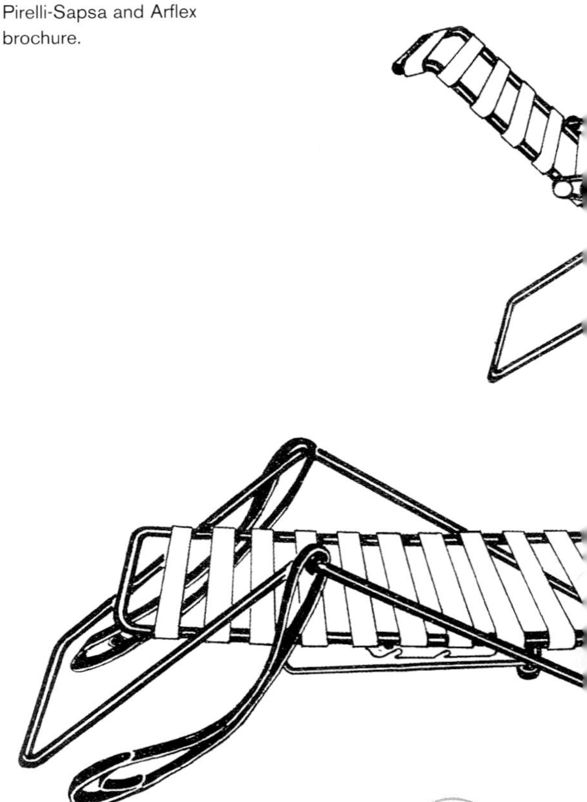

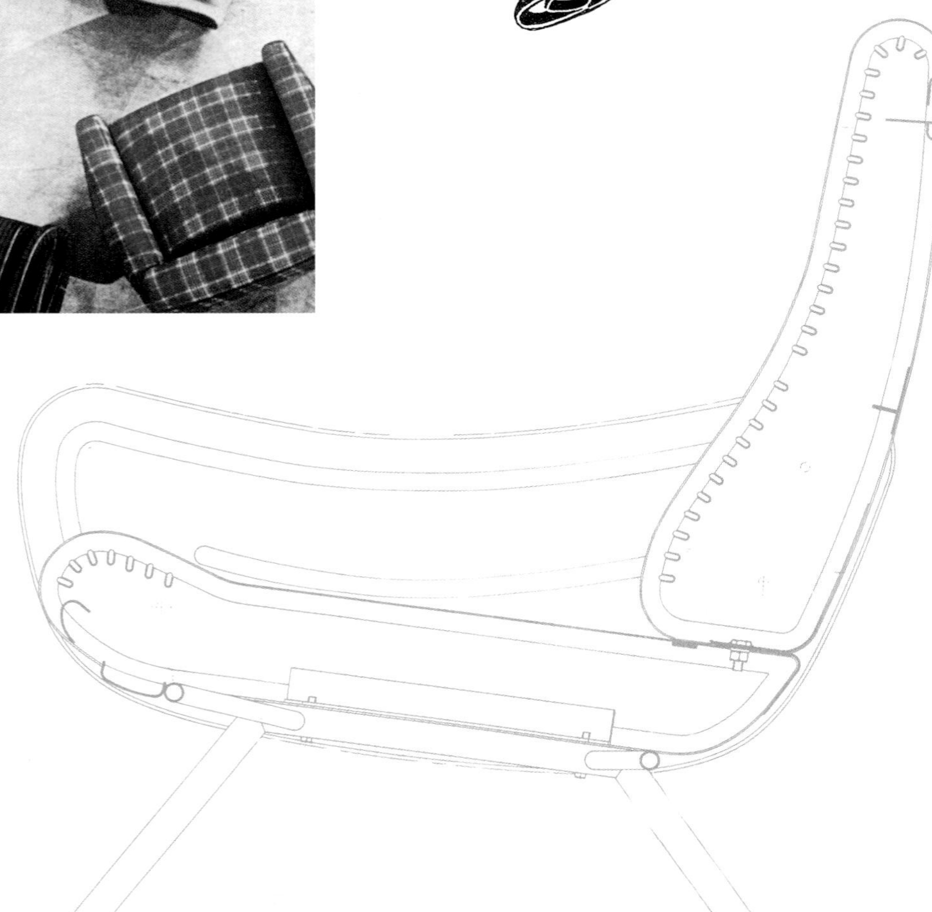

Marco Zanuso, Lady armchair, produced by Arflex, 1951. Design of section where the metal structure, the hooks for the elastic bands for suspension and the thicknesses of the foam rubber padding are visible.

Marco Zanuso, iron tubing and Nastrocord folding sofa-bed, produced by Arflex. Utility patent deposited on 11 March 1954.

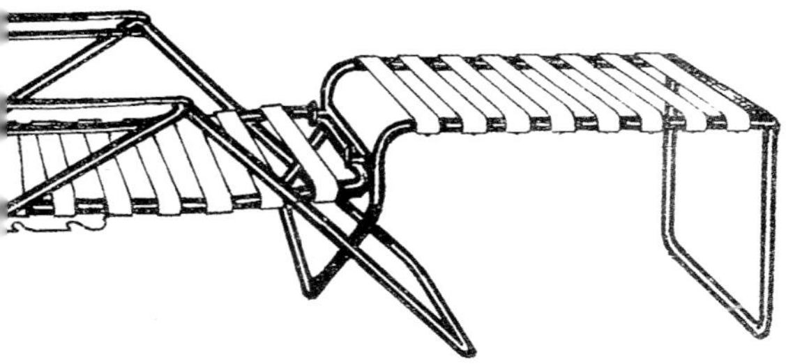

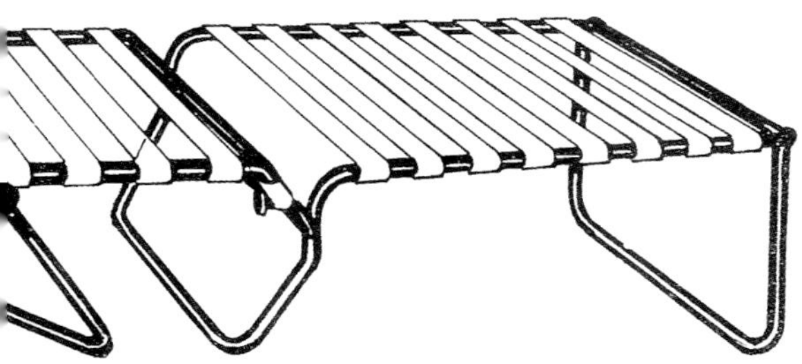

Marco Zanuso, St. Moritz model, iron tubing folding bed, Nastrocord and foam rubber mattress, produced by Arflex, 1951.

When Marco Zanuso (who was among the first to experiment with the use of foam rubber as a modern material for industry) recalls the absolute innovation that the Lady armchair introduced into the slow market of Italian furniture, still dominated by dynamics of production that were, broadly speaking, artisan, he does not hesitate to underline: "Immediately after the Triennial, Arflex [the company that produced the armchair, ed.] carried out a survey at the Fiera Campionaria [Trade Fair] where there was a sector devoted to furniture. From this research it transpired that a hundred copies had been made of the Lady alone, not to mention those that imitated its construction system. Arflex decided to publish warnings in the newspapers. This worked as indirect advertising that established the value of the original. It is no coincidence that the Lady was extensively copied. After years, someone in Brianza candidly confessed to me: 'I bought my first lorry with your Lady.'"

This memory allows us to understand the direct effects, a kind of chain reaction, that the original forms of industrial products could trigger on the productive infrastructure of a given region, in this specific case Brianza, one of the geographical areas with the highest patenting tendency, counting hundreds of patents for armchairs and couches with innumerable shapes and innovative performance characteristics.

The archives that house the patents are a large repertory of industrial forms, whether good or bad. Nobody was to feel left out, every carpenter in the Brianza, every housewife with sartorial skills, every player with a minimum of statistic knowledge, every car body repairer dreaming of being an artist could compete in the lottery to be one of those rewarded by industry. In the archives, as a physical place that embraces all inventors with impartial benevolence, high culture (represented by Gio Ponti, Salvatore Ferragamo, Dante Giacosa, BBPR, Bruno Munari, Vico Magistretti, Leonardo Sinisgalli, to name just a few...) meets that anonymous people of inventors left to their often misunderstood destiny.

It is a huge warehouse of ideas, where inventiveness does not have hierarchies or internal divisions. And if "the idea is the first state of the thing bound to live", the landscape described by the set of patents represents a world of imagination, which, all in all, is different from that later realized.

Just as the indigenous people of Melanesia built simulacra of aircraft in the forest

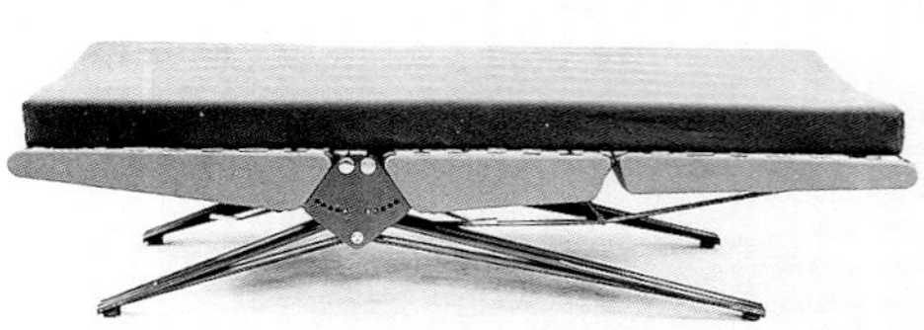

Osvaldo Borsani, model L77 bed with multiple adjustable transversal sections, produced by Tecno, 1958. Ornamental patent deposited on 20 May 1958 and utility patent on 12 May 1958.

with branches and lianas, in the hope that one day the aeroplanes that flew over their heads would settle by them, so, in many cases, the patent appears to be a propitiatory rite, a simulacrum that houses the expectations of a better future for those not waiting indifferently for things to change but getting on with active participation in the preparations for this future that seems to await them.

The patent can be imagined as a sort of identity card of objects: the forms are deposited and entrusted to the community for ratification in a parallel general register of objects (which records the hows, wheres, whens and whys: people, dates, places where the inventions were germinated, summary descriptions of the innovations of the invention itself…).

There is no doubt that it is also a precious source of documentation, on account of the continuance – a little pedantic, to tell the truth – of a method of filing in which every single data item contributes to a larger design like a piece in a mosaic.

In the end, from this unusual and fragmentary design there emerges a portrait of Italian industrial history in a particularly successful period for the history of design: an unusual and fragmentary body of work, like the industrial fabric itself, made of small and medium-sized businesses.

The very structure of the archives – in which authors, designers, engineers, DIYers, curious entrepreneurs are found on the same plane, inspired by an inventive spirit rendered more alive by the mirage of success and the possibility of hypothetically multiplying infinitely their own individual contribution to the solving of the problems of the world – gives preference to a reading where the projects or, to use the legal term, the original forms, of industrial products are inserted into the continuous flow of things as though this were a non-stop concatenation. In the same way, the new landscape of daily life appears as a unitary body where forms – from Ferragamo's shoes to Dante Giacosa's microcars, to Roberto Menghi's or Gino Colombini's plastic buckets, to Gio

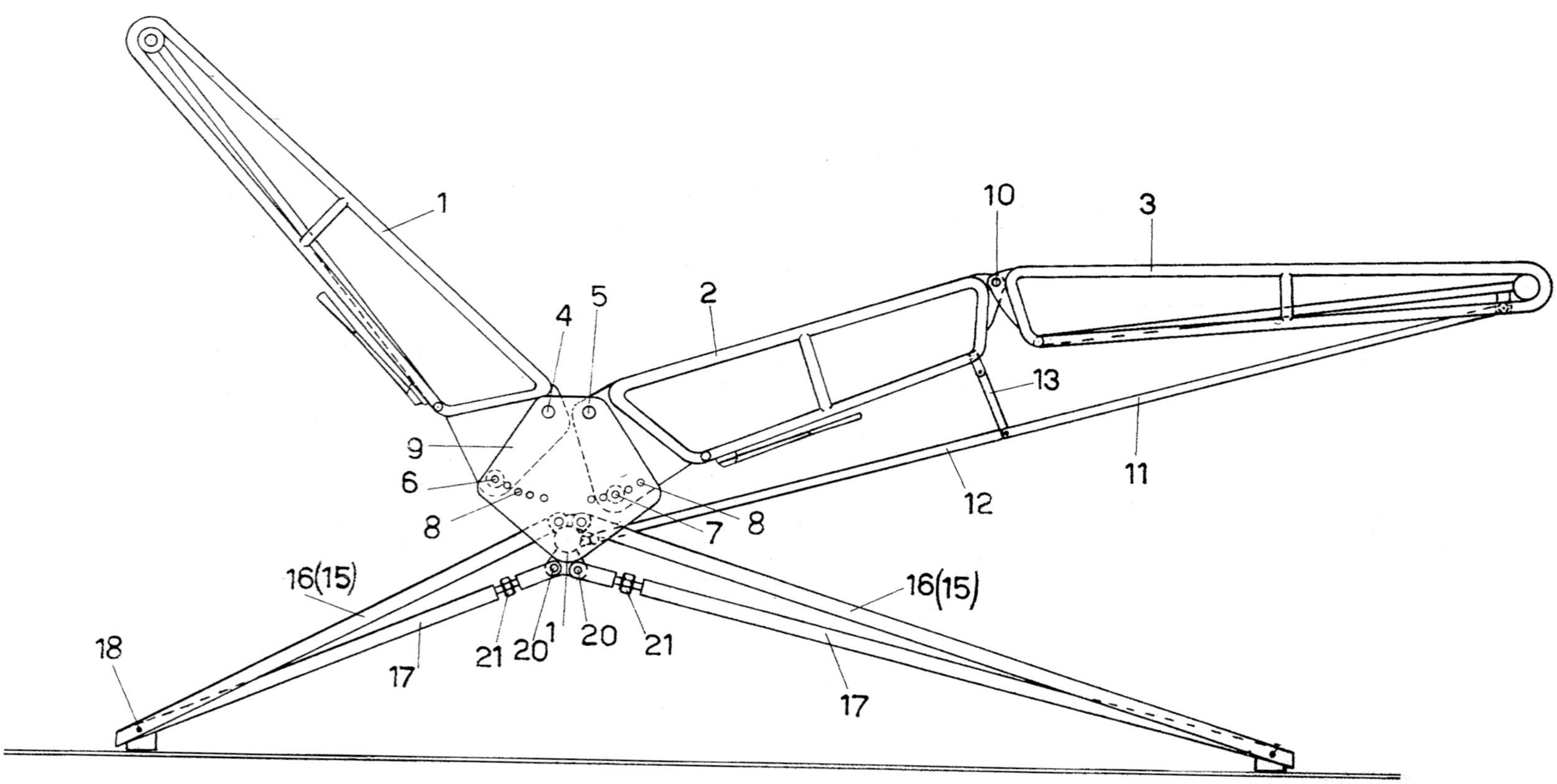

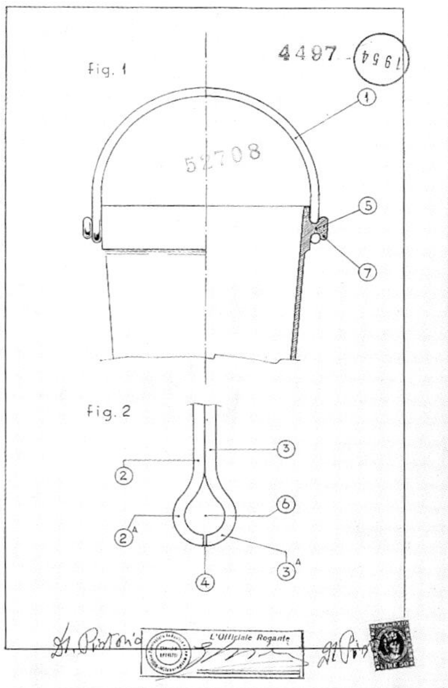

Above and below, right: Gino Colombini, plastic bucket with detachable handle, produced by Kartell. Utility patent deposited on 19 February 1955.

Ponti's bathroom items, to Munari's rubber monkeys (together with their copies, or at least the ranks of products they sparked off) – participate in a common ideal that links them all with a thread. The new landscape was not born by spontaneous generation, but as a result of the programmatic commitment of a generation of intellectuals and entrepreneurs, attentive to the continuity of a tradition and at the same time devoted to a modernity that has its acme in the ideal stated, sought after and wanted with uncommon clarity of intent by Adriano Olivetti, in art, urban planning and production. We need only reread the words of Alberto Savinio, who, in *Ascolto il tuo cuore, città*, writing about Vicenza, a highly conservative, provincial city, recalls how "the only note of glaring modernity [is] the Olivetti shop in Corso Umberto. But in all the cities of Italy the Olivetti shop is the most modern note, even in the Galleria in Milan, a place so rich in modern notes". How could we not cite, then, the opening in New York of the Olivetti shop designed by BBPR and Constantino Nivola on Fifth Avenue, again in the decisive year of 1954.

The windows of the Olivetti shops, like the windows of La Rinascente, devised by designers such as Bruno Munari or Max Huber, and also the pavilions at the Fiera Campionaria in Milan or the décor of the Triennial, disseminated images of a modernity still distant from that which inhabited the "real" domestic environments, if it were not for those industrial products that were the direct emanation of that ideal.

We must not forget, however, that behind those models that we can consider to be the key ones, there was a stream of small-scale artisans and medium-sized industrial companies eager to follow along the new paths, echoing those examples in a smaller scale production that proved decisive in renewing and disseminating the image of a new and, perhaps, finally modern country. Thus the "house of man" of which Rogers speaks or Ponti's "Italian-style house", with the superfluous cleared

Roberto Menghi, plastic containers, produced by Smalterie Meridionali, 1957.

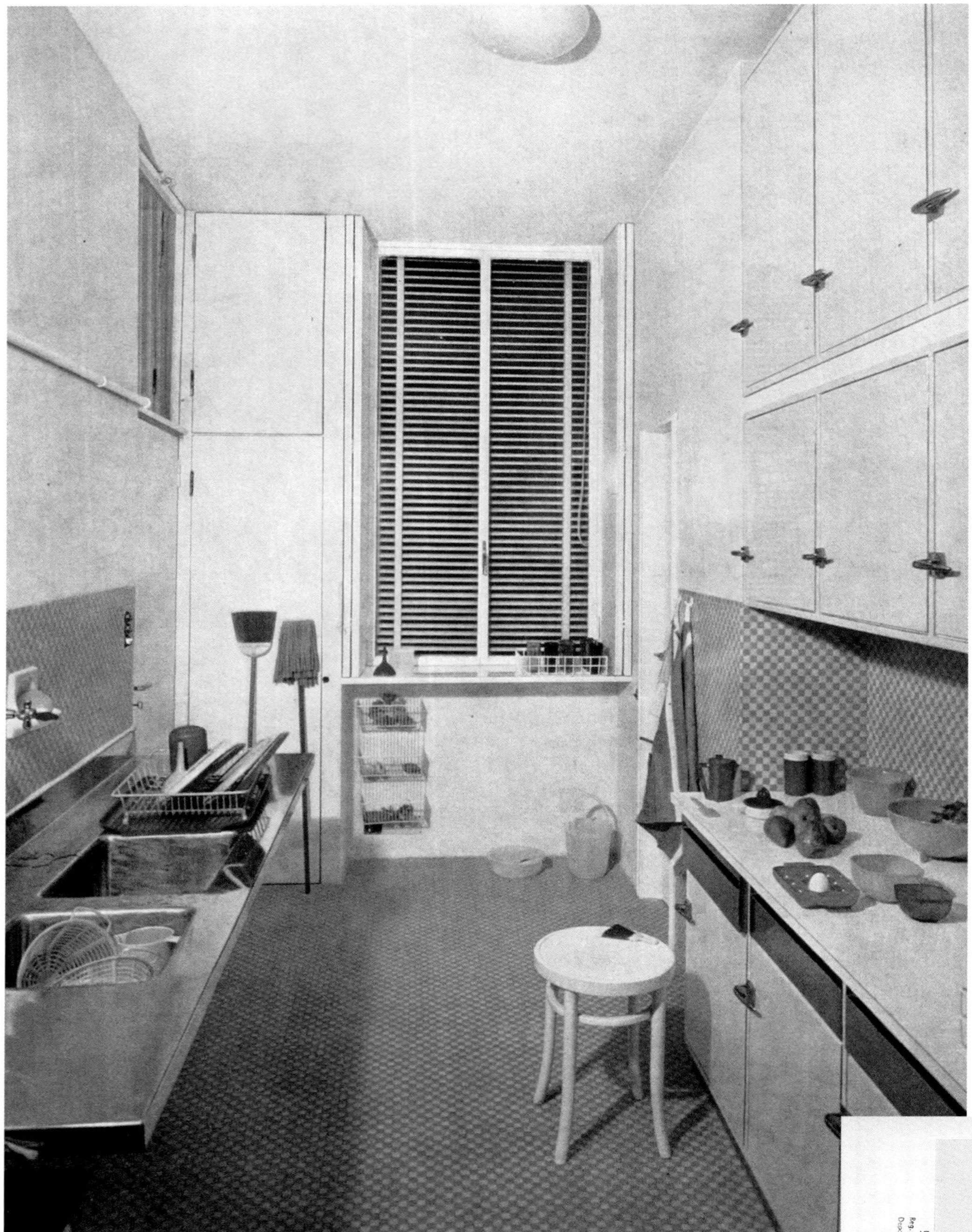

Interior of a kitchen in the mid-'50s in which various plastic elements stand out.

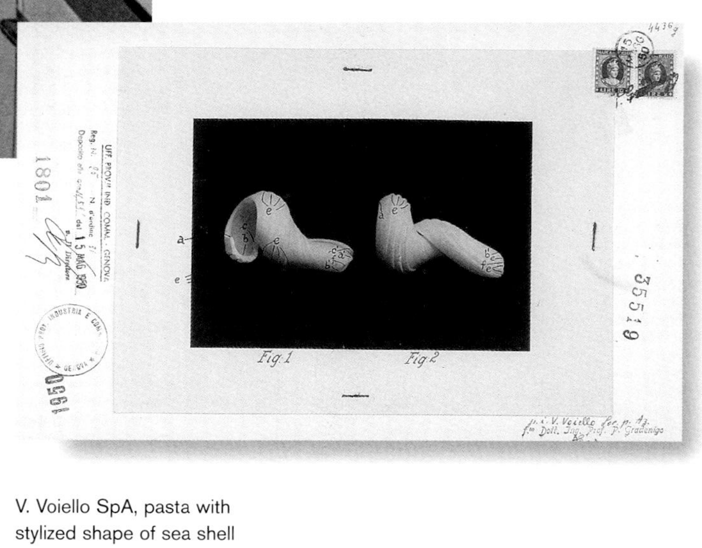

V. Voiello SpA, pasta with stylized shape of sea shell with helical coils. Ornamental patent deposited on 25 October 1950.

Gio Ponti, serie Z sanitary facilities, produced by Ideal Standard, 1954. Ornamental patent deposited on 9 February 1954.

away, airy and flooded with light, was ready to welcome transforming, flexible, demountable furniture, covered with "washable and resistant, economic and impermeable" covers, whether these were the "mechanical furnishings" of Tecno or the "flexible furnishings" of Arflex. Houses inhabited by Nizzoli's domestic machines, smooth as river pebbles, or by Kartell's humble objects made noble by the colour and lightness of plastic, or by Danese's objects worthy of being displayed in an art gallery; houses populated by the lanky lamps of Gino Sarfatti, who studied every detail to diffuse light in every direction, or by the elegant lines of the furnishings of Azucena, founded in 1947 by those sophisticated and resourceful architects Luigi Caccia Dominioni, Corrado Corradi Dell'Acqua and Ignazio Gardella, or by the elegantly experimental couches and armchairs of Cassina (thanks also to Pirelli, who made modern materials such as Nastrocord, Vipla and Plastivir, to name just a few, available on the market).
How can we not remember the experimentations in forms and materials of Gastone Rinaldi, who from Padua offered stimuli to seek new application technologies? (Such as when, inspired by the aerial plots of Harri Bertoia's chairs, he dedicated himself to repeating their plastic transparency, using a type of metal mesh employed for hen-pens and which in the long term proved a rather tiresome semi-finished item to work with.) These people, together with many other enlightened entrepreneurs, undertook to transfer the high quality level reached by centuries-old handicraft production to an industrial production that was finally "modern" and, at the same time, typically Italian.

Roberto Menghi, Libralux lamp, with support fitting on any surface, produced by Lamperti, 1948. Ornamental patent deposited on 30 September 1947.

Achille and Piergiacomo Castiglioni, Toio floor lamp, produced by Flos, 1962. Ornamental patent deposited on 7 November 1962.

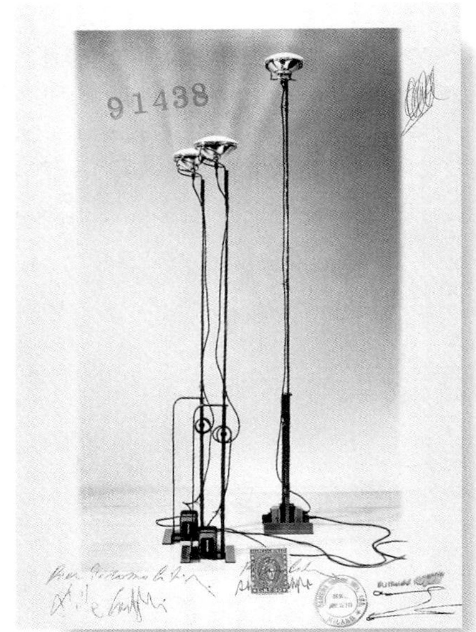

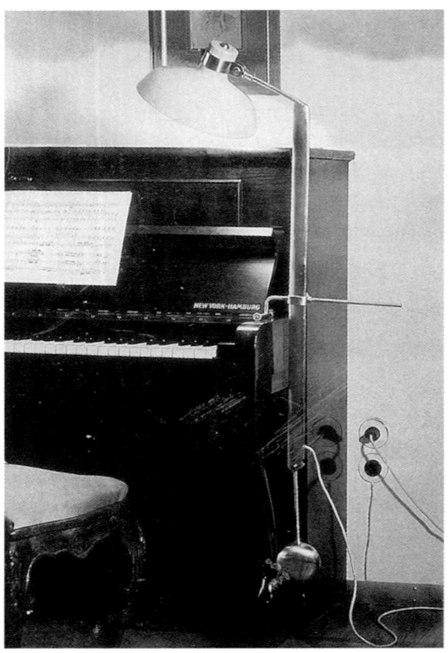

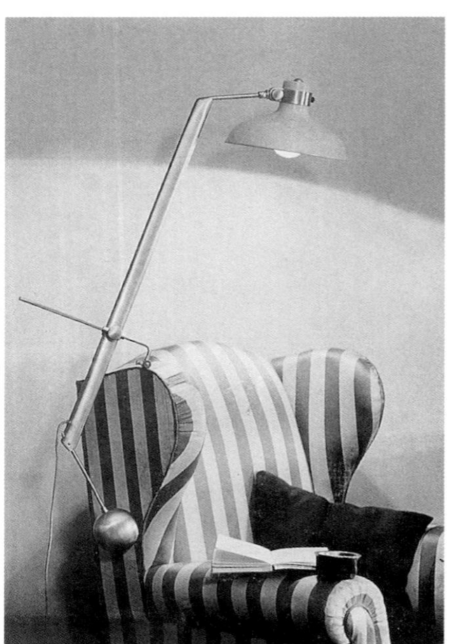

Achille and Piergiacomo Castiglioni, Arc floor lamp, produced by Flos, 1962. Ornamental patent deposited on 7 November 1962.

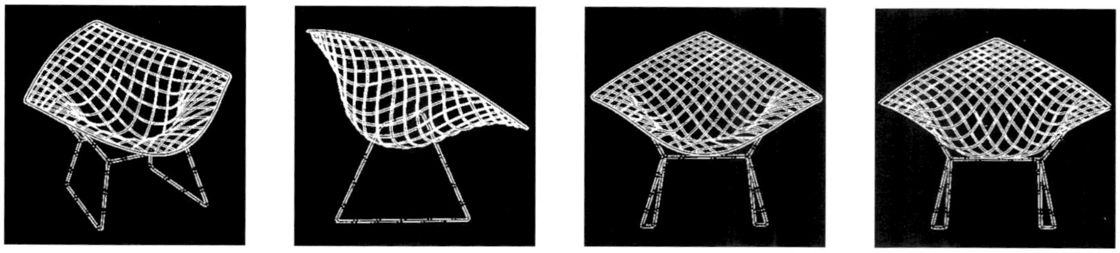

Harry Bertoia, Diamond welded metal wire armchair, produced by Knoll Associates, 1953. Italian utility patent deposited on 27 May 1953.

Gastone Rinaldi, small armchair made of a single piece of metal mesh, supported by legs obtained from a single tubular metal element, produced by RIMA. Ornamental patent deposited on 23 February 1954.

Above and right: Gastone Rinaldi, small armchair for variable use, produced by RIMA. Utility patent deposited on 22 October 1954.

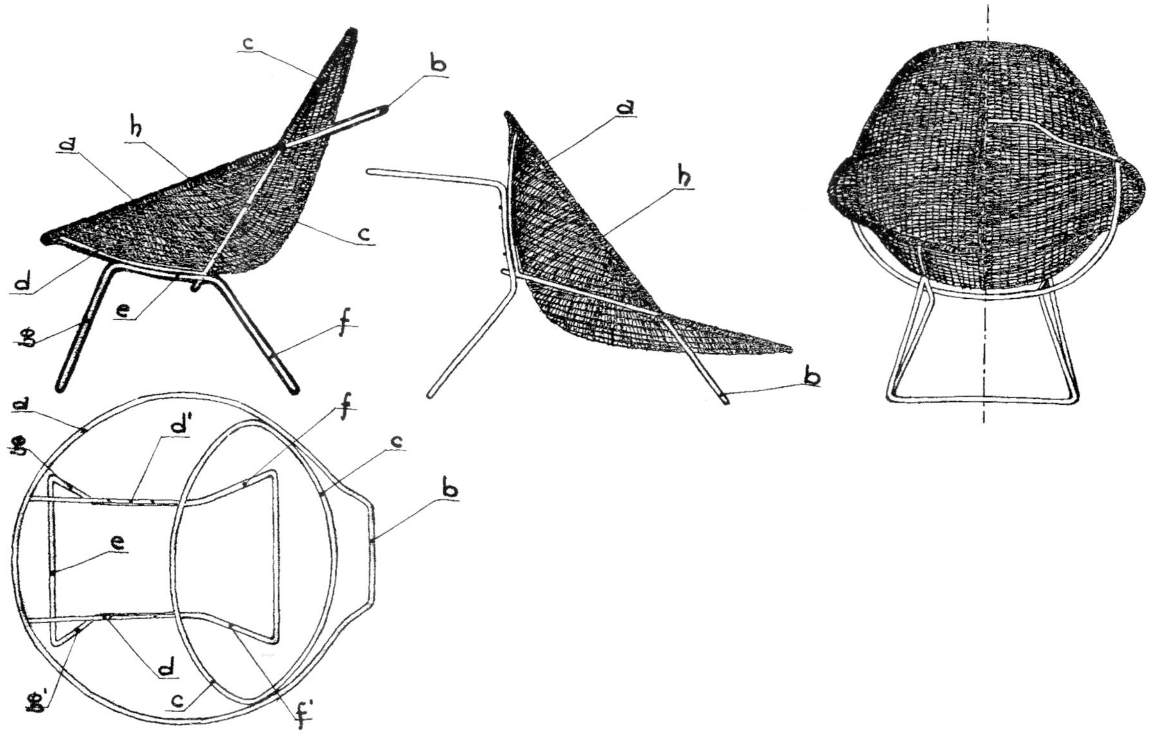

Vittorio Marchis

Machines to Make Home

Some technical features of the Italian product

A. G. Cavalchini and D. Perrucci, Chichibio telescopic standard lamp, produced by Luceplan, 2001.

Epilogue, for use as an introduction

The precedents for a "mechanical history" of the Italian home cannot help being "Classical". The *De Architectura* by Marcus Vitruvius Pollio would not have been a complete treatise had it not included books IX and X, which discuss mechanical clocks, and more besides. The lifting capstans, the hoists, the trestles, the pulleys, the levers and finally the war machines themselves, which destroy the houses, are protagonists alongside the traditional "elements" of building technologies. But this subject strays from design that is intended to represent contemporaneity, or at least those items from the recent past that are still living in the present. The *Nuova architettura famigliare* (Bologna 1678) by Alessandro Capra from Cremona was aligned within a tradition of "theatres of machines" from which only Zabaglia with his *Castelli e ponti*... (Rome 1743) began a new chapter. Yet it was not until the late 19th century that the complex and ambiguous relationship between home and machine found its public manifestation, and above all awareness on the part of engineers and architects. The shining culture reflected by Paxton's Crystal Palace (1851), found again in the most important international Expositions, convinced even the most stubborn and conservative master builders to innovate. *Charpenterie*, *maçonnerie* and *bâtiment* are terms that were destined to disappear, while new sciences and techniques of construction found their accreditation in the "polytechnic" universities.
The paradigms changed and the French verb, *bâtir* (which almost seems to be a play on words), which in Italian metamorphosed into the *bastimento*, explains how a machine – the transatlantic liner, now made entirely of metal and with a steam engine – was to become the model of reference of the *machine à habiter*.
The collective imagination too was nourished with new myths and scientific romance was populated with *maisons à vapeur*, *Stahlstädte*, iron and glass towers. To make the *machines à habiter*, engineering discovered a virgin terrain and threw itself headlong into not only inventing devices, but also those machines without which building homes would have remained a handicraft technique in an industrial world.
New canons and rhythms were imposed on a scientific organization of the building site work and the very protoindustrial nature of the "factory" saw engineers and civil architects as the new stage managers. Rich in contradictions, building technique – more than any other production activity – maintained improvisers and planners, technicians and artisans altogether in a way that is difficult to explain in a simple technological dimension. The home as a manufactured article, in every social stratum, remained the first and most conspicuous asset of family investment. Around this there revolved the very technological dimension of life; the home is always the witness of irreversible metamorphoses. An anthropology of the home, but, more cohesively, an ethnography of construction, cannot think of leaving the machine in the wings.

Homes for machines

With the industrial revolution, or rather, with the technological renaissance which was widely witnessed in Europe beginning in the mid-19th century, building technology was renewed, also because all machines needed a home and no longer a simple refuge, a roof under which to take shelter from bad weather. The distribution and control of energy (hydraulic, mechanical, electrical, but also thermal and chemical) needed infrastructures and gave the *usine* a new face. Everywhere the shed (*charpente*) of the mill now became a multi-storey building, where, helped by

A. Bianchetti, G. L. Giordani, C. Pea and M. Nizzoli, partial view of the diorama of the QT8 experimental district, 8th Triennial, Milan, 1947.

G. Mucchi, vertical section of a prefabricated housing element for QT8, made using the Blocco Togni water and sanitary system, 8th Triennial, Milan, 1947.

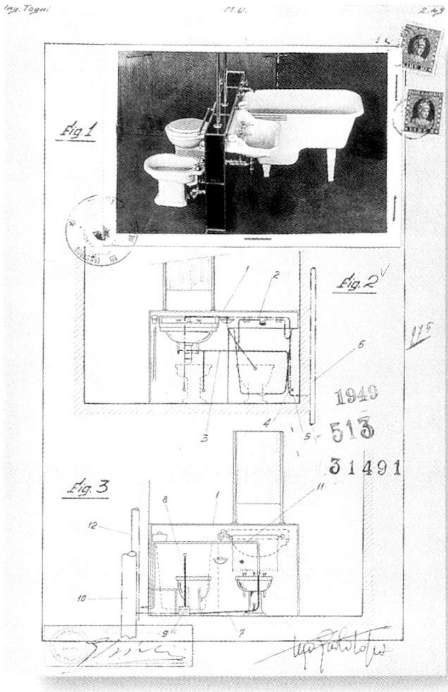

Blocco Togni, utility patent deposit of 31 May 1949.

Giulio Minoletti, Better Living bathroom unit, 1949.

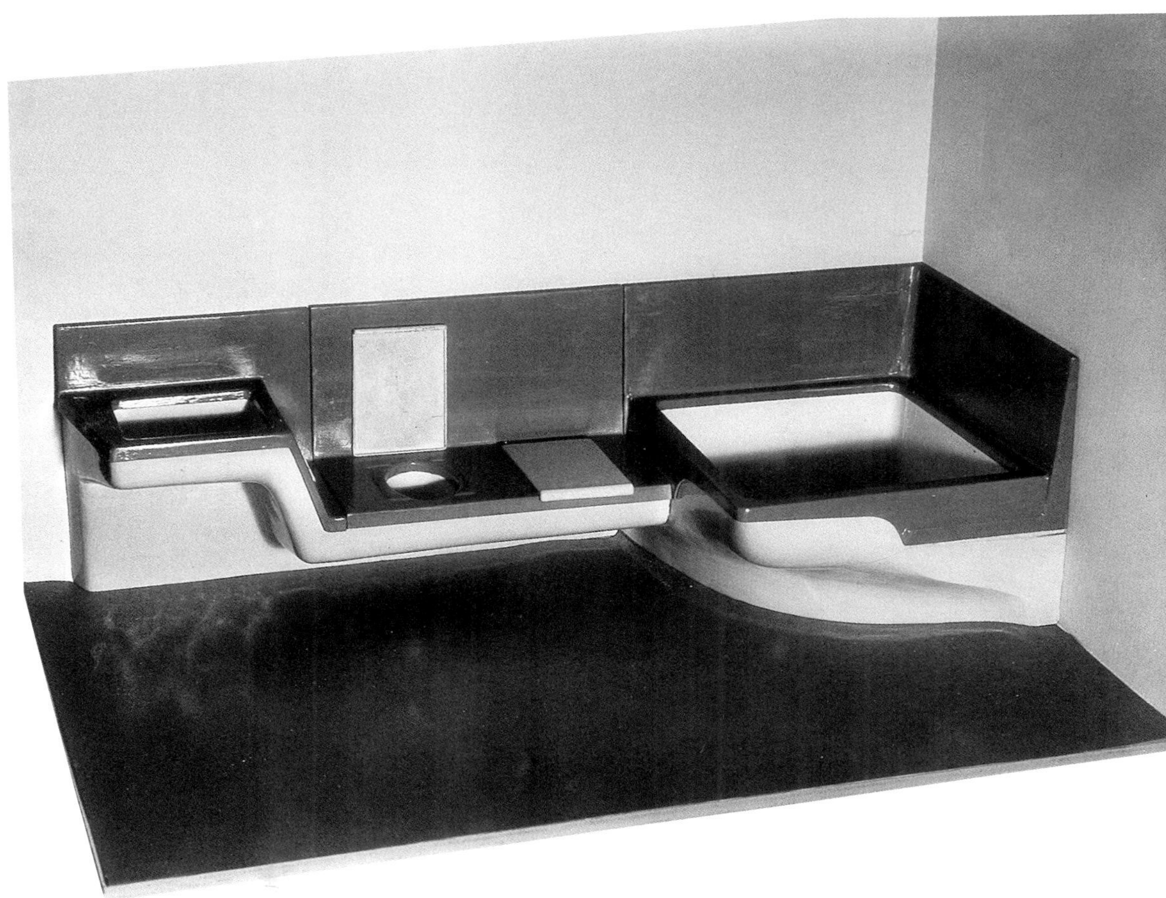

Alberto Rosselli, reinforced polyester bath unit, produced by Montecatini. Ornamental patent deposited on 16 November 1957.

gravity, the wheat came down from the tallest floor and was transformed into flour. Everything was made-to-measure for the machine: water-wheels, capstans, cochleas, millstones, cogwheels. This structure, better exposed to the light, with large windows, was soon to provide the model for the vertical factory, adopted by weaving factories and mechanical workshops, which in the '20s was best represented by the Lingotto in Turin. But beyond this aspect, private homes too took on the form that the loom or some other machine imposed on it. The silk twine plants influenced the housebuilding in Bologna from the 16th century onwards, forcing the houses to cross sluice-gates and *balatroni* to carry water to move the machines, even with priority on hygienic uses.

The symptoms that can be detected in Daniel Defoe's reports in 1726, in his *A Tour through the Whole Island of Great Britain*, are clear: running water arrives for the machines, not for people. He writes: "Wherever we passed any house we found a little rill or gutter of running water, if the house was above the road, it came from it, and crossed the way to run to another [...] and at every considerable house was a manufactory or work-house, and as they could not do their business without water, the little streams were so parted and guided by gutters or pipes, and by turning and dividing the streams, that none of those houses were without a river, if I may call it so, running into and through their work-houses." Every house is provided with water and fire "so that no hands being unemployed, all can gain their bread, even from the youngest to the ancient; hardly any thing above four years old, but its hands are sufficient to it self" (Defoe, 1971, pp. 492–493).

In the same year, Jonathan Swift also states that "he had a very convenient Mill within Half a Mile of his House, turned by a Current from a large River, and sufficient for his own Family as well as a great Number of his Tenants. That, about seven Years ago, a Club of those Projectors came to him with Proposals to destroy this Mill, and build another on the Side of that Mountain, on the long Ridge whereof a long Canal must be cut for a Repository of Water, to be conveyed up by Pipes and Engines to supply the Mill: Because the Wind and Air upon a Height agitated the Water, and thereby made it fitter for Motion: And because the Water descending down a Declivity would turn the Mill with half the Current of a River whose Course is more upon a Level. He said, that being then not very well with the Court, and pressed by many of his Friends, he complyed with the Proposal; and after employing an Hundred Men for two Years, the Work miscarryed, the Projectors went off, laying the Blame entirely upon him; railing at him ever since, and putting others upon the same Experiment, with equal Assurance of Success, as well as equal Disappointment" (*Gulliver's Travels*, ch. IV).

In Italian houses a place of honour was reserved for the loom, where the weavers toiled away on piecework, fitting into new family dynamics of the Biella or Brianza areas. And in the years of the reconstruction, before the economic miracle, knitting machines looked very impressive in the small dining-rooms of working class houses.

Today certain prophets of the "intelligent home" and the "global village" hope to find in flat liquid crystal screens and in integrated data processing systems the key elements of a new "wired home", as others already see for the city.

Corrado Beguinot (1998–99) affirms: "Technological innovation and the new way of communicating that it proposes may represent the point of departure for a different way of conceiving the architecture of the city, of experiencing mobility inside the urban space and recomposing the dichotomy between the 'city of places' (that of stone) and the 'city

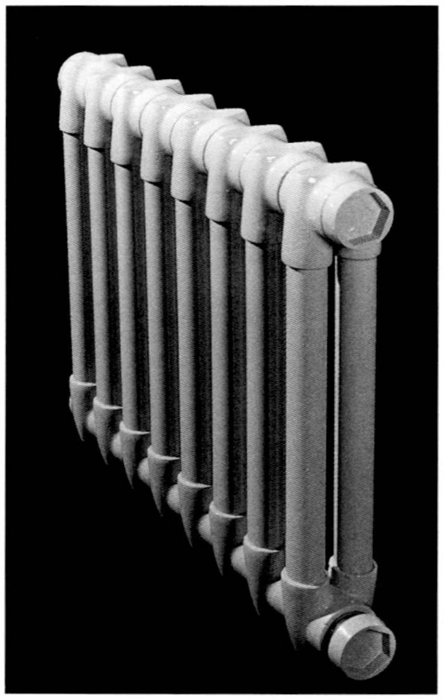

AFL radiator, produced by Falck, 1960.

of flows' (the non-material one of relationships). This means that the 21st century opens up ample and innovative prospects for the recovery of the semantic values of the city, under the condition, however, that a full-blown interactive process is established between the use of information and the invention of new architectural spaces. Only like this, by developing a new design and planning culture, will it be possible to give life to an architecture for a society that is profoundly changing people's way of communicating and therefore of interacting. Today, our task is to prevent the city of electronics from following in the wake of the city of the car, bringing the human condition to even higher levels of complexity, insecurity and unliveability". The house is not built but assembled; it is wired, connected, and *Wired* is not only the title of a computer science magazine. Already in the early 19th century, the French engineer Girard, the inventor of a new hydraulic turbine, conceived the house as a tangle of pipes. "Before describing the perfected equipment employed by us for the use of natural hydraulic forces and the creation of artificial forces, we must describe the objective we have set ourselves to achieve; namely, through the distribution of a driving force to the home, to be able to divide up all work – using water as the driving force for all local industry. [...] There, at the end of the pipe, a motor is fitted that uses the energy of the water [...] it will also be possible to achieve the objective we propose utilizing a series of steam-engines that are efficiently linked. [...] Through this transformation of work, a small number of extremely powerful steam-engines, placed outside towns, will be able to satisfy the demands of all the industries, by placing at the disposal of each a portion of the driving force received via a simple, small unit that is completely free of any risk" (*Publication des brévets*, 1868, p. 291).

Construction phase of one of the first examples of a prefabricated building, realized in Milan in the early '50s to a project by Giuseppe and Guido Bigontina. From *Edilizia Moderna*, no. 51, 1953. Graphics by Albe Steiner.

The technology changes, the "fluid" vector of power and information changes, but the new technological and mechanistic dimension of the home remains, and "you cannot go back", as always happens in every revolution. By now the myth of "Adam's home in Heaven" could no longer make reference to "natural" models, and civil disobediences *à la* Thoreau have little bearing on the new rules of the game. However, "among the causes of the state of deterioration of the built environment, Olgyay clearly identifies the domination of technological air-conditioning systems, which have eliminated the traditional 'symbiotic' relationship between built environment and physical/climatic context. In ecological terms, today we would say that the culture of the *machine à habiter* has contributed to cancelling out the differences and complexity of housing developments, therefore making them very fragile" (Gianni Scudo); little remains of the degrees of liberty of a system that evolves according to dynamics of enormous inertia. The intrinsic instability of biological systems does not leave great margins for the optimistic perspective of some utopians. Conceiving the city of the future without air-conditioning or lifts is absolutely illusory, unless there is a return to the "Medieval near future". The citizens of today's world are machines.

Machines that make homes

There would be no machine-homes without machines-that-make-homes. Rather, it is precisely the "machinic" nature of the building product that gives the imprint to the new home. *Plug-in* could be the new motto. It is necessary, however, to take a step back: arriving before the plugs and electric cables there are the bricks and chains.
The brick, which, as a modular element, has accompanied building since antiquity, demands new production dynamics. Even

Marco Zanuso and Alberto Scarzella, contoured floor tile consisting of circle arcs. Ornamental patent deposited on 16 March 1955.

Marco Zanuso and Alberto Scarzella, enamelled earthenware tiles, produced by Cedit, 1959.

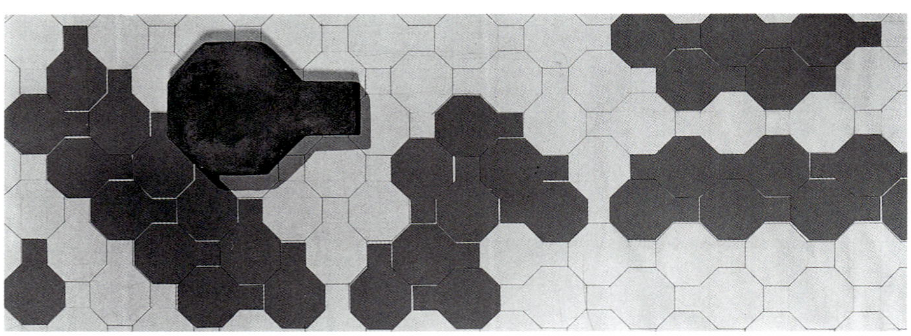

Achille and Piergiacomo Castiglioni, terra-cotta floor with sectional tile, produced by Ruggeri della Cà Tortona, 1956.

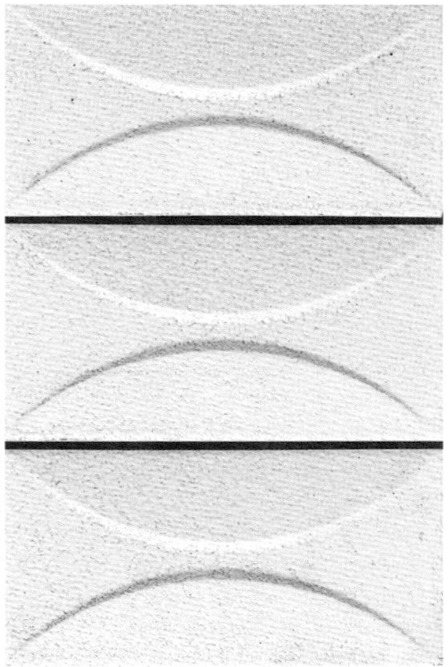

Gio Ponti, grès tiles
in enamelled relief,
produced by Joo Gresite,
1960.

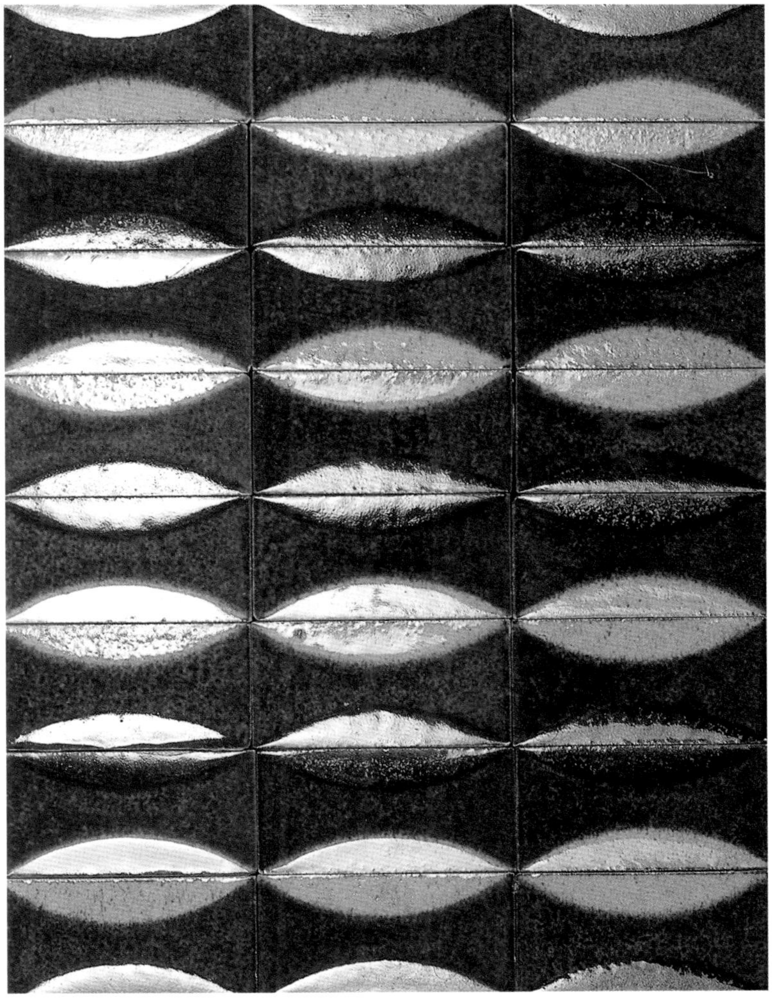

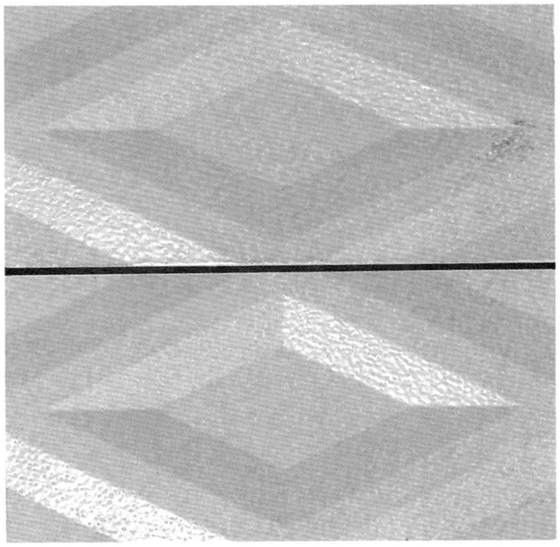

if Hoffman continuous rotation furnaces were already in operation, manual manufacture was no longer a sustainable process. The innovation of the technologies applied to housebuilding more than doubled in the thirty years of the 19th century prior to Italy's unification. The first presses for manufacturing tiles were soon joined by dods for perforated bricks and grès pipes. The rationalization of the tile product was gradually standardized and lost that diversification of forms that had characterized it in the multiple artisan firms.
In the districts in Milan and Turin, some centres specialized in the production of binding materials (Bergamo and Casale), while tile production remained more widely spread over the territory, also for geographical reasons. The machines for this industry already had an international market. The producers knew of them through the industrial fairs and the advertising information became increasingly powerful and effective.
The best machines for working tiles in the last years of the 19th century came from France, and the efforts of those who on this side of the Alps struggled to invent (and copy) alternative solutions were in vain. In Italy too scalers, mixers, presses, dods, moulders and tiling machines had the names of G. Pinette à Chalon-sur-Saône, Schnierber à Mulhouse and others besides. The good tiling machines were the Boulets of Paris. Soon, however, our own competitors would also arrive.
Also, and above all, iron – first quietly, almost hidden out of modesty, then increasingly displayed to show bare structural essentials – was soon centre stage. It almost seems that the *domus* was to stay anchored to the past and that the workshop lent itself more placidly to the new experiments, but this was not so.
The bathroom was the first "technological" room in the *fin-de-siècle* house. The alibi of the health enthusiast, supported by illustrious scientists, among whom the renowned Louis Pasteur, changed the home, transforming it into a body traversed by lead veins carrying flows of water, steam, warm air, illuminating gas, sewage, smoke. The fireplace, or rather the rows of chimney-flues, that sagittally crossed the skeletons of houses, made way for heaters and radiators, which, for the greater safety of their future users, had long been experimented with (and highly successfully) in the greenhouses of botanical gardens and in prison dormitories.
Even before electrical current brought light to every room of the house, thin

Alberto Rosselli, enamelled ceramic tile, produced by Joo. Ornamental patent deposited on 18 February 1960.

Two types of enamelled ceramic tile, produced by Joo. Ornamental patent deposited on 18 February 1960.

Wallpaper with pattern of vertical and horizontal lines, produced by Braendli & C. Ornamental patent deposited on 23 May 1959.

Opposite: Interior of the Candy washing-machine factory, 1965.

Angelo Mangiarotti, living-room arrangement created with CUB 8 sectional system, produced by Poltronova, 1967.

Enzo Mari, enamelled *cottoforte* and silk-screen tiles, produced by Gabbianelli, 1968.

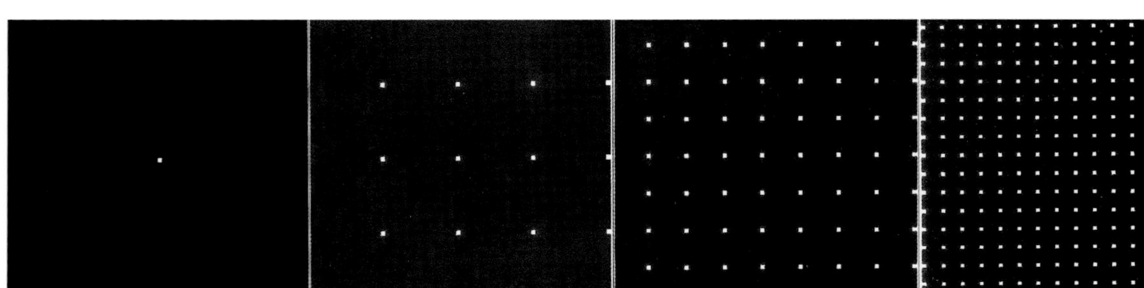

Antonia Astori, Oikos sectional system with flat elements, produced by Driade, 1973.

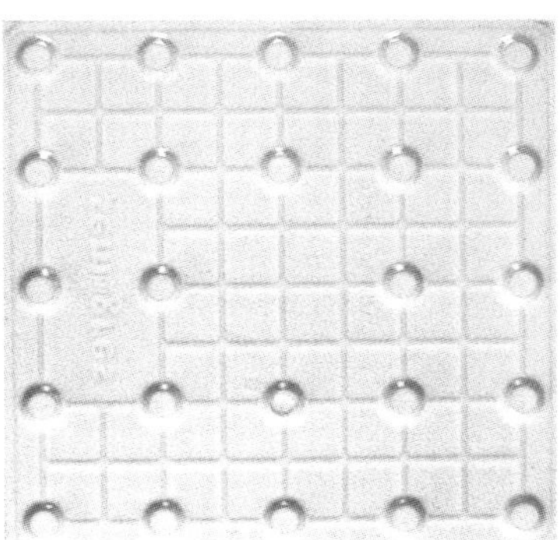

Alfonso Leoni, *cottoforte* tile with enamelled relief, produced by Maioliche Faentine, 1975.

Bruno Munari, enamelled *cottoforte* and silk-screen tiles, produced by Faetano, 1976.

copper wires connected Daniel batteries, housed in the closets of antechambers, to electric bells to send orders and messages to the servants. The telephone, perhaps more than the electric light, was to contribute to wiring and interconnecting the city of machines. Radio too. The washing machine and the television were the new centre of gravity of the miraculous home of the '60s: Italo Calvino's *Marcovaldo* was perhaps the best and most reliable witness of this.
The economic boom turned the home upside down: the multi-storey buildings of the peripheral districts and building speculation had to come to grips with the new tenants that an industry produced with endless assembly lines. The space for the washing machine in the bathroom and the garage under the house not only marked the houses of the middle class. The ranks of the *petite petite bourgeoisie* and the *Mimì metallurgicos* all demanded these inalienable rights.
The materials too, no longer "natural", invoked renewed professionalism: polypropylene and polyvinyl, stainless steels and light alloys, polycarbonates and synthetic rubbers, epoxy paints and silicone adhesives, almost make us forget that houses are made with iron and cement, tiles and bricks.
The worksite was populated with machines and, only in the French language, but *de facto* also in every industrialized country, entrusted its activity to the *engins de chantier*, which Villard de Honnecourt relied upon so much in the 13th century. The *engin* – none other than the English *engine* – has in *ingenium* not only its etymon but the very essence of engineering.

Homes that become machines

From Bauhaus to the ideal house of Fillia, Pagano, Sant'Elia, everything was transformed technologically through the fault of engineers, who almost forgot architects. The concerns of those who wished to save the past, or to preserve artistic canons, were not heeded. The engineer Leonardo Sinisgalli – so linked to his archaic land of Lucania as to bear the work and art of a tinsmith, who makes lamps of all kinds by hand, as the emblem of man's industriousness – perceived that by then society was a "civilization of machines". According to Le Corbusier (1926): "A home has two purposes. First of all, it is a machine for living; that is, a machine whose aim is to assist us to be fast and accurate with our work, and a diligent, considerate machine to satisfy the requirements of the body: comfort. But it is also well-suited to meditation, and is also the place in which beauty exists and brings an indispensable peace to the spirit; I do not expect art to provide nourishment for all, but I say simply that, for some people, the home must impart a feeling of beauty.
Everything that regards the practical purposes of the home is provided by the engineer; as for what concerns meditation, the feeling of beauty, the order that reigns (which will be a bulwark of beauty), this will be architecture.
The engineer's work on the one hand, architecture on the other."
The house is a machine for living, said Le Corbusier. His "five points": 1) adoption of *pilotis* to leave the ground floor free; 2) roof-garden, replacing pitch roofs; 3) adoption of the open plan, freed from the old supporting walls; 4) adoption of continuous windows (ribbon windows); 5) façade free from any structural conditioning transforms the house into something else. As an ideal reference, transatlantic liners, the *bâtiments*, were considered, but also the Lingotto in Turin, designed by engineer Mattè Trucco, which was intended to be a machine even when it was supposed to be a little bit like a house. And for this the French architect astounded, not managing to grasp the spirit of the Olivettis of Ivrea. But the

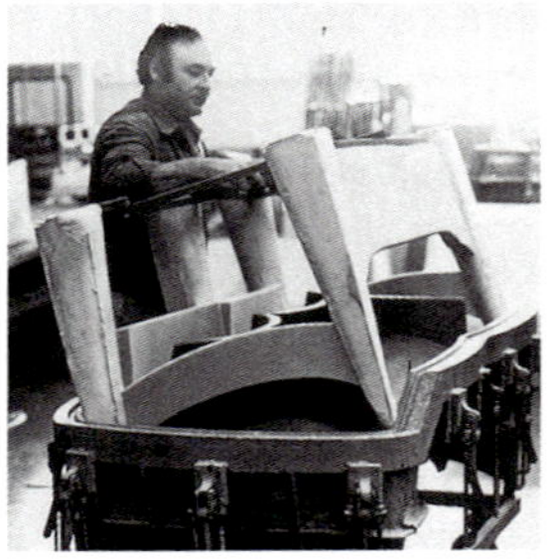

Some phases of construction of the Le Bambole padded sofa designed by Mario Bellini. Produced by B&B Italia, 1972.

iron logic of progress does not spare anybody, not even those who would have liked history to move differently.
Typewriters, "machines for writing", which invaded offices and houses, but showing *ante litteram* the relationship with the body that was later to be called ergonomics. Metal wardrobes, desks with technological prostheses, a new concept of furnishing.
In the wake of Le Corbusier there was no lack of innovating experiences, such as Prouvet's *pavillon* or the new utopias, which in truth were rather bizarre, of the engineer from Pavia, Gaetano Ciocca (1882–1966).
Transforming Le Corbusier's "house as a machine for living" into an authentic "machine-house" assembled with 5,436 prefabricated parts, Ciocca hoped for the triumph of an "aesthetics of uniformity" characteristic of the new corporate order, imagining the harmonious urbanization of a landscape characterized by housing nuclei connected by roads and cars, serving collective structures of leisure and action. A philosophy of the car applied to the "mass planning" of the home (Schnapp, 2000).
Wim Wenders' *Tokyo-Ga*, which traces these deep transformations of dwelling and living in an age that is ahead of our own times, might serve as a warning. Yet history is not the teacher of life.

A prologue for the future

Without technology, man would have remained a primate and would still be living in caves and natural shelters today. Machines, those that have made the home, have also profoundly changed man, defining new paradigms for living and above all living together. The machines that make homes are no different from the machines that are homes, and they will soon be assimilated into the machines that will be prostheses of people and homes. What fantasy perhaps grotesquely projects into strange future worlds is not so far away. Are the images of urban sprawl and its chaotic housing spaces, to which *Blade Runner*, *Neuromante* and *Amrita* are accustoming us, the voice of new mute prophets?

Mario Bellini, Le Bambole sofa, produced by B&B Italia, 1972.

Research into new housing models coordinated by Dante Donegani and Giovanni Lauda, with the assistance of Jae Kyu Lee, project by Hyung Jae Maeng, Exposed technical installations, Domus Academy, Milan, 1997.

Ora-Ïto, Cappellini house, Cologne, 2001.

Raimonda Riccini

The Appliance-Shaped Home

From the electrified home to the wired home

Marco Zanuso and Richard Sapper, Grillo telephone, produced by Sit-Siemens, 1966.

The electrical and mechanical home

It has been said that "a form that ignores its technical context absolutely cannot welcome a balanced life" (in Bettinelli, 1991). That is why, in delineating a profile of habitation culture in Italy, we cannot ignore the role and meaning that electrical appliances have played in it. Rather, the technical context of the home enables us better to understand not only the organization of the space, but also the subtle bond that technology and its objects for the home have established with the plants and installations, with the furnishings, with the lighting equipment. "For numerous architects of the first half of the 19th century, the Neo-classical house is a 'lifeless skeleton', a dead thing." Then, it will have to be "flooded with a series of flows (water, gas, heated steam, etc.) that transform it into a living thing [...] everything that renders the home a 'well tempered environment' (pipes and piping, drains, air conditioning systems, cables, aerials, meters, switches, etc.)" (Bellini and Teyssot, 1986, p. 11). Then came the machines, the domestic terminals for work and entertainment; finally, today, the most prodigious of networks, the combination between information technologies and those of demotic communication.

If the image of the Italian home has its own precise physiognomy as regards furnishings and accessories, it is perhaps less clear as regards its technical form. Less clear but no less important. Indeed, in Italy the dream of a technically equipped home accompanies the developments of architecture and interior design and qualifies some of its historical passages up to today, to the point of sometimes conditioning its results.

Beginning in the '30s, when people started to consider the possibilities of introducing electrical fittings and equipment into houses, Italian architects were among the first to detect the wind of change brought on by technology. In those years, at the 4th Triennial in Monza in 1930, an Electrical home was proposed, designed by Luigi Figini, Guido Frette, Adalberto Libera and Gino Pollini. The project for the kitchen was created by Piero Bottoni, who studied its organization like a full-blown laboratory containing twenty or so small and large electrical appliances. The project, executed with the support of Edison, had a significantly experimental and promotional character. For this reason, also because of its high costs, it remained an isolated and unrealized episode. Nevertheless, beginning from this experience there began to form in Italy the design culture around technology in the home that was to have such influence in the postwar design of electrical appliances; it also prefigured domestic scenarios of great evocative fascination.

Alongside the visions and realizations of planners, another fragment of this history concerns a second dream: that of the American kitchen, which Italian women had cultivated for many years through the movies and, subsequently, television. It was a dream that the Italian production system, assisted by a design culture ready to meet the challenge, was capable of interpreting in the best of ways, reinventing it with a care and an imagination that were 100% Italian. Until the '50s "Italian women had only seen 'American' kitchens in American films. The leading actor returns home in the evening, goes to the fridge, takes out a sandwich and a bottle of milk, makes a silent snack. And around him the shiny, aerodynamic kitchen, a homogeneous array inserted into which are furniture items above and below, sink, oven and hobs, appliances. The women sighed and said: 'Now *that* is a kitchen'".

This dream was discussed in these terms in an article in the magazine *Casa Novità* in June 1961, devoted to the American kitchen and its introduction in Italy. The

Luigi Figini, Gino Pollini and Piero Bottoni, nocturnal view of the Electrical home, 4th Triennial, Monza, 1930.

Piero Bottoni, view of the kitchen in the Electrical home, 4th Triennial, Monza, 1930.

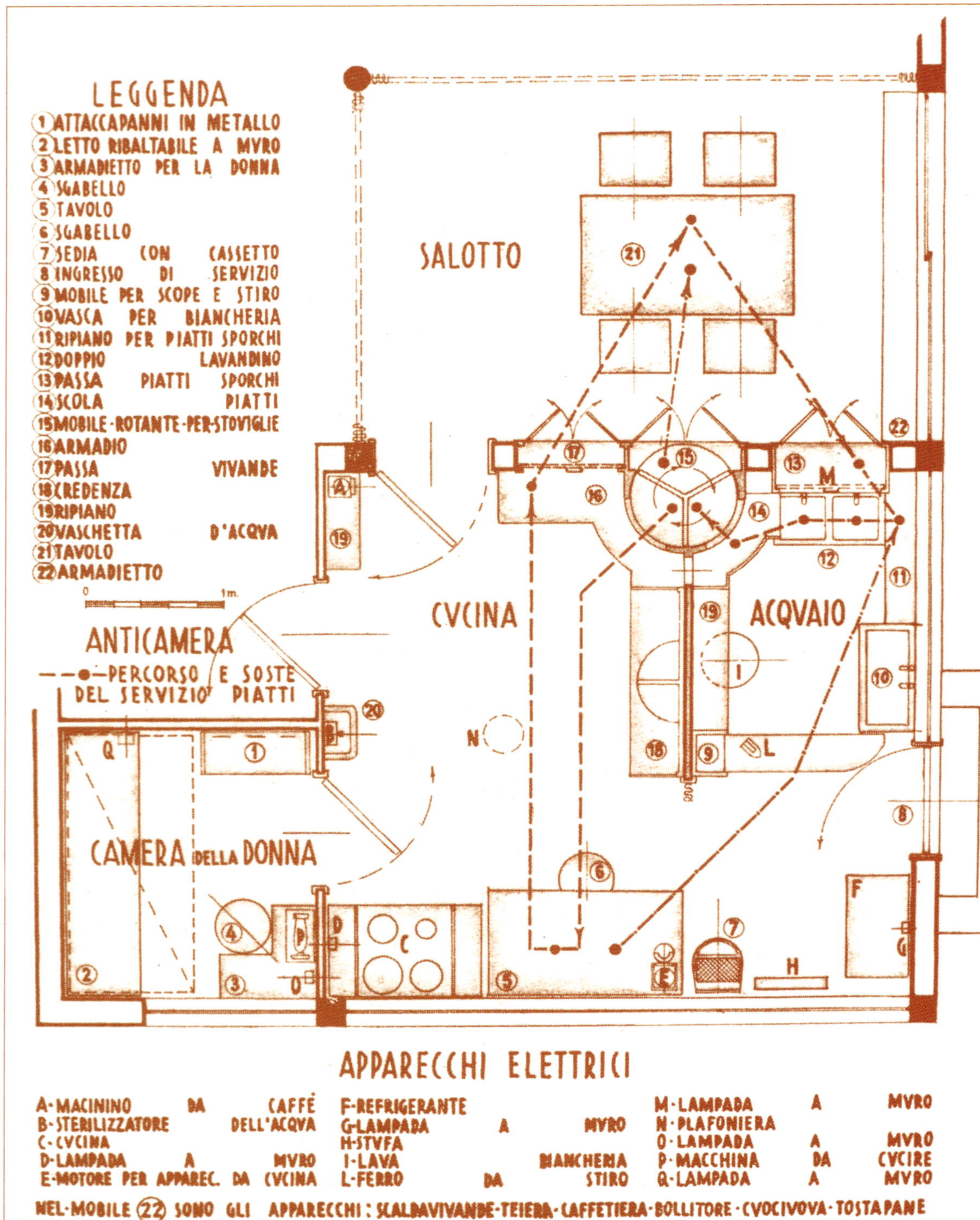

Piero Bottoni, plan of the dining room, kitchen and utility rooms in the Electrical home, 4th Triennial, Monza, 1930.

Some advertising images of American-style kitchens of the '50s.

Top loading washing machine, produced by Candy, early '50s.

Giulio Minoletti, minimal kitchen, produced by Breda, 1951.

Roberto Menghi, sectional kitchen, produced by Saffa, 1954.

Gian Casè, T12 sectional kitchen, produced by Boffi, 1960.

Refrigerator, produced by Indes. Ornamental patent deposited on 6 February 1957.

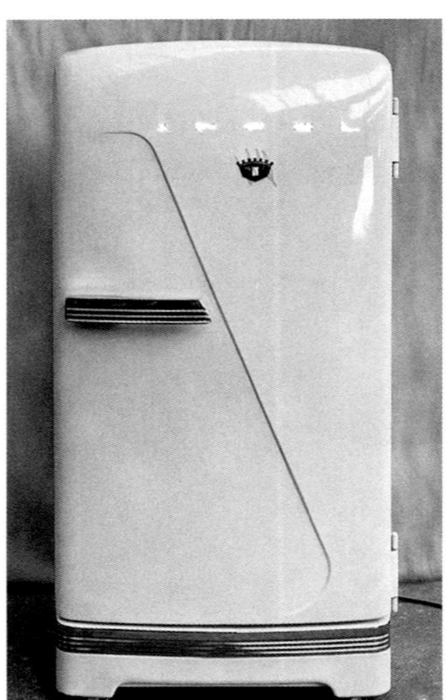

Advertising for Phonola televisions, late '50s.

Advertising of furniture with audiovisual equipment, produced by Geloso, late '50s.

Sergio Berizzi, Cesare Buttè and Dario Montagni, model 17/18 television and adjustable cinescope, produced by Phonola, 1956.

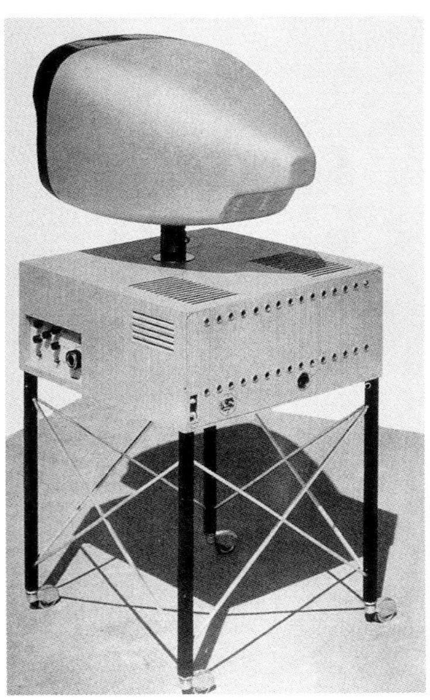

young interior design magazine, which was later to become *Abitare*, illustrated the national production of kitchens with a long feature. It is here that the concepts of sectional structure and rationality appear, accompanied by the insertion of electrical appliances, but with a wholly Italian taste for colour and precious materials.

We must not forget, however, that throughout the '50s Italy was a poor country, in which conditions of housing, hygiene and space were still very backward. Many houses still did not have an independent kitchen space (24%) nor a bathroom (73%), and many still did not have running water (48%). Only 7% of families possessed a telephone. On the other hand, great expenditure was certainly not possible, aside from that for primary necessities, as the average per capita income was around 380,000 lire a year in the North and 190,000 in the South. Then a Fiat 500 Topolino cost 675,000 lire (approximately 13-15 million lire today).

Despite this reality, beginning precisely in that crucial decade, in Italy a production system was constructed that was strongly oriented towards goods for the home. Already in those years the range of refrigerators on the market was extensive, due to the presence of foreign brands, but also numerous Italian manufacturers. The national brands concentrated on small absorption refrigerators, with lower yields but with reduced dimensions and affordable prices, pursuing the policy of "a fridge for all" that had already begun in the automotive field with small utility cars. In 1951 only 18,500 refrigerators were produced in this country, in 1957 the figure had jumped to 370,000 (Ginsborg, 1989, II, p. 290).

At the same time, specialist publications, trade fairs and trade associations started to spread and publicize the application of modern technology to the home. Appliances – large and small – were "the means that progress offered for making domestic chores fast, light and easy to do" (*Enciclopedia delle 3 B d'oro*, 1948).

So it was that, through women's publications, architecture and design magazines, the images of American

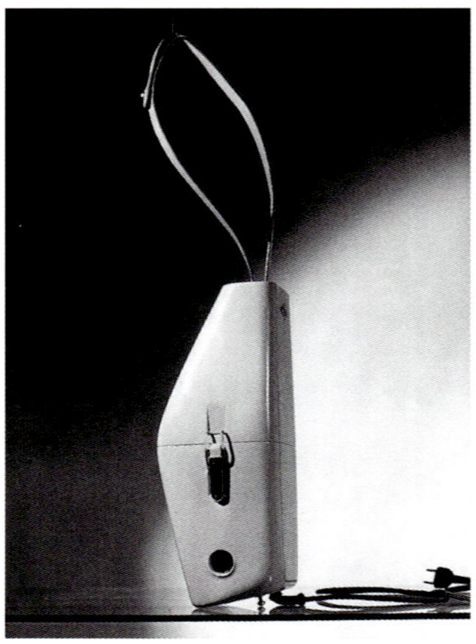

cinema and television advertising, a culture of domestic modernity previously unknown in Italy was built. This modernity prevalently concerned the spaces of the kitchen and the living room, which slowly adapted to the presence of the refrigerator and the washing machine, the radio, TV and telephone. Already certain small appliances began to take their place as objects of domestic worship and design practices; they were increasingly featured in advertisements and in practical demonstrations in the most prestigious shops selling goods for the home.

In the sector of electrical appliances and their uses in domestic life, initiatives of various kinds proliferated. There were, for example, national exhibitions of appliances which acted to attract demand and promote what was to be one of the key sectors in the Italian economic boom. Appliances were offered as prizes in various contests including, alongside the ordinary fare of radios, sewing machines, televisions, irons, blenders, gas and electrical cookers and hobs, floor polishers, cheese-graters, gramophones, refrigerators, and washing machines, the "jewels" of Italian industrial design, newly emerging but fast taking hold: the Necchi's Mirella electrical sewing-machine and the Lettera 22 portable typewriter, both designed by Marcello Nizzoli.

The Triennial in Milan in 1954, devoted to the home, revealed that architectural and design culture knew how to appropriate the new climate favourable to the applications of electricity in the home.

As Siegfried Giedion said, mechanization entered homes, with a series of machines, great and small. And it entered fast, since in Italy in those years we witnessed a rush to purchase appliances that, together with the advent of the car and television, remains as one of the most characteristic phenomena of the period, the phenomenon through which the change in Italians' daily lives was best measured.

In first place was the refrigerator, that cornerstone of the change in the whole food preparation and consumption

Achille and Piergiacomo Castiglioni, Spalter vacuum cleaner, produced by Rem, 1956.

Marco Zanuso, studies for refrigerator doors, produced by Homelight, 1955.

process; in the '60s it was the most widespread appliance, together with the television, present in 77% of homes and followed quite a distance behind by the washing machine (54%). In Italy, as they had been in the America of Raymond Loewy and Henry Dreyfuss, these items, which appeared destined for formal and stylistic anonymity, become the training ground for designers, who made them strongly characterized objects, first and foremost the refrigerators of Gino Valle for Zanussi and Marco Zanuso for Homelight. The way Italian designers interpreted the designing of new appliances accompanied and facilitated the transcendance of suggestions for women: "Today's tendency is towards colour, obtained both with the use of plastic laminates and with woods printed in various shades. Appliances too, in the search for an increasingly pure and rational line, and in a by no means insignificant technical progress, have now been inserted in the furniture and so the eye falls upon continuous, smooth surfaces, orderly to the maximum degree, with lively and cheerful shades, creating an extremely pleasant and functional overall effect" (*I mille consigli di Casa mia*, 1969, p. 52).

Yet it would be a mistake to think that the home as an electrical appliance was

domestic models of a rigidly rationalist (or rather, substantially poor) mould, characterized by white surfaces and the use of Formica and metal. In the '60s the hierarchical and specialized organization of the kitchen, understood more as an accessoried laboratory away from the rest of the flat, was left behind. Here there emerges the idea of the kitchen as a liveable space, usable not only by the family but also by friends, equipped therefore not just with antiseptic containers, but with real pieces of furniture; the kitchen started to impose itself as the place for new forms of socialization, the place of a changed sociability (Tosi, 1994, p. 35).

Let us see what the characteristics of the kitchen were at the end of the decade, as described in a manual of practical

ultimately reduced to the kitchen environment. In reality, other technical artefacts have profoundly affected the traditional orders of habitation in Italy and marked our domestic landscape with their presence. The triumphal entrance of the television into the home as a full-blown totem in every proper living room inaugurated the progressive introduction of technical elements (hi-fi, "industrial"-type lighting) that was to have its consecration later in the season of high tech.

It is no novelty to speak of radio and television as symbolic objects, icons of our time, but the fact is often neglected that they contributed to that rather accentuated change in the conception of interior spaces beginning in the '70s. Especially in the newly constructed

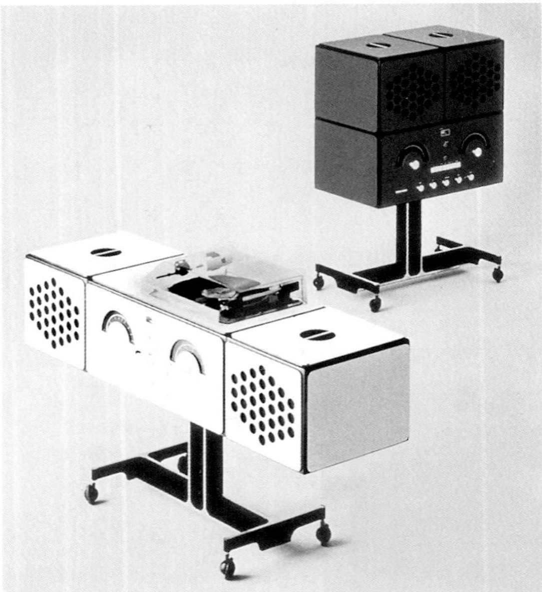

Achille and Piergiacomo Castiglioni, RR 126 stereo radiophonograph, produced by Brionvega, 1966.

Franco Albini and Franca Helg, Orion television, produced by Brionvega, 1962.

Marco Zanuso, Doney television, produced by Brionvega, 1962.

residences, elements of flexibility in the organization of rooms and their functions were particularly valued, something also made possible by a new conception of utilities, which themselves began to become an aesthetic element.

The separation between zones (night, day, services) and the rigid specialization of the individual rooms were attenuated.

The rooms interpenetrated each other, the spaces became multi-functional, there was a growth in non-closed places for receiving. The living room definitively lost its sacredness, sometimes incorporating the kitchen in a single room, proof not only of less rigidity in the furnishing, but also of a greater boldness in providing settings for technology.

There has not been sufficient meditation on the fact that this new way of conceiving spaces ended up increasing the presence of lighting equipment, which left the fixed points in the middle of the ceiling, to invade the corners, walls, furniture surfaces. And they were ever less inclined to conceal their technical nature. This is the case of exemplary lamps such as the Castiglioni brothers' Tojo (1962) and Arco (1962) for Flos and Parentesi (1971) designed with Pio Manzù.

A similar role was performed by television sets, such as the Algol (1964) and the Black St 201 by Marco Zanuso and Richard Sapper for Brionvega.

Looking at the '70s and early '80s, the average character of the residence that emerges from this brief portrait is in contrast with an element typical of the cultural climate of those years: the utopian tension that is encountered not only in the political and mass movements, but also in design and architectural culture, and especially in the imaginative conceptions proposed for homes by the more radical and provocative designers (Branzi, 1984).

In 1972 at the Museum of Modern Art in New York, there opened the exhibition, co-ordinated by Emilio Ambasz, symbolically entitled *Italy: the New Domestic Landscape*. A milestone in the history of Italian design, the show brought together a series of objects, furniture and furnishings, designed in the '60s and early '70s, that have remained in our cultural and visual patrimony: from the Grillo telephone by Marco Zanuso and Richard Sapper to the lamps by the Castiglioni brothers, to the Valentine typewriter by Ettore Sottsass, to the production of plastic furnishing elements by Anna Castelli, Giotto Stoppino, Rodolfo Bonetto and many others.

Also still very much alive from that exhibition are a series of design-reflections on habitation and technology, which are translated into intuitions and projections on our domestic destiny. Skimming through the pages of that event today, what is striking is the experimental daring of many of the designs on display. One of the most interesting themes was that of the "furnishing systems", such as the kitchen block, small units that contained a whole system in a single volume with measurements reduced to a minimum: the hobs, the worktop, the sink, the refrigerator, the chopping board, a small extractable table, sockets for the small appliances. On this same theme, other designers developed provocative proposals through which all the functions of the home were recomposed in a single block: from sleeping to cooking, with an absolute integration between technology and furnishings. I am referring in particular to the total furnishing unit by Joe Colombo, but also to the self-sufficient housing unit for collective and emergency use, designed by Marco Zanuso and Richard Sapper, and finally to the housing cell with audiovisual microenvironment by Ugo La Pietra.

On one hand we imagine a superorganization, situated freely in space, even freed from the walls of the house. On the other, in these superfunctional habitats, understood as

Achille and Piergiacomo Castiglioni, Luminator floor lamp, produced by Gilardi & Barzaghi (1955), Arform (1957), and Flos (1994).

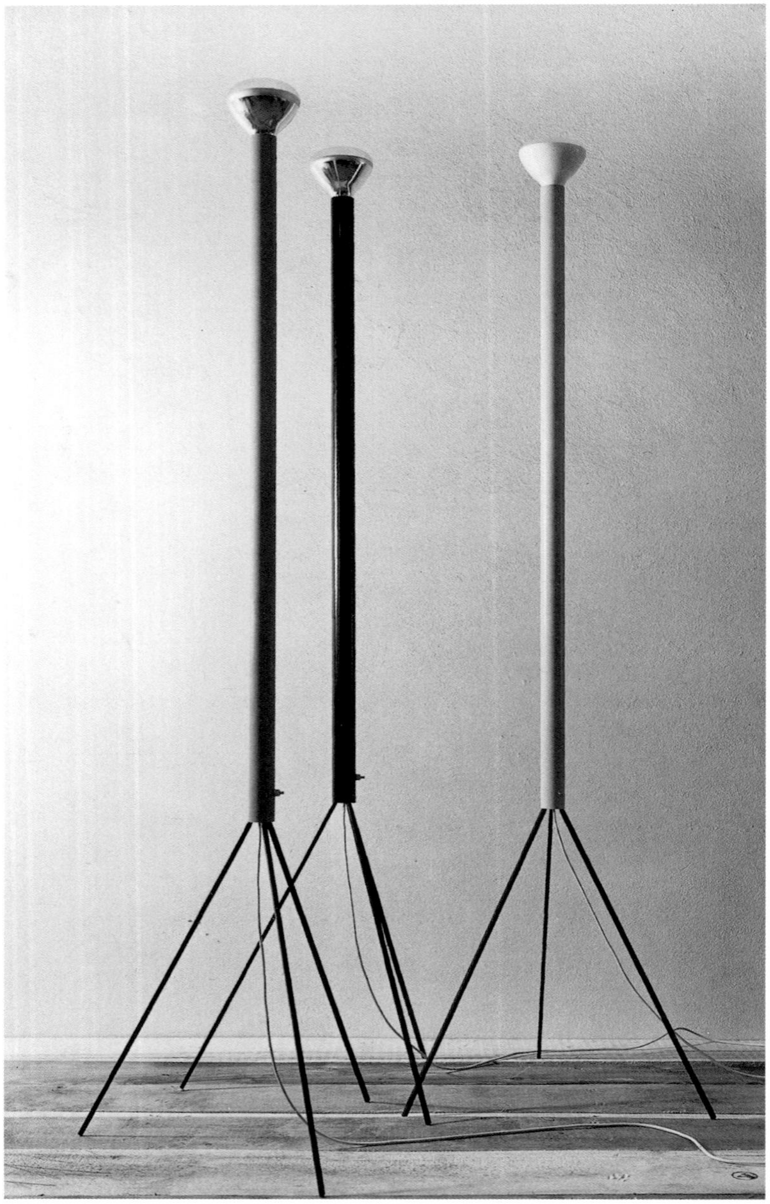

Marco Zanuso and Richard Sapper, Algol television, produced by Brionvega, 1964.

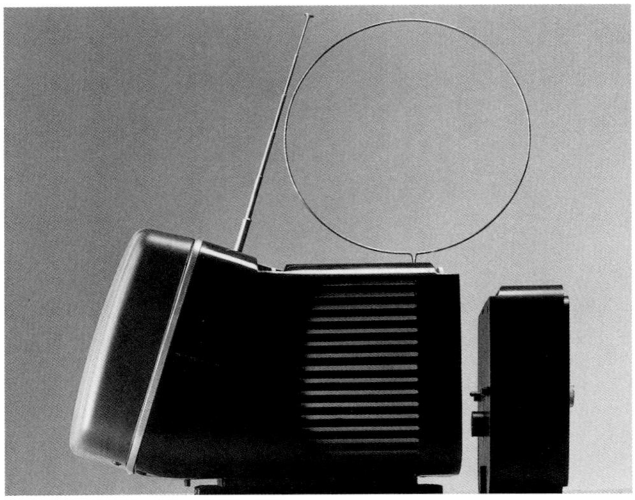

Marco Zanuso and Richard Sapper, 12 Black St 201 television, produced by Brionvega, 1969.

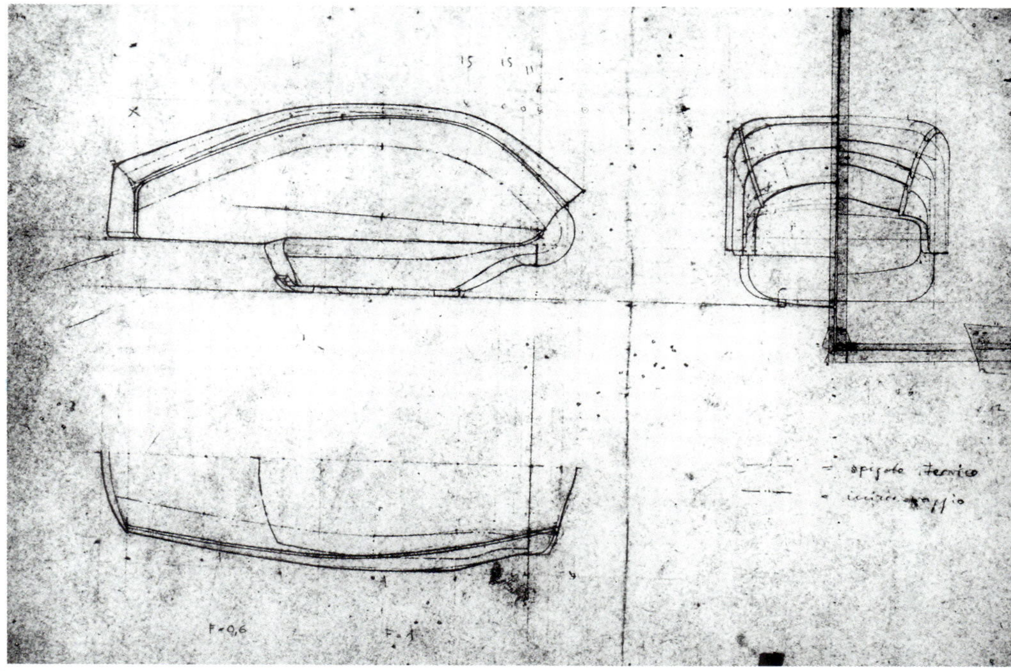

vaguely claustrophobic technological plastic shells, we also sense an implicit criticism of the desocializing elements of the home. "Let us say that the underlying hypothesis could be formulated as follows: the new technologies, arriving in the domestic environment, would contribute to the mutation of the inhabitants themselves" (Teyssot, 1992, p. 96).

The mechanical housewife

If we leave the emphasis of the enthusiasm or the criticism, it is rather evident that technology now became an integral part of the ideal home of most Italians. As has already been said, together with the increasingly numerous equipment items for entertainment (alongside the television and radio, now also appearing in strength were the hi-fis, small tape recorders, portable radios), white appliances were now an integral part of the domestic landscape. However you wish to furnish the kitchen, there must be a refrigerator, sometimes with a freezer, the group that includes the hob, oven, hood, and finally the dishwasher, an essential item. It was also in these years that "fitted" appliances took their definitive place. Precisely in the logic of favouring as far as possible the free choice of a kitchen furnishing designed to one's own taste, the manufacturers provided increasingly standardized technical elements, without body, so as to be adapted inside the furniture, almost disappearing amid the mouldings of the old style wood or under the shiny plasticized surfaces. Naturally, in the transition from the pages of magazines to reality, things went rather differently: the number of appliances was not always so complete. Nevertheless, with the exception of the freezer and the dishwasher, almost all Italian families now possessed the other white appliances. Not to mention the more traditional small appliances, such as the iron or electrical sewing machine, but also less usual ones, such as the vacuum cleaner. In short, the housewife became mechanized.

Also for the preparation of food, spaces opened for the assistance of small appliances: blenders, beaters, grinders, whisks, electrical graters entered the market in large quantities, and also with an infuriating variety of functions, many of which, to tell the truth, were purely illusory. In this segment of domestic

Marco Zanuso and Richard Sapper, Grillo telephone, produced by Sit-Siemens, 1966.

Joe Colombo, Mini-Kitchen on wheels, produced by Boffi, 1963.

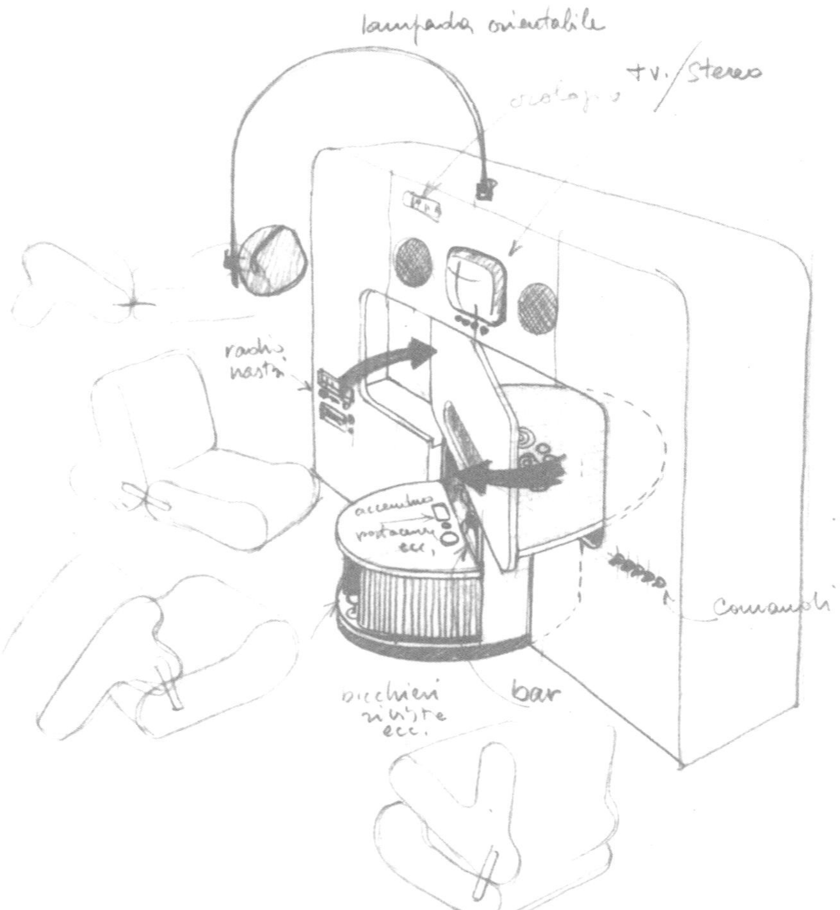

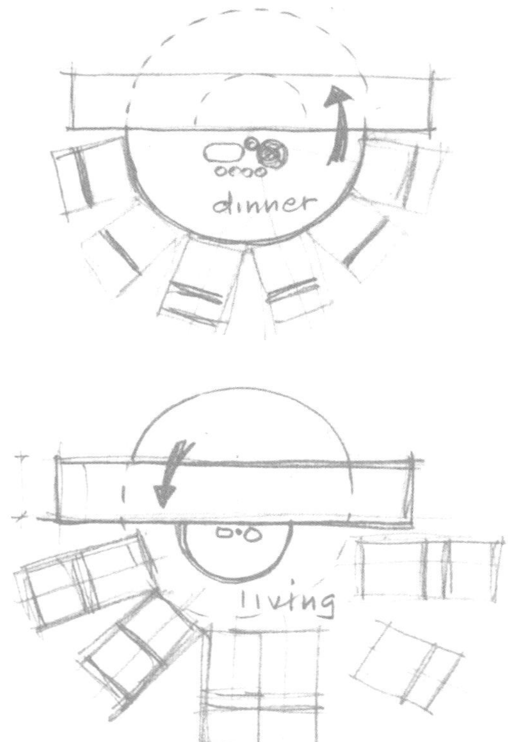

Joe Colombo, Rotoliving monoblock, 1969.

Ettore Sottsass, experimental domestic space designed for the exhibition *Italy: the New Domestic Landscape*, New York, 1972.

PastaMatic advertising in *Apparecchi elettrodomestici nella casa moderna*, August 1980.

technology, since the early '80s, another specific trait of Italian design came to the fore, one that was to long enjoy good fortune: conferring a playful and friendly aspect on technology. This aspect is well represented by the small round colourful appliances by Michele De Lucchi for Girmi.

The joviality achieved by technology makes the distribution of spaces more uninhibited and the various proposals of combination between furnishings and technical equipment less standardized and increasingly flexible. Just consider the sometimes surprising positioning of appliances, even in the living room, as suggested by some models of refrigerator, conceived as furnishing elements. This is the case of the Black fridge by Roberto Pezzetta for Zanussi (1986), transformed into a small "bathing resort" construction with its own flag even, or his more recent Oz refrigerator (1998) and Zoe washing machine, conceived as biomorphic presences that want to move away, at least externally, from the traditional typology of the square parallelepiped.

So we have the "young", colourful home, one of great compositional liberty; and also the high-tech, almost professional kitchen, into which out-of-scale elements are introduced, such as the appliances produced for large restaurants or professional hoods for oven extraction; or even the accessoried kitchen, with its abundance of clever solutions to meet even the most diverse needs. The models multiply, the rooms of the home are populated with ever more numerous items of equipment. This is a phenomenon that follows the fragmentation of lifestyles and the pulverization of the nuclear family. Without losing its role as the institutional, co-operative and solidarity centre of society, the family has been divided up into so many small subunits, consisting for the most part of the single individuals that compose it. To each a television, to each his own walkman, to each his own hair dryer, to each his own time for returning home, his own time to eat, to use the refrigerator or the microwave oven.

The proliferation of technologies and their personalization strengthens the individual relationship with the fitting-out of their own home. The fact must not be forgotten, for example, that – in contrast to what happens in other countries, where kitchen equipment is experienced as an integral part of the home, as fixed elements like those of the bathroom – in this country the kitchen space is always fitted out with furnishing elements acquired *ad hoc* (Dell'Acqua, 1993, p. 136). This fact is also closely connected with the extraordinary development of the industry of furniture for the kitchen that sees this country in a

Michele De Lucchi, design of a kitchen interior, standing out in which are the "soft technology" elements of the Girmi small appliances, 1979.

Michele De Lucchi, model of fan, produced by Girmi, 1979.

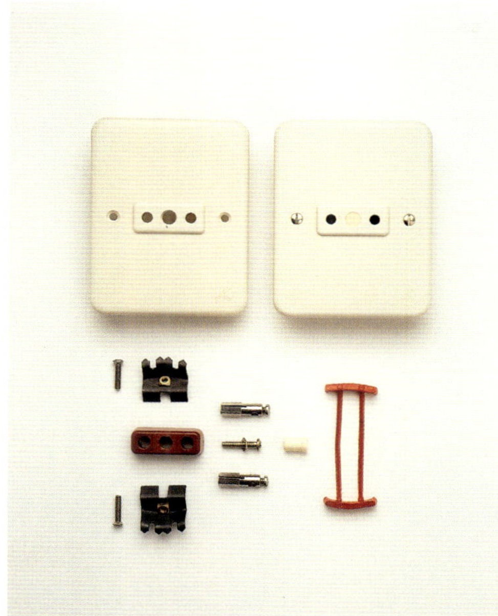
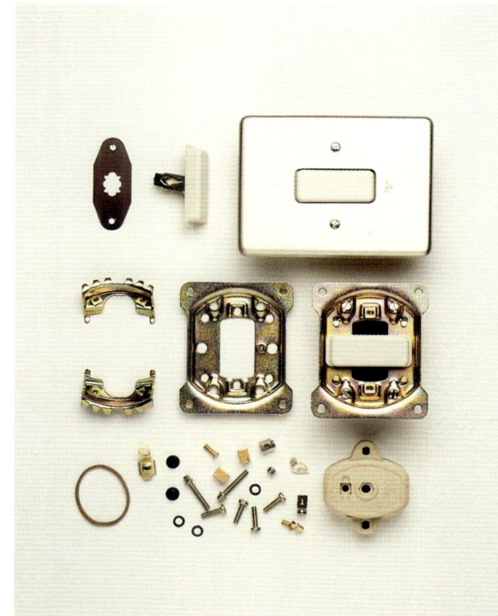

Series of historical light switches produced by BTicino, '50s-'60s.

A modern BTicino light switcher (2000) installed in MY HOME house-web, Piazza Diaz, Milan.

Denis Santachiara, Ines domestic robot for the exhibition *Il progetto domestico*, 15th Triennial, Milan, produced by Kartell, 1985.

leading position. The design factor, which counted for so much in the appliances sector, has also sustained the sector of skilfully crafted furniture combined with the production processes of sophisticated industrialization.
In this context, a tendency has developed to charge the physical world with visual value, even the small things, even the most minute details of the technology. Everything is superbly functional, but every technical object, every utensil must appear loaded with aesthetic values: it is no longer sufficient that impeccable performance is guaranteed; they must have attractive forms, always new and amazing.
The final chapter of this history is that of the most recent and pervasive dream of the intelligent home, the one that sees the move from the electrical to the electronic appliance, and to the functional and communicational integration of equipment for control, safety, comfort and information. Born in the United States in the late '70s, following the invention of an actuator capable of turning electrical equipment on and off at a predefined time, the automation of the home soon conquered a significant place in research in Europe too, as well as once again suggesting material to architects and designers for domestic scenarios seen as allegories of the presence of technologies in the human environment. We are thinking, among others, of the Telecoms house by Ugo La Pietra, Gianfranco Bettetini and Aldo Grasso from the 1983 Milan Trade Fair or the Remote controlled house by Andrea Branzi or Ines, the Terminal house by Denis Santachiara, both for the exhibition *Il progetto domestico* at the 15th Triennial in 1986.
From the '80s to today, the whole concept of habitation has been rethought following the shifting of attention from the home in itself (understood as a complex of structures) to the integrated and systemic functions of communication, comfort and safety. On the basis of this new conception, habitation as a whole is considered as an organic complex of service structures, rationally and efficiently integrated, to meet the manifold requirements of use (Enea 2001 Automation). The idea that lies at the basis of the research and experimentation going on all over the world is that all the technical equipment in the home could be connected up and controlled by the user through small centralized control stations.
In this context, it appears clear that there is a different and more highly structured function for installations and their terminals, beginning with the traditional switch, developing into a full-blown system of instruments, with interfaces for videos and consoles.
Once again Italian creativity is faced with a challenge coming from new technologies, this time fleeting, immaterial, pervasive.

Andrea Branzi

A Homeless Country

Experimental models for the domestic space

Bruno Munari, Abitacolo polyfunctional structure, produced by Robots, 1971.

Middle class interior, Germany, mid-19th century.

To talk about the Italian research into innovative residential models between 1945 and 2000, we need to begin with a consideration of a historical nature.
This theme in fact has an important and specific origin in the events of this country in the modern era, and has had a great importance in Italian design's way of operating.
Italy's delay in the initial phases of the industrial Revolution weighed heavily on its current design culture, and especially in the formation of the idea, more theoretical than practical, of the modern home.
The home as a real lived-in space has never been present in the history of Italian society, nor has a sure typology of reference ever been defined for design culture.
It was in Britain, in the Victorian reformist climate, that the first true residential models of the middle class emerging from the Industrial Revolution were formed; these models laid the foundations for a lifestyle different from that of the aristocrat, which was to remain an important reference point for the whole of European modernity. In the Victorian mansion, certain templates were established for a sophisticated and intellectual taste: the sunlit sitting-rooms opening onto the garden, the fireplace, the library, the large hospitable kitchen, the children's room, the attic. It was then that the true basic typology of the contemporary home was born, and together with this the search for the fundamental commodities to which new-born design made reference.
At the same time, in Paris, the restoration of Napoleon III defined the canons of the urban home for the new middle classes, attentive to decoration but also to technological innovations and changes in taste. Through the 19th century the bases were therefore laid in Europe for habitation linked to new political and cultural statutes; the first museums of design and the applied arts were born then, such as the Victoria and Albert Museum in London and the Österreisches Museum für Kunste und Industrie in Vienna, the places of an evolutionary vision of the morphology of domestic objects, and also the place of maintenance of archetypes of a world that industrialization threatened.
The foundation of the home of the new modern middle class was entirely missed in Italy; and this absence constituted the premise for a shifting of all the processes of modernization, of behaviours and habitation, which – as we will see – happened not on the basis of transformations already under way, but on their proposal by the avant-garde movements.
From then on the home became a hypothesis of research, a space that belonged more to the imagination that to daily routine: a hypothetical laboratory of experimentation of evolutionary behaviours. So, many homes for the future, none for the present.
The process of renewal of the applied arts under way in Europe during the 19th century was a battle to safeguard the dignity of the home and living there; Morris's Red House can be considered a symbol of this. At the beginning of the 20th century, the battleground shifted to architecture, which seemed to be the place of recomposition of a new civilization.
This long season of debates was concluded with a vast programmatic recomposition when in 1907 the Deutscher Werkbund, in plenary session, directed an appeal to artists, intellectuals, architects and poets, to collaborate to make the world inhabitable again, devastated as it was by the expansion of industrialism, according to a collective project to which industry, craftsmanship and the applied arts could furnish important tools.
In 1928 Walter Gropius proposed the recomposition of the major and minor arts in the unity of the building, that is, in the

Giovanni Muzio and Mario Sironi, Graphic arts room, 4th Triennial, Monza, 1930.

inhabited house as a central and positive place for a new design culture, born within industrialization.
In Italy modernity did not propose any of these recompositions, but produced two great models of aesthetic thought: Futurism and Metaphysics, and neither of these movements made reference to a possible model for the home.
Futurism proposed a scandalous, dynamic modernity, capable of producing a kind of permanent revolution, inside "a city that rises", without destination and without form, and in homes crossed by uncontrollable flows of information and transformations.
For the Futurists, technology was not the bearer of new systems of certainties, but of a permanent instability, a progress that created imbalances, fast transformations, scandals and fractures. Theirs was an idea of discontinuous progress and a permanent growth in the crisis and uncertainty of domestic values and rites.
Futurism performed the first shift of the focal point of cultural and aesthetic production in Europe, from the home towards the city. If in Europe, from the World Exhibitions to Bauhaus, the place of a possible cultural recomposition had been sought in production for the home as the sample sector of a renewed universe, for the Futurists the point of reference became the city, understood as a structure open to modifications and conflicts, in which the project signalled the vortices of divergent and incompatible drives. Public and private, home and city, intimacy and technical development had entered into an incurable contradiction, to which Futurist culture testified.
The "words in freedom" of the Futurist visual poets, such as Francesco Gargiulo and Filippo Tommaso Marinetti, or the set designs of Anton Giulio Bragaglia, are very clear in this sense: not even the space of a page, of a home, can be defended from the continuous flows of information, noises and signs that cross the city, disrupting the order of metrics and furnishings from the outside.
In its turn, Metaphysics sought in modernity the traces of a classical identity, the memory of a humanistic root, which made the home an uninhabitable theatre of an existential discomfort.
Both Futurism and Metaphysics warned in different ways of the failure of the dawning modern civilization.
Metaphysical painting came about from the immobility of the present, closed between the failure of the past and the failure of the future: it looked with irony at both the myth that history brought to us, devoid of meaning, and a future without direction and values. The man that Savinio

Giorgio de Chirico, *The Enigma of the Day*, 1914. Museum of Modern Art, New York.

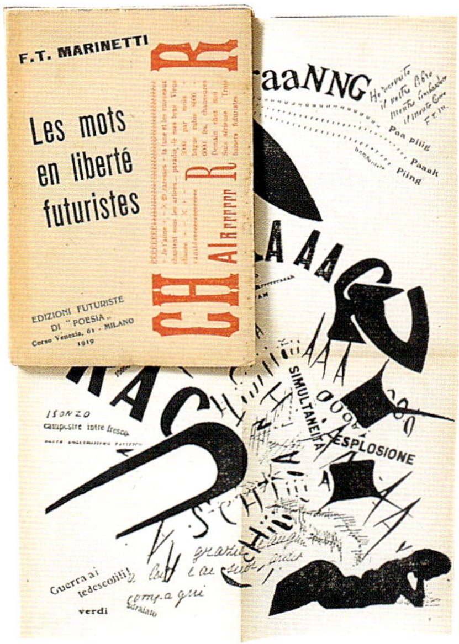

Filippo Tommaso Marinetti, *Les mots en liberté futuristes*, Edizioni Futuriste di "Poesia", 1919.

paints is an antiquarian, hoarded in whose abdomen are indigestible fragments of the past, inside a modernity without Enlightenment and without progress.
Domestic items were the embarrassing testimonies of an unjustifiable inheritance and the insides of bourgeois rooms were ironic theatres of battles of argonauts who had never existed.
In this sense Metaphysics was the child of a country struggling to find the energy for a total modernization, and drawing from this state of indeterminateness a continuous suspension and a wholly original deposit of logical contradictions.
Metaphysics developed an Italian model of enigmas, as missing answers to missing questions. A world of theatrical scenes for a homeless man.
Even Gabriele d'Annunzio's house at the Vittoriale was an example of the literary conception of the environment, as eclectic as life itself, which contrasted originally with the rigour of European modernity.
In his mausoleum d'Annunzio affirmed the very Italian idea of a home that belongs to autobiography, a store of testimonies and symbols, extraneous to any pre-arranged and repeatable model. A place both unconfessable and at the same time the

Giacomo Balla, *Screen (with Speed Lines)*, 1917. Beatrice B. Davis collection, Kansas City.

Giuseppe Terragni, interior of first floor meeting room with decorations by Mario Radice, Casa del Fascio, Como, 1936.

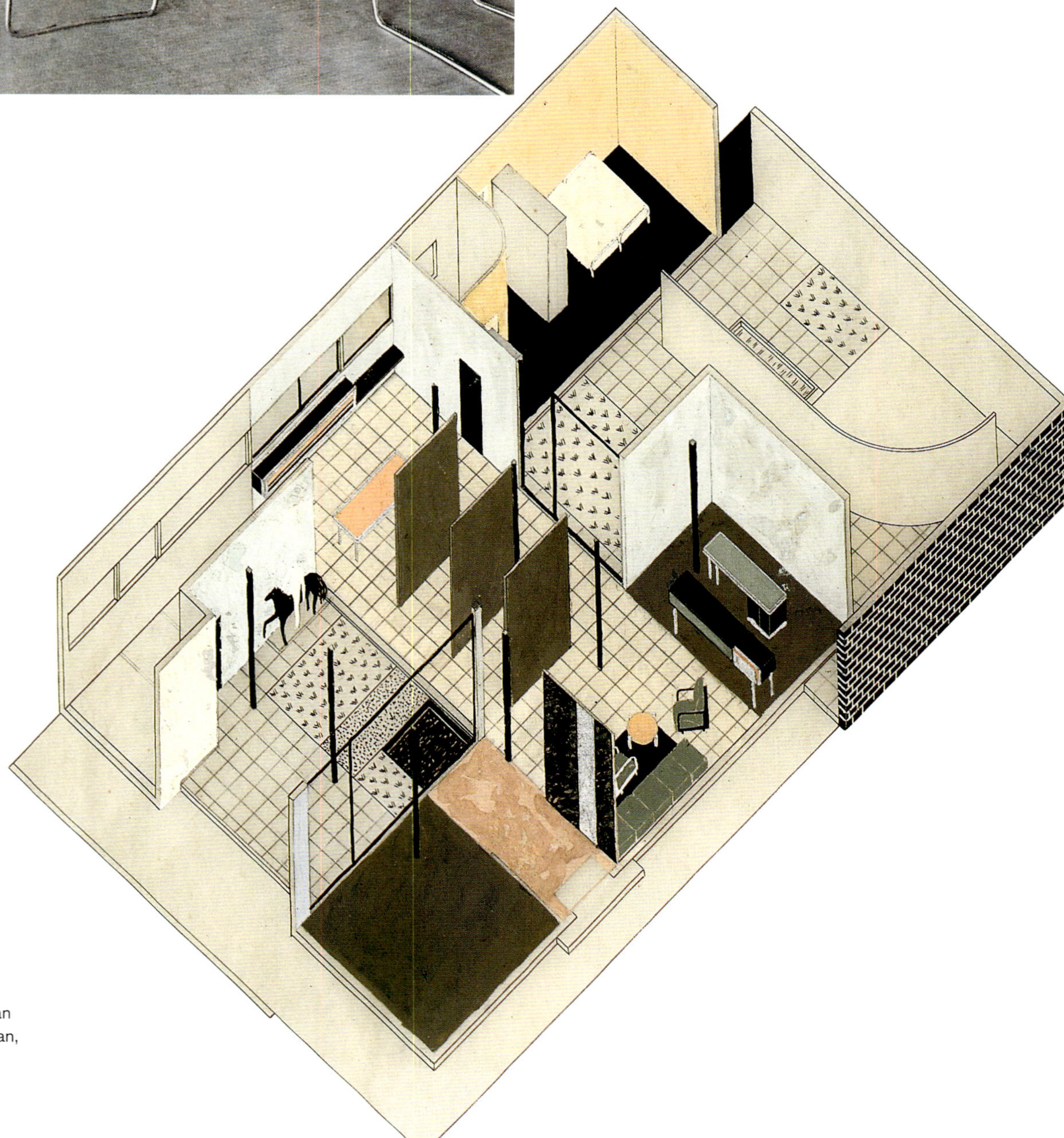

Luigi Figini and Gino Pollini, Villa-studio for an artist, 5th Triennial, Milan, 1933.

BBPR, Manetti apartment, 1933.

BBPR, Premoli apartment, 1935.

theatre of its own most daring self-presentation.

The works of the so-called Italian Rationalist-Fascists, even if of extraordinary quality, were the fruit of isolated figures such as Giuseppe Vaccaro, Ignazio Gardella, Franco Albini, Edoardo Persico, Giuseppe Terragni, Luigi Figini and Gino Pollini, Giuseppe Pagano, and then Adalberto Libera, Luigi Moretti, Mario Ridolfi, Giovanni Michelucci and Ludovico Quaroni.

These were architects who moved on the faultline that divided the two continents of Futurism and Metaphysics, of which from time to time they bore obvious traces. It is no coincidence that Manfredo Tafuri talked rather of Surrealists when referring to the protagonists of Italian Rationalism.

The first work of so-called Italian Rationalism was the furnishing of Casa Zampini in Macerata, by Ivo Pannaggi in 1925, and presented by Marinetti as an orthodox Futurist work. This work testifies to how Italian Rationalism was generated from the interior of the irrationalist movement (Futurism) that had preceded it.

Italian Rationalism consisted wholly of exceptions, of theoretical, uninhabitable, provisional, experimental houses and heterodox methodologies, which used art for its technological possibilities and technology for its artistic possibilities.

The Italian Rationalist movement laid the foundations for the distinct characteristics of modern Italian architecture today: oscillating between structuralism and monumentalism, between methodology and ideology, producing isolated works in discontinuity with the context, bringing out the polemical and critical component rather than aiming at vast operations to gain consensus and habitability.

The relationship between Terragni and Italian design is an important one, because, as the major exponent of Italian Rationalism, he never proposed a simple functional solution for furnishing objects. They presented themselves rather as sarcastic presences, almost ironic exercises in reason that challenged the conventions of good taste; objects close to the gesture of the artist, who invents forms and functions together. This autonomy of the furnishing object with respect to the space that contains it, this discontinuity between the small and the large scale, were the testimony of how Italian Rationalism worked outside the idea of the unity of the project and aimed rather to create multiple, often conflictual, design circuits,

Franco Albini, Living room in a villa, 7th Triennial, Milan, 1940.

View of the Housing Exhibition curated by Belgiojoso, Diomede, Mattioni, Rusconi Clerici and Ciocca, fitted out by Marco Zanuso, at the 8th Triennial, Milan, 1947.

able to produce differences of potential inside the inhabited space.
Also Terragni therefore, as Giacomo Balla before him, and then Franco Albini and Gio Ponti, proposed the rebellion of the object that Manfredo Tafuri discussed: a rebellion against spatial hierarchies, against functionalist aridity, to produce that "cruel elegance of pre-war Italian avant-garde design".
The young Gio Ponti also drew inspiration from the climate of a surreal neo-classicism; Ponti was the Italian designer who most completely developed the themes of the relationship of mutual animation between innovation and tradition, between religious faith and modernity, between architecture and design, between profession and promotion, also acting as a bridge between the pre-war and post-war periods.
His professional success consisted in a particular interpretation of an innovating but non-enlightened modernity, which combined Futurist unpredictability with the classicism of "Novecento", yet without believing in either one or the other, but in the end only in himself, and in the liberation of his own creativity.
Presenting his "Italian-style house" in *Domus* in 1928, he said: "Beautiful as a crystal, but perforated like a grotto full of stalactites." As a true Catholic he therefore saw together the temptation of form and salvation from it in light. Dark caves and bright crystals were sides of the same coin, parts of the same play. Everything was a game, and so the game was the only serious thing; rather, it was life itself.
In the '50s the powerful political hegemonies that emerged from the war of Liberation (Catholic and Communist), for various reasons did not favour the starting of a real process of modernization of the country.
The Italian design of the post-war period was also born out of the strange alliance between intellectuals (expelled from both the government and the opposition), and small- and medium-sized company owners, historically extraneous from and dissatisfied by central government. In given geographical areas, such as Milan, they established a kind of operational

Marco Zanuso, experimental dwelling with folding foam-rubber padded seats and bed, 9th Triennial, Milan, 1951.

Gio Ponti, Habitable windows, 8th Triennial, Milan, 1947.

alliance that chose to begin immediately, starting with industrial products, the transformation of society and structures that Rome was so slow in planning. This tactical alliance was born out of the faith that in the "real" country there existed an unanswered demand for modernity, to which it could respond with good economic results.

Between 1946 and 1947, the first exhibitions (the RIMA and the 8th Triennial) were organized in Milan for the production of popular furniture. Those first exhibitions were very important for the development of Italian design; and not only for social and industrial reasons.

We can in fact note that, according to the Italian tradition, well represented by the Triennial itself, the theme of the exhibition was proposed not to document an existing state of fact, but rather to suggest it as a work theme for planners and industrialists. The result of these exhibitions was in fact not to construct a catalogue of productions at the market's disposal, but to illustrate what the production of popular furnishings could have been. At the basis of these initiatives, therefore, was not the solution to a problem, but rather its presentation to the public, and to the industry that would have had to produce it.

The project therefore illustrated the theme, urging the solution to it, but did not confront its real and immediate practicability. If we analyse those projects by Vico Magistretti, Gardella, Michelucci or Albini today, we see that their furnishing programmes, motivated by the desire to intercept a popular realism, practised a kind of domestic landscape that did not have any reference to the real

Achille and Piergiacomo Castiglioni, living room prepared for the exhibition *Colori e forme nella casa d'oggi*, Villa Olmo, Como, 1957.

Ettore Sottsass, Kama Sutra bedroom, installation at the exhibition *La casa abitata*, Florence, 1965.

behaviour of users, much less to mass-scale productivity.
Italian design was therefore born in a figurative form, hypothesizing a cultural evolution of use, starting with the proposal of basic furnishing, artisan and economic systems.
Yet in this evident absence of realism, Italian design and its industry paved the way for a different value for the concept of the project, understood as an autonomous reality, reflecting the market but never entirely corresponding to it; yet precisely for this reason capable of organizing an equation rich in variables, experimental, to which a zero never corresponded, but which produced a difference, a surplus to be used as energy of communication and as stimulation for a new expansion. If at the first RIMA exhibitions and the Triennial they wanted to connect the dawning Italian design with the themes of the reconstruction of the country and with a possible industrial planning, the apparently unusable response that followed it was – if we look closely – endowed with its own realism; it signalled the major complexity that existed in the theme, which went well beyond the optimism of the politicians, and vindicated the autonomy of the designer in also developing the question, and not only the answer.
If we look at the exhibitions on modern furnishing that followed each other with growing success in Italy, during the '50s and '60s, we can ascertain that despite the great programmatic commitment, the idea of the home became ever more elusive. In 1957 the Castiglioni brothers, participating in the exhibition *Colori e forme nella casa d'oggi* (Colours and Forms in Today's

Achille and Piergiacomo Castiglioni, living room, installation at the exhibition *La casa abitata*, Florence, 1965.

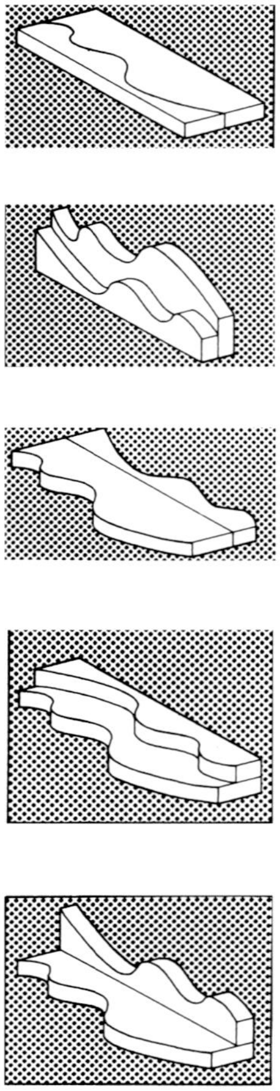

Home) at Villa Olmo in Como, proposed a kind of furnishing of residual space, an Italian home under the staircase, the inhabited closet, where modernity is defined as liberty, the provisional, the accidental. A kind of clever DIY of great elegance and looseness, entirely out of position with respect to the rigours of European Rationalism, but capable of making explicit that state of permanent uncertainty that Italian design has always ridden, since its birth in the Futurist avant-gardes.

In 1965 the exhibition *La casa abitata* (The Lived-In Home) was organized at Palazzo Strozzi in Florence, as part of the Triennial of Modern Furnishing, in which, among others, Spadolini, Mario Zanuso, De Carli, Angelo Mangiarotti and Vittorio Gregotti exhibited, with settings for the first true industrial, mass-produced items. Ettore Sottsass presented a room devoted to the Kama Sutra, with a double bed placed at the centre of the home: a sort of erotic foundation for living outside the functionalist line laboriously proposed in the intentions of the exhibition.

From then on, Italian design developed housing models that had no comparison, the fruit of a culture that saw the home as the place of maximum social and planning diversification, favoured by the very indeterminateness of the Italian term *abitare* (to live, inhabit).

In the late '60s groups of young people and less young architects took shape in the various cities of Italy (Florence, Turin, Milan, Naples). Launching a sort of early Pop-design, they came together in the radical movement that constituted the first front critical of the certainties of classical modernity (Archizoom Associati, Superstudio, Ufo, Ziggurat, Strum). This placed itself on the threshold of an epochal transition, one that saw the end of the context in which the historical avant-gardes had operated and the dawning of an age in which it was the whole of society that adopted an avant-garde logic, definitively burning all its standards, every root, living from innovation and advanced technologies.

The radical movement signalled the impossibility for the historical avant-garde

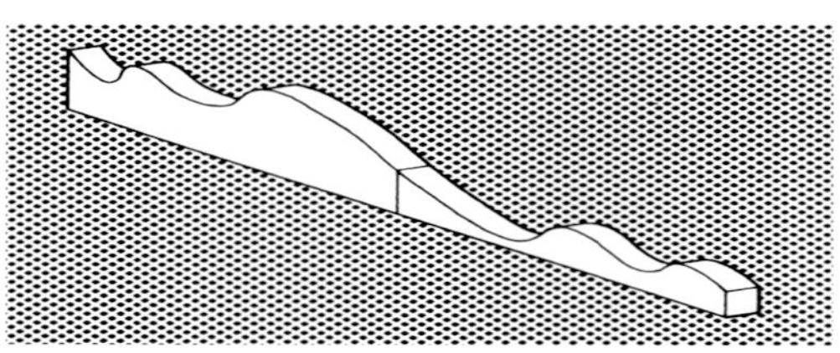

Archizoom Associati, Superonda sofa, produced by Poltronova, 1966.

Archizoom Associati,
La Superficie Neutra
habitable wardrobe,
1972.

Ettore Sottsass, Grey furniture, presented at the Eurodomus, Milan, 1970.

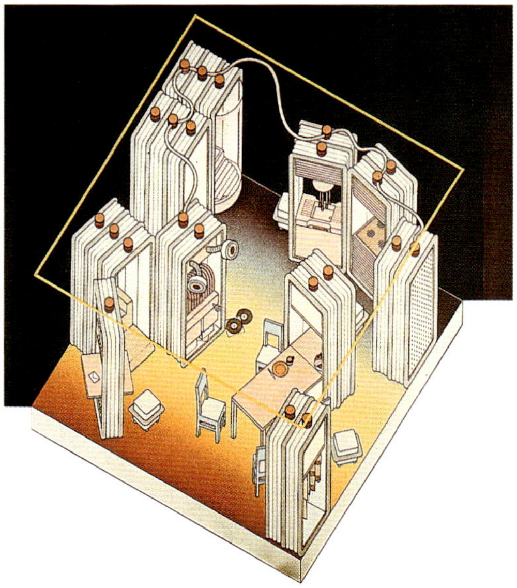

Ettore Sottsass, experimental domestic environment for the exhibition *Italy: the New Domestic Landscape*, New York, 1972.

to live in an age when the avant-garde was widespread among contemporary society: the radicalism marked society's definitive uprooting from its albeit weak traditions and from its albeit weak modern theorems. The movement refused any unity, any recognizable linguistic and methodological code, to act instead as a movement operating within itself, to definitively burn any residual trace of the old modernity, to free its creative energy in search of new orders for the project in a hybrid metropolis and society.
The idea of a home as the place for recomposition of classical modernity passed away definitively all over the western world: for everyone the home became the true theatre of post-industrial complexity, where standard and one-off products, advanced and primitive technologies, mass languages and sophisticated signs, and codified and anarchistic behaviours all coexisted.
A warm home, therefore, definitively experimental and provisional.
Between 1964 and 1972, therefore, changes occurred in Italy that in just a few years made its design the most interesting phenomenon, also at international level.
In 1972 Emilio Ambasz organized the exhibition *Italy: the New Domestic Landscape* at the MoMA in New York, with the design of a nation being introduced to the world public for the first time. And the scenario that emerged in that first great exhibition was the one that, with secondary variations, was to characterize the decades that followed.
Present in fact at that exhibition were the generation of masters and the new protagonists of the radical avant-garde, the theorists, the historians, the industrialists, and the problematic themes typical of that culture, that is, the relationship between the home and new technologies.
Italian design emerged there as a phenomenon deeply rooted in the contradictions of a country that had never been the true protagonist of modernity, a design not definable in a style (as the Scandinavian or the German), deprived of a unitary methodology, consisting of opposing tendencies, personalities and politics, and produced by a weak but rampant industry; data that as a whole defined its originality and actuality, as well as its substantial strategic unity.
This strategic unity was defined by Emilio Ambasz with the term "new domestic landscape", indicating that the general novelty that Italian design presented from the rooms of the MoMA was a domestic scenario already very different from those proposed by Le Corbusier, Charles Eames or Richard Neutra, which were all based on the permanence of a stylistic and functional code, to be placed in a rigorous urban context for an enlightened, Calvinist society.
Italian design, however, proceeded along in fits and starts: it mixed mass production with artisan products, experimental prototypes with modular systems.
The new Italian domestic scene consisted of incomplete segments, expressive fragments of a partial modernity, inserted within which could be historical fragments and qualities linked to the art of habitation, in deteriorating suburbs, or the open Italian landscapes: a domestic scenery that communicated with the art of dressing and eating, according to an evolutionary model of modernity, free and uncodified; a modernity that fed on its internal contradictions, its political limits – on its references to a poorly defined market – to respond to behaviours more imagined than real.
Also the technical objects on display and designed by the masters of Italian design manifested their reference of use to unlikely gestures: radios portable like bags, typewriters like schoolbags, televisions to stand on the floor, take-apart couches, endlessly sectional armchairs, habitable cars, space cockpits for destructured homes (Zanuso, Sottsass,

Alberto Rosselli, experimental domestic environment for the exhibition *Italy: the New Domestic Landscape*, New York, 1972.

Vico Magistretti, Selene chair (1966) and Vicario armchair (1971), produced by Artemide.

Marco Zanuso, experimental domestic environment for the exhibition *Italy: the New Domestic Landscape*, New York, 1972.

Enzo Mari, Sof-Sof chair and Frate table, produced by Driade, 1972.

Bellini, Gae Aulenti, Cini Boeri).
Yet this high functional and commercial improbability, instead of providing Italian design with an appearance of a pure formal exercise, gave it a positive charge, an aggressiveness that transcended the elegance of the forms, describing less canonical relationships between product and user, between project and non-project, between home and city; leapfrogging architecture, it left the spaces of the home undefined and open to the user's free intuition.
The theme of the *abitacolo* (polyfunctional structure) had already been developed in 1969 by Joe Colombo (present at the MoMA) for his exhibition *Visiona* in Frankfurt; already then it was a kind of "lived-in machine" that proposed the integration of all dwelling functions within a single volumetric organism, created in a large white plastic case.
Joe Colombo's idea not only heralded the possibility of mass-producing domestic systems and service technologies, but, also, through this compacting, freed up the surrounding space, making it an available territory for activity not controlled by the project. The theme of an unplanned habitation was taken up in New York by the Archizoom group, who proposed a grey, empty room inside which a child's voice described a bright and colourful house, which every visitor could freely imagine.
For the American market – stuck with the myths of mass diffusion of comfort and optimism in a standardized modernity –

Jonathan De Pas, Donato D'Urbino and Paolo Lomazzi, Shanghai clothes-stand, produced by Zanotta, 1973.

and for the European market – uncertain and traumatized by the devastating effects of youthful revolt and its terrorist followers – the image of the Italian "new domestic landscape" had a major importance in terms of culture and market, because it pointed out a road that, instead of bemoaning the shattering certainties, seemed decided upon riding that crisis, changing its sign, transforming it into a positive opportunity for the release of new energies.
In other words, the diagram that appeared of the MoMA exhibition was that of an effective surpassing of modernity and its idea of linear development: it was the birth, *de facto* and from below, of a second modernity: an unbalanced, unenlightened modernity, less unitary but more enjoyable.
This context, so profoundly renewed, was called (ten years later) post-industrial civilization, and too many essays have been written on it for us to analyse the phenomenon here.
The fragmenting of the great mass markets into niche markets directed at semantic and fashionable groups – and therefore the demand for ever more sophisticated expressive qualities – the capacity to manage the soft and sensorial structures of space and the product already belonged to the history of this discipline in Italy, even before the new operational conditions imposed with urgency a global renewal of design all over the world.
When in the late '70s the crisis of

Ugo La Pietra, Telecoms house, Milan Trade Fair, 1972.

Alessandro Mendini with studio Alchymia, Proust's armchair, produced by Alchymia (1978), today produced by Cappellini.

Michele De Lucchi, Holiday home, in the exhibition *Le case della Triennale*, Palazzo dell'Arte, Milan, 1983.

Paolo Deganello and Alberto Magnaghi, Shared home, in the exhibition *Le case della Triennale*, Palazzo dell'Arte, Milan, 1983.

modernity became the central theme of the whole culture of western design, Italian design had already internalized the post-modern question, avoiding those serious revolutions into which architecture ended up falling.
Italy was therefore the only country in the world that continued to experiment with housing models until the end of the 20th century, following a strategy of stylistic research into its components, but also following the path of functional transformations, intercepting those subtle but profound mutations that happen inside the contemporary city.
Placed at the crossroads between the universe of the new information technologies, the intelligent objects, the new professions, and the scenario of contemporary cities where all the traditional functional goals dissolve and blur, the contemporary home presents itself as a landscape in which production, commerce, promotion, and residence coexist. It is a space that is relational, therefore, reversible, part designed and part available for unforeseen actions, an incubator of the new economy for an entrepreneurial, planning society, which often needs to change the modes of use of space.
When Italy is referred to as a "homeless country", it is not at all intended to underline a negative aspect; on the contrary, the intention is to indicate its capacity to envisage the configurations of contemporaneity well in advance, prefiguring a world like the current one, one that no longer has a sure point in the home, but sees it rather as an opportunity, an openness towards social and technical change.
Only cultural systems like the Italian one, that for a century have considered the home as an open problem, as an order in evolution, are today capable of providing architecture, urban matters, and also design, with the information necessary to face contemporaneity.
If once there was much talk of the "home of the future", today we have to speak of the "home of the present", because the future is an out-of-date category. The adaptation of the project to meet the mutations that have occurred and are occurring has become the central problem of our weak and diffused modernity: many mental and political delays risk creating an unbridgeable gap with respect to the real times of the economy and changing society.

Dante Donegani and Giovanni Lauda, Hideaway effect, 1997.

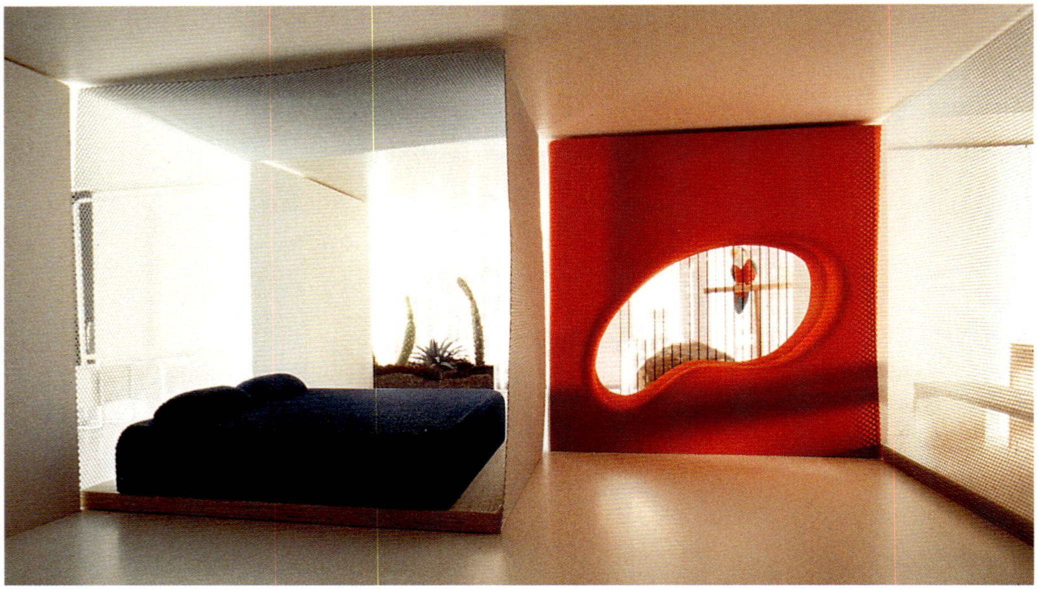

Andrea Branzi, Vertical home, 1998.

Research into new housing models, coordinated by Dante Donegani and Giovanni Lauda, with the assistance of Jae Kyu Lee, project by Carole Chabert: the Horizontal home, Domus Academy, Milan, 1997.

Giuseppe Finessi

Laser Deviations*

Visual arts and interior architecture in Italy 1938–2000

Ettore Sottsass, detail of a wall in ceramic tiling for a Milan house, 1955.

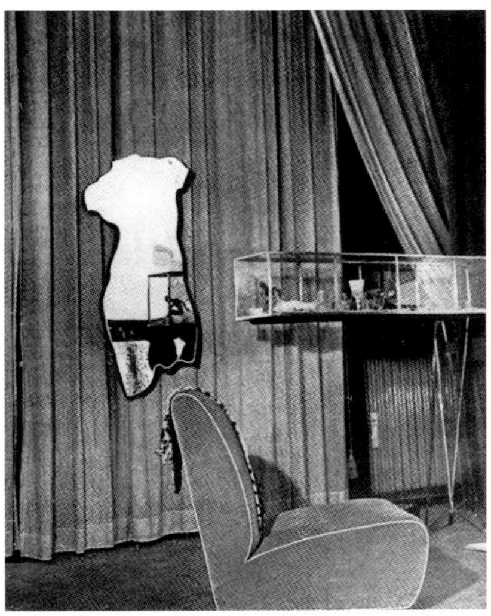

Carlo Mollino, Miller house, Turin, 1938.

This is a difficult history to recount. A naturally difficult, necessarily difficult one, formed of friendships, interconnections, habits, complicity, passion, betrayals, reflections, rebounds, corruptions. And much else besides.
The relationship between visual arts and interior architecture in Italy from the Second World War to the present day is a story made of many tiny links, fragments and episodes. It is a story made of many architects in love with art, and of the work of many artists/friends in tune with their projects, a story characterized by an outsider *par excellence* who evades catalogue definitions and professional/disciplinary boxing-in such as Bruno Munari, and strung between the reasoning of two artists who have given a fundamental contribution to modern architecture (and not only Italian) – Lucio Fontana and Gianni Colombo – and clarified by the work of three architects/artists who have provided texts: Getulio Alviani, Gaetano Pesce and Corrado Levi. Mingled in with all this were, pleasure, luck and excitement, and there are many things to be read between the lines.

Let us proceed by pointing our laser on the variegated world of these deviations and omissions from the history of architecture as it is normally told.

Carlo Mollino, Miller house, Turin, 1938
Untiring and open-minded, explosive and genial, a representative of the rare category of true outsiders, Carlo Mollino followed in his father's footsteps in Turin from the middle of the '30s. Able to shuffle the cards of modern architecture like a true magician, or perhaps a highly talented cardsharp, Mollino concentrated upon interior architecture for at least twenty years, making it his preferred venue for experimenting with and focusing his personal style. Often this took the form of autobiography, often for his own spaces (family homes) or for an extremely restricted circle of acquaintances, these interiors were far from any possible rapport with the prevailing architecture of other architects. "Architecture in one's free time. A full-time hobby", wrote Mollino's first biographer, Giovanni Brino, to describe the multitude of passions that passed through the life of this architect,

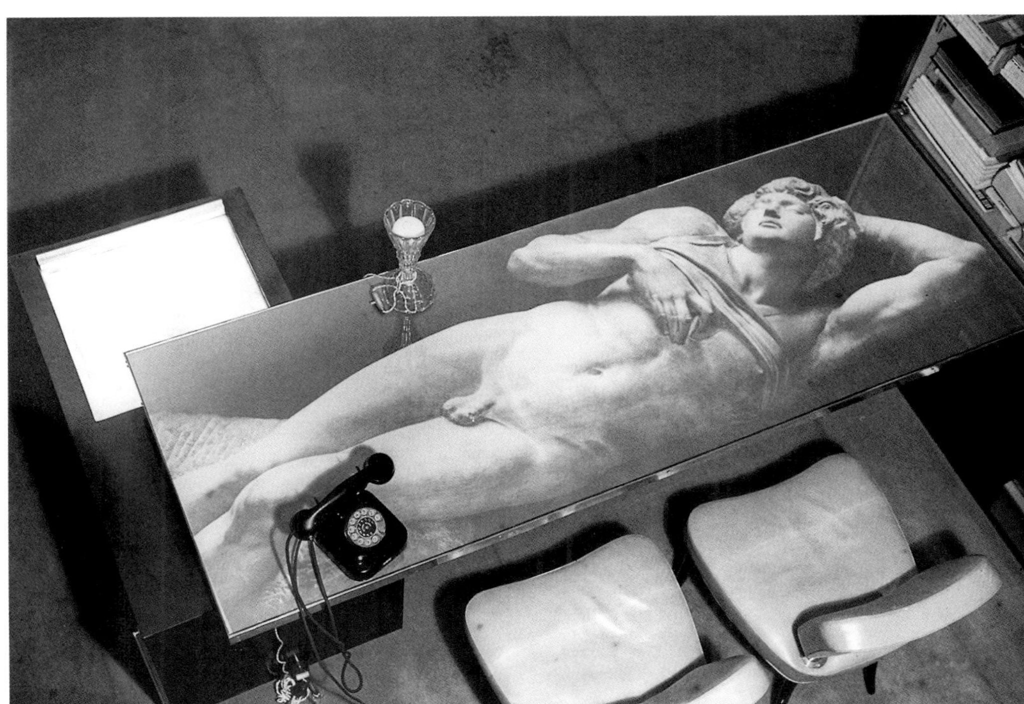

*"Deviazioni laser" is the title of an essay by Corrado Levi on Filippo de Pisis published in *De Pisis*, exhibition catalogue (Palazzo Grassi, Venice 1983), Milan 1983, pp. 34-35.

Marco Zanuso with artists Dova and Ballocco, library of the College of Architects, Milan, 1952.

rendering it volcanic, but enabling him to include in his architectural project all the things he would be doing away from his project table. Hence his passion for flying, for motor cars and speed, for skiing and mountains, for fashion, literature, travel, eroticism and women, and for photography (which in terms of results and volume produced can be placed on a par with his architecture). All passions that Mollino actively pursued and lived intensely as true arts, to be honoured with the greatest commitment. He would write important treatises on photography, patent instruments for aircraft, race in the Millemiglia on a Bisiluro designed by himself, publish novels and take tens of thousands of photographs. Passions (and arts), these, that Mollino would bring in some way into his interiors, each time making them spaces for experimentation and interdisciplinary contamination. In the Miller house, designed immediately after his first masterpiece (Società Ippica Torinese), a setting in which Mollino invented a lamp that ran along an electrified rail on the ceiling – designing a slalom in the rooms – to position itself always in the most suitable place; his love for classical art is exemplified by a giant photograph of a Michelangelo *Prisoner* which becomes the studio table.
Thus writes Elena Tamagno: "In this arrangement of interiors, Carlo Mollino continued his poetic view of architecture, overturning the viewpoint and making it the setting for his own encounters, his own photographs, his own fantasies. Here, he seems to test some assumptions that he would subsequently develop in his interior architecture, whilst he almost ingenuously declares his cultural and affectionate bonds with [artists] Italo Cremona and Piero Martina". It might be a disrespectful shifting of priorities, perhaps, to place a telephone (!) on a masterpiece, but the point of non-return has by now been passed. From that moment on, classical capitals become side-tables, female profiles become tables or mirrors, views of landscape and architecture become giant photographs to

Luigi Figini and Gino Pollini with Fausto Melotti, lamp for the office and residential building in Via Broletto, Milan, 1947–48.

Main stairway in the 9th Milan Triennial, 1951, above which hangs Lucio Fontana's *Spatial light*. Design by Luciano Baldessari and Marcello Grisotti.

Carlo De Carli with Lucio Fontana, Galli apartment, Via Pontaccio, Milan, 1951.

apply to walls in order to contribute to the narrative and setting. Art is a 360-degree narrative for this first hero of contamination, and in this sense he is the first true modern Italian architect.

Roberto Menghi and Marco Zanuso with Lucio Fontana, "Spatial friezes" for office building, Via Senato, Milan, 1947
An emblematic example of "integration of the arts" between the art of Lucio Fontana and the work of Roberto Menghi and Marco Zanuso. A series of panels fitted beneath the window and made from glazed pottery with manganese, this is a *Spatial frieze* that shows off and adds value to the architecture, being placed in specially defined spaces, rendering them more noble and making them stand out and vibrate with its material informality.

Luigi Figini and Gino Pollini with Fausto Melotti, office and residential building, Via Broletto, Milan, 1947–48
It was in the fertile, rich setting of the Triennial exhibitions that the young Figini and Pollini began working with the artists, with Lucio Fontana and with Fausto Melotti before him. It was the latter who would design the lamps for the building in Via Broletto, imagining them as a long, ruffled leaf ready to screen the light-source.

Carlo De Carli with Lucio Fontana, Galli apartment, Via Pontaccio, Milan, 1951
With the Galli apartment in Milan, Carlo De Carli wrote an important chapter regarding his idea of interior architecture, an idea that sprang from sophisticated reasoning about the distributional/spatial setting, built with the help of a great love for wood as a material of choice ("Tarlo De Tarli" – Woodworm De Woodworm" was the teasing nickname given De Carli as a result of this hidden passion) and sealed by an unconditional love of contemporary art – in particular of sculpture – that drove him to work with some of the most important figures of Italian contemporary art, including Aligi Sassu, Umberto Milani, Gino Cosentino, Alessandro Nastasio, Luisa Premuda, and Agenore Fabbri. However, it was above all with

Angelo Mangiarotti with William Klein, *Endless construction*, Bignardi home, Milan, 1951–52.

Lucio Fontana that De Carli worked: important projects such as the large *Madonna* in Vicenza stone made by the artist for the Cimiano complex of 1958–60, and "minimal" ones, such as the lamps in the living room of the Galli house that Fontana designed for the wooden wall separating this room from the studio, an original contribution for an emblematic fellowship. In the same house, in the dining area that is enlivened by De Carli chairs covered in fabrics of different colours, we find a sculpture by Agenore Fabbri.

Angelo Mangiarotti with William Klein, "Endless construction", Bignardi home, Milan, 1951–52

In the design of the Bignardi home in Milan, Angelo Mangiarotti designed a diaphragm with mobile walls in the form of four pivoting panels running on rails in order to permit ever different positions. The decor, an abstract collage by the American painter William Klein, executed in white, black, cream and yellow, is the factor that helps multiply the number of possible combinations. As Lisa Licitra Ponti, who presents the project of the "young, gifted architect", explained in *Domus*: "The various positions of the panels provoke a series of unexpected points of view and perspectives. The rail on the ceiling runs along the wall, branching off so that the diaphragm can be opened out partially or flattened completely against the wall (alternating the order of the panels, if so desired), and enabling the space to become a single room again." "A minimal machine with maximum effects", "a new fact", that "draws together painting, sculpture and architecture".

Franco Albini, Marcenaro apartment, Genoa, 1954

Franco Albini, the greatest Italian architect of the century, as Alessandro Mendini defines him, makes use of art – including classical art – with respect. And in a measured manner, which is the identifying feature underlying his form of interior architecture. The "detachment" of Franco Albini, his lyricism, his syntax,

Franco Albini, Marcenaro apartment, Genoa, 1954.

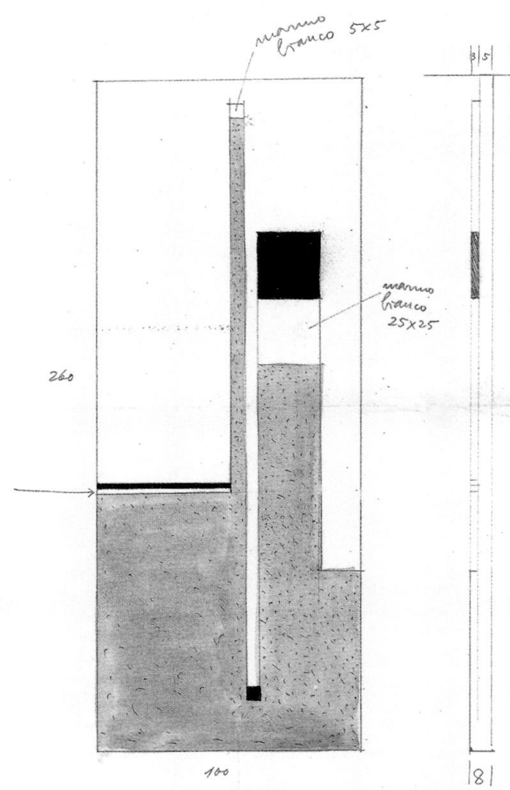

Ico Parisi, Silvio Longhi, Luigi Antonietti with Bruno Munari, *Negative-positive* bas-relief/mosaic for the Padiglione di Soggiorno, 10th Triennial, Milan, 1954, now Biblioteca del Parco.

Gio Ponti (Ponti Fornaroli Rosselli studio) with Bruno Munari, *Negative-positive* decorative panel for the National shop, Milan, 1955.

geometry, and rhythm will all be discussed, and it was said that the heroic season of museum architecture in Italy was never again to reach the levels of his Genoese museums, Palazzo Bianco and Palazzo Rosso. These are moments in which care, control and respect are elements of strength in Albini's architecture of details (and large-scale knowledge), applied there, emblematically, in the relationship with the works of art. Little details to exhibit, hang, illuminate, protect, archive – the verbs which Albini was to adopt as his own and for which he would become a shining example. In his work for the apartment of the councillor, Caterina Marcenaro, on the last floor of Palazzo Rosso in Genoa, Albini recreated a true fragment of a museum, in which the internal divisions are wings and the works of art are hung from a track that (as in the museum) runs through all the rooms; but the elements of architecture are also handled as though they were works of art: chimneys and stairs are suspended from beams and steel cables and emblematically (and theoretically, Albini would add) do not touch the ground. They seem, and indeed are, works of art. Albini transformed the architecture of the interior in the setting and domesticity of art, or vice versa, as he had already done for *Living room for a villa* at the 6th Milan Triennial in 1940, a watershed as far as modern design is concerned. In it, in a light and at the same time rigid setting, rich in pure inventions (an aviary made of netting "formed" around the theory of the hyperbolic paraboloid, a pair of suspended armchairs derived from those used in chair-lifts that are correctly balanced when used, a hammock in metal and cord netting, etc.), art was set with meticulous, but never banal, attention: the sculpture of a reclining woman by Genni Mucchi placed on a crystal floor suspended above a flowery meadow, almost a Michelangelesque statue; the metallic table with a mosaic and glass top from a design by Carlo Del Bon; a painting by Gabriele Mucchi hanging away from the wall thanks to a metal device which also illuminates it for correct vision…

Ico Parisi, Silvio Longhi, Luigi Antonietti with Bruno Munari, "Negative-positive" bas-relief/mosaic for the Padiglione di Soggiorno, 10th Triennial, Milan, 1954, now Biblioteca del Parco

In that origami made architecture, in that folded sheet of reinforced concrete, in that which is the true – perhaps only – masterpiece of Ico Parisi, the Padiglione di Soggiorno, for the 10th Milan Triennial, now aptly transformed into a public library, Bruno Munari, Umberto Milani, Mauro Reggiani and Francesco Somaini were invited to produce mosaics, bas-reliefs and sculptures for the architecture that was being constructed. But whilst Milani, Reggiani and Somaini participated in a traditional manner, simply by overlaying their works over the skin and spaces of that architecture, Bruno Munari interpreted the ideals of that invitation to best effect (it was the Triennial of the "Integration of the Arts"), and designed a bas-relief/mosaic using his (already) famous negatives-positives, a decorative element that was perfectly integrated with the architecture, a play upon perception and space, a design obtained in the thickness of the wall of reinforced concrete, to which little inserts of black and white marble were simply added. A work of art that is still unknown to most people, but which still exists.

Gio Ponti (Ponti Fornaroli Rosselli studio) with Bruno Munari, "Negative-positive" decorative panel for the National shop, Milan, 1955

In a double-height space designed by the Ponti studio and destined for a shop and offices, Munari – invited by the generous Ponti – was asked to decorate the wall of

Gio Ponti with Fausto Melotti, Ponti apartment, Via Dezza, Milan, 1957.

Achille and Piergiacomo Castiglioni with Giuseppe Aimone, living room, *Colori e forme nella casa d'oggi* exhibition, Villa Olmo, Como, 1957.

the mezzanine containing the offices (with a blue-green and black *Negative-positive* composition). Some of the squares and rectangles transform themselves – in their integration with the architectural elements – into transparent windows allowing views and the passage of air.

Gio Ponti with Fausto Melotti, Ponti apartment, Via Dezza, Milan, 1957

One of the most important homes in the history of the architecture of Italian interiors: Ponti apartment in Via Dezza, Milan, 1957. Gio Ponti designed a plan in which he played with thresholds and visual telescopes, with his modern idea of space and settings, and continuous, open spaces one after the other, but yet independent and private. Furnished window, self-illuminating furniture... An emblem for Ponti's "total work", the result here was produced in company with Fausto Melotti, who designed and produced a frieze for the ceiling and floors with a diagonal design of textures, graduations and highly refined, light colours.

Achille and Piergiacomo Castiglioni with Giuseppe Aimone, living room, "Colori e forme nella casa d'oggi" exhibition, Villa Olmo, Como, 1957

In the Villa Olmo exhibition, a fundamental milestone in the history of Italian interior decoration, the brothers Achille and Piergiacomo Castiglioni (Cicci and Popo to their friends) showed their masterpiece, the lodestone from which every one of their future projects would draw inspiration. In a setting of just a few square metres, they presented screens of cardboard, armchairs entirely in foam rubber with enigmatic profiles, a television suspended from cables which could be pushed up out of the way, a bicycle seat transformed into a stool for the telephone, a tractor seat transformed into a sprung stool... and many other

Enzo Mari, *Passage*, *Colori e forme nella casa d'oggi* exhibition, Villa Olmo, Como, 1957.

Marcello Nizzoli, decorative panel for the Domosic offices, Castiglione Olona, 1959.

things. The Castiglioni brothers also invited the painter Giuseppe Aimone to work with them. And in what we might define a style "in the manner of Castiglioni", the decoration created by Aimone was produced using perforated moulds. A technique far removed from any form of painting loaded with cultural baggage, a simple but not banal system that was fresh, unusual, non-decipherable and almost abstract, yet achieved by an extraordinarily concrete technique and reasoning.

Enzo Mari, "Passage", "Colori e Forme nella casa d'oggi" exhibition, Villa Olmo, Como, 1957

The then 25-year-old Enzo Mari, fresh from the one-man show *Esperimenti Colore-Volume* (Colour-Volume Experiments) at Milan's Studio b24, participated in the *Colori e forme nella casa d'oggi* (*Colours and Forms* in Today's Home) exhibition by concentrating his attention on a *Passage* between the various spaces hosting the projects of the architects invited. The work, which won him the silver medal (the international jury was formed of André Bloc, Felice Casorati, Alfred Roth and Alberto Viani), was closely linked to the research that Mari had realized, such as *Instruments for research into the relationships between colour and volume* (1951–52) with which "to explore directly the phenomenology of three-dimensional space", or the better known and later *Structures*, which were fundamental in that Programmed Art of which Mari and Munari were the first protagonists.

In the *Passage*, one wall became a composition of identical cubes, painted in black and white with ever-different backgrounds and rhythms. "The origin is of a purely scientific character: several identical volumes, if coloured differently, take on different sizes in our perception." This was a way to reason about space working in essence with just two dimensions. It proved a fundamental experience for Enzo Mari, a true case of "passage" between art and "architecture for interiors/decoration" (here, we happily use the title given to the courses at the Italian architecture faculties at universities in the '50s and '60s).

Marcello Nizzoli, decorative panel for the Domosic offices, Castiglione Olona, 1959

Marcello Nizzoli is considered by many the father of Italian industrial design for his work done with Olivetti – which recalls the emblematic work done by Peter Behrens for AEG. He began with painting, and moved on to illustration, graphic work, publishing and decoration, to arrive subsequently at design and architecture. Clearly, what came later did not cancel out what came before: thus, for example, some of the elements in his typewriters seem to recall, indeed are, highly refined sculptural forms, an association confirmed by this decorative panel for the Domosic offices. Likewise, some of his architecture of the '50s and '60s is marked by a graphic and chromatic sensibility evidenced from his work in neighbouring arts.

Nanda Vigo with Lucio Fontana and Enrico Castellani, Pellegrini house, Milan, 1959–63

Nanda Vigo received her training in Milan in the '50s, working alongside Piero Manzoni, Lucio Fontana and Gio Ponti. She harboured a great passion for glass as a material offering unique characteristics, and she was an experimenter *ante litteram* with the use of artificial light in a manner that is never obvious. She has always undertaken architectural research that aims to integrate the arts, defining "global" settings with an idea of space that is completely new. "Then the encounter with Piero Manzoni; we see each other from afar and recognize each other immediately. Competition with

Above and right:
Nanda Vigo with Lucio Fontana and Enrico Castellani, Pellegrini house, Milan, 1959–63.

Luigi Caccia Dominioni with Corrado Corradi Dell'Acqua, apartment in Via Vigoni, Milan, 1961.

Piero is hard, with no quarter given; he was working on painting, on the conceptual philosophy of objects, and I on the setting. In '59, I produced the first white residential unit, made of light, with glass walls and the neon that changes colour with the changing of daylight; in those years, the architects (there was no mention as yet of designers) were influenced by the North and only used to make wooden furniture, cumbersome, rational boxes…" It was the Pellegrini house, a dry, ordered, never obvious setting, for which Fontana produced one of his shining *Spatial concepts*, which was hung in the conversation area of the living room, perfectly calibrated to those tones, that light, that atmosphere. In the dining area, just as appropriately, there was a large *Surface* by Enrico Castellani, whose play of textures and lights/shades echoed the work of Nanda Vigo.

Luigi Caccia Dominioni with Corrado Corradi Dell'Acqua, apartment in Via Vigoni, Milan, 1961

A corridor from an interior by Luigi Caccia Dominioni with a floor from a design by Corrado Corradi Dell'Acqua. An emblematic example of integration and collaboration between these two friends (other times, Caccia Dominioni would work often with Somaini), this provided a concentrated case of a distribution of an apartment in space: those corridors and rooms leading the one into the other give a clearer idea of Caccia Dominioni's view of interior architecture than the main rooms. For him, spaces normally considered purely in terms of connecting become places to test, to work upon, to live. And even more emblematically, the artist's contribution (is Corradi Dell'Acqua here more artist or more architect?) seems to follow the signs of Caccia Dominioni's sinuous and smooth itineraries on the plan of the apartment, translating them into naturalistic forms.

Vittoriano Viganò with Bruno Munari, Cinema Cavour, Milan, 1963

The history of the true collaboration between Bruno Munari and Vittoriano Viganò has still to be written. It needs to

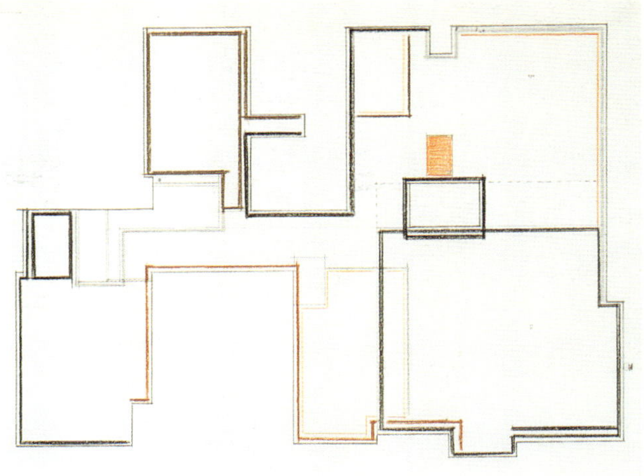

Vittoriano Viganò, geometric ground-plan of Viganò home which in form and colours recalls the compositions of Bruno Munari in his *Negative-positive* series, Milan, 1956.

Vittoriano Viganò, Viganò home, view of the entry to the bathroom, Milan, 1956.

Vittoriano Viganò, interior view of Viganò home with a *Negative-positive* by Bruno Munari in the foreground, Milan, 1956.

Vittoriano Viganò with Bruno Munari, Cinema Cavour, Milan, 1963.

Getulio Alviani, renovation of the Brollo house, Grado, 1964.

Gianni Colombo, *Zoom Squares - Cromodromo*, La Città gallery, Verona, 1970.

be seen not simply in terms of the Viganò home in Milan (1956–58), in which the ground-plan of the house and its axonometry reveal a "negative-positive" work brought into a third dimension with the theorization of the famous architectural stalagmites-stalactites, and where there is an original Munari just there, next to the chimney: an important, unknown, unpublished work, that seems to be the plan of the house, perhaps at one of the different levels, perhaps at ceiling level. It must also be seen in terms of the decoration of the walls that Viganò created in the Istituto Marchiondi at Baggio (1953–57), at the apex of his (our) Brutalist season. This is not quite "negative-positive", but it is clearly linked to Munari's projects. What is certain is their collaboration in this interior project, the refurbishment of the Cinema Cavour in Milan, 1963, marked by the play on the exterior sign (white squares in which the letters have "drifted" to the edges) and by the exchange (certainly energetic) as regards the choice of "strong colours in the decoration of the ceilings, walls and floors" (Viganò).

Getulio Alviani, renovation of the Brollo house, Grado, 1964

Getulio Alviani, a plastics designer, draughtsman, theoretician and collector, began very soon – towards the end of the '50s – to take an interest in art, architecture and design. Like many other young people at the time, he frequented Fontana's studio, worked an apprenticeship in the studio of Marcello D'Olivo and became a friend and collaborator of Konrad Wachsmann, Max Bill and Bruno Munari. As an artist, already in 1961 he began exhibiting the *Vibratile texture surfaces*, a series of works that brought immediately him international fame. In the renovation of the Brollo house, we find elements that recur in the later architectural works of Getulio Alviani: rigour, rhythm and mathematical scansion, the relationship with works of art (not just his own), the chromatic presence of just black and white, the extreme cleanliness of every detail, the attempt to reduce every mark to a minimum. This is an architectural project that is particularly aligned with the minimal in art of that period, and was way in advance of the minimal architecture that is in vogue nowadays.

Gianni Colombo, "Zoom Squares - Cromodromo", La Città gallery, Verona, 1970

The great architect of Italian art Gianni Colombo in one of his emblematic projects between art and architecture. Luminous thoughts about space, ideas to overcome its traditional obviousness, authoritative examples to question balances and stabilities that are often stifling. Forcing one to be astonished.

A G Fronzoni and François Morellet, "Ambiente 1980", Genoa, 1980

A G Fronzoni, which is written without full stops because even they would be too much: the Italian testament to the idea of less being more, the self-taught pioneer of ornament as crime, the paladin of a global design of all aspects of communication, architect, designer, draughtsman, teacher, "designer" as he loves to define himself. During the years he worked as consultant to the Genoa city council, he designed a white display structure that could be laid out in a space in different ways to generate different forms of equilibrium. François Morellet, invited to take part in the *Arte e città* exhibition (Genoa, 1980), decided to intervene on four of these elements, setting them together in an unorthodox, almost disjointed manner, and then "tidying" them with a horizontal stripe of black self-adhesive tape. A sign able to ensure a new order, an indication for the subsequent disorder, a minimal sign of great art which in an instant tells

A G Fronzoni and François Morellet, *Ambiente 1980*, installation at the exhibition *Arte e città*, Genoa, 1980.

of spaces and perceptions. Rarely has so much been seen to be done with so little…

Gaetano Pesce, Hubin apartment, Paris, 1985–86

For an Art Deco interior in avenue Foch, with friezes, columns and all the rest, Gaetano Pesce – a pure artist who thinks about a project as a place to fight against the monotonous idea of the one-off piece – imagined a project made of phrases/fragments that did not necessarily match. Pesce is a theoretician of design projects as a place of experimentation, a paladin supporting the use of materials of one's own times, artist/craftsman committed in the front line as regards the completion of his works. He blended together in the constitutive elements of interior architecture (floors, doors, fittings, handrails, containers, furnishing) his thoughts of the world – no rules, no predictability, no diktat, no repetition, never banality – reinventing form, material and structure of every element: the doors become hands to brush against, the floors a flow of multicolour resins, the banisters a disjointed dance of light sources. This interior is the emblematic demonstration of how art can be a way of thinking in every direction of the compass.

Umberto Riva, ceiling design for Insinga house, Via Arena, Milan, 1987

Much could be said about Umberto Riva: about his proverbial calmness, his millimetric and personal attention to each tiny detail of a project, about his unique capacity to capture, seek, exploit and express natural light in his architectural interior projects. The story that concerns us here and which brings Umberto Riva's architectural project direct to art is his love for painting, which he practised personally and which enabled him to reflect upon forms, colours and materials directly, with the slowness that in the case of Riva is only an advantage. Fragments of this art, which he claimed was influenced by Léger, can

Gaetano Pesce, Hubin apartment, Paris, 1985–86.

Umberto Riva, ceiling design in the Insinga house, Via Arena, Milan, 1987.

Toni Cordero with Gilberto Zorio, Blumarine clothes shop, Milan, 1990.

be found in some of his architectural works. In the Frea house, a fundamental restructuring project, in the main bedroom, on a white wall, a small horizontal mark, a rectangle of glossy blue enamel paint, encloses tremendous knowledge and astuteness in just a few square centimetres.

In the Insinga house in Via Arena in Milan, a few plaster shapes mark out salient passages on the ceiling – similar stratagems are used also in the floor design – thereby provoking plays of light and shade, and cancelling out the tedium of the horizontal surface that normally sits above our heads. This was a device already used by Riva in his house in Via Paravia, Milan (1969), where the exposed reinforced concrete ceiling was divided by sections of different colours in an unusual composition that ultimately derived from the ceiling of the Bloc house, the heroic masterpiece of Villa La Scala (1957–58) that Viganò had courageously designed on the hill of Portese del Garda.

Toni Cordero with Gilberto Zorio, Blumarine clothes shop, Milan, 1990

The heritage that was handed down to Toni Cordero in terms of freedom enabled him in his '90s interior designs to match his Turinese predecessor, Carlo Mollino, in imagining interiors that were full of signs, none of which needed to worry about being in tune with the other. In these high-speed circuits, in which the lighting installation is a tangle of cables and bulbs, where the structures for displaying the clothes are halberds, the floor seeks help from the master of Arte Povera, Gilberto Zorio, and becomes one of his stars, full of energy, light and colour.

Marco Romanelli with Massimo Noceto and Marta Laudani, Borea-Lombardi house, San Remo, 1995–98

A design by Marta Laudani realized with geometric backgrounds of water-based paint and different coats of paint applied by roller over templates, to bring a delicate, almost imperceptible decoration in this interior by Marco Romanelli,

Above and right: Marco Romanelli with Massimo Noceto and Marta Laudani, Borea-Lombardi house, San Remo, 1995–98.

Manolo De Giorgi, renovation of an apartment in Viale Bianca Maria, Milan, 1997–99.

which, in its subdued tone, enriches the already successful refurbishment.

Manolo De Giorgi, renovation of an apartment in Viale Bianca Maria, Milan, 1997–99

To solve this difficult enigma, an architectural ground-plan that is as little felicitous as it is interesting, Manolo De Giorgi has imagined a theory of itineraries, a multitude of spaces that are more or less articulated, and a privileged relationship with (objects from) the history of design, about which he is expert. Moreover, we see here a highly personal manner of transferring the signs of contemporary art into his fragments of interior architecture: close to the bookcases, after a long corridor in which spaces are multiplied by the reflections of two mirrors derived in their measurements from the "perfect" ones by Michelangelo Pistoletto, an enamel paintwork in two different tones of grey, giving formal rise to the repetition of the basic module of the thickness of the parapet of the bookcase itself, in an irregular design that communicates with some of the heights of the space. Signs that could have been born from the art of the Polish artist Julije Knifer, were it not for their simple derivation from an almost mathematical datum – derived itself from architecture – and repeated by adding or subtracting.

Massimo Curzi with Mario Airò, renovation of an apartment in Pavia, 1997–98

The collaboration between the architect Massimo Curzi and the artist Mario Airò is a result of a friendship and a reciprocal esteem between these two young creators. Curzi, here tackling his first work, invited Airò – a well-established artist – to collaborate in refurbishing this apartment in Pavia. Their work together is the fruit of interminable discussions on materials, finishes, tactile sensations, perceptions, transparencies, colours, light and atmosphere. Once the rigorous ground-plan had been designed by Curzi, every other decision was subjected to this fertile exchange between the two artists, sometimes so tense and dense as to

Massimo Curzi with Mario Airò, renovation of an apartment in Pavia, 1997–98.

Fabio Novembre, Bar Lodi, Lodi, 1998.

render Airò's characteristic style indecipherable: panelling in green Plexiglas as a background for the large bookcases, walls in waxed iron, furnishings in English leather, floors in Indian coir, elements in stainless steel, walls in sanded glass, walls plastered with mortar. A sampler born of the reasoning of two indissoluble minds.

Fabio Novembre, Bar Lodi, Lodi, 1998

The young Fabio Novembre, who dedicates his research to public rather than private spaces, in this small project for the Bar Lodi, has achieved a happy peak in his free, energetic work. After transforming Da Vinci's *Last Supper* into a mirrored wall for the restaurant area of the Café l'Atlantique in Milan, and discotheques in Italy and elsewhere, here, in redesigning the elongated rectangle of the Bar Lodi – which features the barcode of a recently published book by him just after the entrance – Novembre illuminated the space with a wall made from recycled mirrors, drawn from a photograph of Avedon from Warhol's Factory. The profiles of the protagonists have been sanded and become illuminating "bodies", whilst their shadow on the floor becomes a decoration that can be walked upon. The public, which likes being at the centre of attention, drinks cocktails surrounded by the (virtual) presences reflected/reflecting in the star system.

Bruno Vaerini with Alberto Garutti, restaurant in Bergamo, 1998–99

A restaurant in Bergamo has been the latest of the works undertaken by Bruno Vaerini in almost twenty years of design, an activity preceded by a career as an artist/sculptor following training at the Academy of Fine Arts. There, Vaerini developed his first thoughts about forms and materials, which he then translated into architectural form in interior design, comprising some of the best Italian work in the '80s and '90s. Projects in which to find, for example, an active dialogue with art and artists themselves, as in the case of this restaurant in Bergamo with Alberto Garutti – one of Italy's leading artists – and this must be seen not so much in a particular fragment or work, but in the overall direction a project takes: in a hard, dry, raw staircase that looks as though it could have been made by Richard Serra and Donald Judd jointly; in a system of lighting that against every custom projects external light from outside up towards the ceiling, and which is from there reflected into the room. (Legend has it that Vaerini brought a reproduction of a Caravaggio painting as an example to the site, to the lighting engineer who had to resolve a particular request…) In a floor made of large slabs of different marbles – of irregular forms betraying an intermediate stage in their production – joined by a grout of grit: a succession of "coloured rugs" laid with astute energy and courage at the end of the restaurant. All choices which are the result of comparisons, criticisms, advice, intuition, swapping around, complicity.

Stefano Testa/gruppo Cliostraat, renovation and decoration of the Micronido e Istituto di Psicoterapia Psicologica for the Cooperativa Sociale Icaro 2000, Sesto San Giovanni, 1999

Stefano Testa, a Milanese architect awake to social problems and also a designer open to the world of art, imagined a tactile cupboard as the setting for one of the play areas for children, with the doors covered in ever different materials to arouse the curiosity of their little users and stimulate their sensations. This is faced by a wall decoration inspired by one of the most famous *Negatives-positives* by Bruno Munari, the artist who always appealed to Testa and with whom he had had a direct link via the Faculty of Architecture in Milan. A homage, therefore, that was also motivated by the type of location, a kindergarten (it seems superfluous here to recall the fifty years of activity undertaken by Munari as an educator who was especially involved with small children), but also a way to break the monotony of the box without intervening (or being able to intervene) on the structure, and using Munari's teaching to best use.

Corrado Levi, Roca's Pub, Milan, 1999

A transverse career, that blends love for art and the practice of architecture, is what distinguishes the work of Corrado

Bruno Vaerini with Alberto Garutti, restaurant in Bergamo, 1998–99.

In this page and opposite, above: Stefano Testa/gruppo Cliostraat, renovation and decoration of the Micronido e Istituto di Psicoterapia Psicologica for the Cooperativa Sociale Icaro 2000, Sesto San Giovanni, 1999.

Levi. The pupil of Franco Albini and Carlo Mollino, the friend of many contemporary artists (amongst whom Alighiero Boetti, Aldo Mondino, Carol Rama and Mario Schifano), and a teacher in the Faculty of Architecture at the Milan Politecnico, Levi has brought into his recent architectural projects some personal artistic/political/didactic and social experiences, succeeding in bringing to them a sensibility towards things of the world that are usually ignored.

In planning a project for the Roca's Pub in Milan, a bar in which a considerable crowd regularly meets to watch football matches live, Levi planned for the ceiling – the part of the premises that was freest and at the same time most visible to the public – a decoration made by painting 18 football tops carefully and as many socks from the most popular clubs. The stars of football in the sky, astral bodies above the heads of the fans, and always at the centre of their thoughts. Socialization, desire, eroticism, passion, humour. All with a simultaneously measured and prejudice-free theatrical drum-roll.

All this to close in an emblematic fashion this firmament of stars seen in a bright flash of light – independent, free, "non-categorizable" – ready to shine and light up a history that is still being written every day, between the folds of evidence, in the gaps between the disciplinary settings, every time that architecture accepts – intelligently, necessarily, opportunely – to return with vibrant energy and touch upon the freest emotions, those daughters of intuition, smiles, freshness, wit, courage, desire to live and breathe the world.

Corrado Levi, Roca's Pub, Milan, 1999.

Frida Doveil

New Materials and New User Values for the Home

From foam rubber to casual and high-tech models

Piero Gatti, Cesare Paolini and Franco Teodoro, Sacco armchair, produced by Zanotta, 1968.

When Gatti, Paolini and Teodoro proposed the Sacco armchair to Aurelio Zanotta, it was only 1968 and we were still far from the idea of a padding whose ergonomics could lie in the fact of not having a shape: it was the material (pre-expanded polystyrene beads) that offered the possibility of adapting to any interpretation in use.

Materials represent a central theme of the contemporary culture of objects. Indeed, a great deal of the design experimentation of recent decades has passed through new materials. And many of the most representative objects of recent history owe their extraordinariness to the use of innovative technologies. New materials are also taking on a significant role in defining the new qualities of the contemporary home.
However, this theme has not always been investigated correctly. All too often new materials have been considered synonymous with innovation proper, as if material innovation could be sufficient in itself. This is the mistake that some of those involved in technical culture have made, believing for a long time that they would succeed in making technical innovations acceptable simply by the fact that they were bearers of functional innovations. This has partly also been the mistake of those in marketing, who have used material innovation as a gadget of progress, banalizing the profound contents in favour of a "surprise effect" considered, for purchasing purposes, to be more important than real innovation. The result has been that of slowing down rather than promoting the diffusion of new materials in everyday life. To be accepted, any material innovation must be capable of being the expression of a broader transformation. It must succeed, that is, in being an instrument of change in user cultures or expressive languages, contributing to modifying the established vocabulary.
More than the victory of technology, the growing diffusion of new materials in daily life indicates an important cultural revolution: it is the sign of the affirmation of the culture of research design directed at finding a meaning for technology, over traditional technical culture, accustomed to only considering materials as an instrument for the practical realization of objects.

A humanistic vision of technology

Italian habitation culture has made an important contribution to this cultural revolution: first, in the early '50s, by experimenting with new materials together with the beginnings of Italian industry, and later, in the '70s and '80s, with the experiences in colour and surfaces, contributing to making the design of expressive languages the new strategic objective of the whole advanced industry of these years.
Its contribution falls within a broader design scenario, which has been able to construct an original path of research and experimentation into new materials through forty years of dialogue with technical and production culture, and has had an enormous influence on the material culture of the late millennium. What has distinguished it, also in the variety of the different languages, has been the type of approach to technology. In the Italian approach, new materials have never meant simply a problem of constructive correctness, as much as a potential of expression and use to be revealed. It offers a humanistic vision of technology, through which to express new habitation qualities, such as dimensional flexibility or easy transformability, as well as new formal languages, capable of changing the very meaning of comfort, the bearers of new forms of emotional relationships with the habitat.
The experiences with foam rubber in the '50s, and a little later with polyethylene and polypropylene, the vanguard of new plastic materials, which in the mid-'60s made plastic the protagonist of the new themes of the domestic habitat: sectional furniture, multi-purpose furniture, affordable prices, these are all part of that research path into materials. These are the same themes of which Gio Ponti spoke when presenting his wood and plastic Superleggera chairs, which today, forty years later, have

Gaetano Pesce, Up series of padded furniture, C&B (1969), currently produced by B&B Italia.

Following the thread of lengthy research into expanded polyurethanes, in 1969 with C&B Gaetano Pesce completed the Up armchair, sold as a "flatpack", contained in a special PVC wrapping, to then take shape, by being inflated, only at the moment of use, once the wrapping is removed.

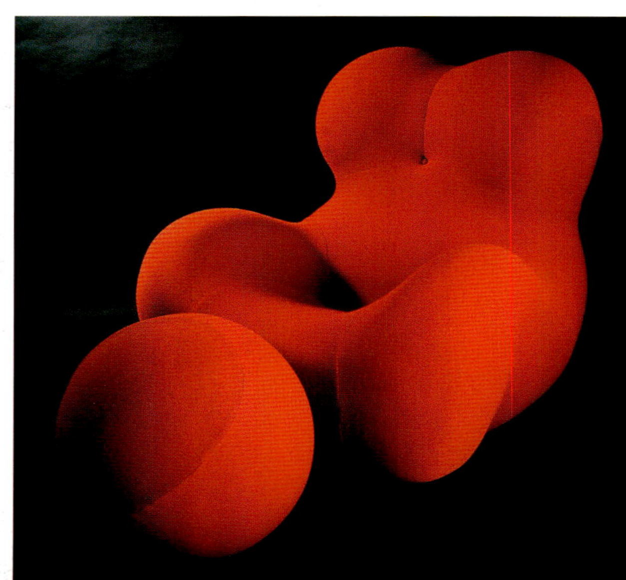

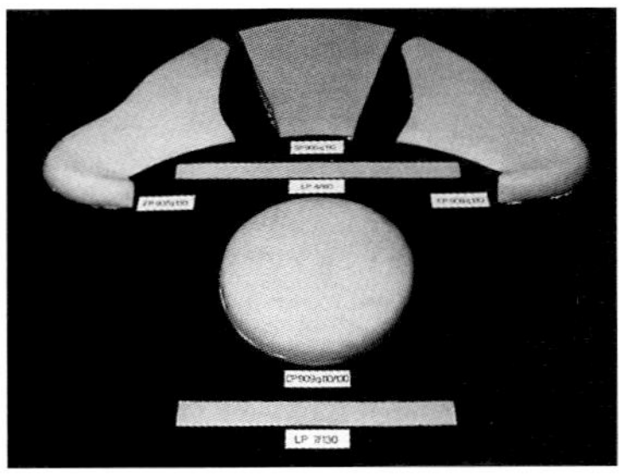

Marco Zanuso, Lady armchair (*above*), produced by Arflex, 1951, and Martingale armchair (*left*), produced by Arflex, 1954.

The Lady and Martingale armchairs by Marco Zanuso, made of foam rubber and elastic bands, belong to the Arflex experience of the use of new Pirelli synthetic materials for making padding industrially, starting with experimentation with new production technologies.

Cover of *Stile Industria. Forma e stile nella produzione* magazine, no. 7, 1956.

Issue completely devoted to the aesthetics of plastic materials.

once again become the protagonists of international design.

The centre of interest of this research was not the use of new materials, as much as that of combining the production experimentation with an important linguistic experimentation. The search for technical and formal alternatives to the materials of the domestic tradition was driven by the search for alternatives to the old lifestyles and the old languages of domestic design.

There was a type of approach that was intuitive and often irreverent towards new materials, which – going beyond their engineering role – managed to grasp their symbolic aspects, giving them new dignity according to a humanistic vision of technology, which indirectly influenced the approach of the whole of the production industry towards the theme of materials, well beyond the domestic confines.

The Italian contribution to the theme of new materials

The idea that we can speak of an Italian path to material innovation, that most of the values of which Italy became the standard-bearer pass through the history of Italian production directed at the theme of habitation, is little investigated.

Yet we need only reread carefully the different contributions that Italian design has made over the years to the theme of materials to realize that they have offered the clear and cohesive premise for most of the strategic themes of today's production culture: the attention to the expressive value of materials, the control

Right: Joe Colombo, Additional Living System series of padded items, produced by Sormani, 1967.
Far right: Cini Boeri, Serpentone sofa, produced by Arflex, 1971.
Below: Marco Zanuso, Lombrico sofa, produced by C&B, 1967.

The Lombrico "infinite" sofa, by Marco Zanuso for C&B from 1967, made of fibreglass and polyurethane foam, a research into the possibilities that are ideally connected to Additional Living System by Joe Colombo, from 1967, made of polyurethane foam and a metal comb structure, and the Serpentone by Cini Boeri for Arflex from 1971, 100% polyurethane elements simply glued together. Monocoque seats rather than seating, often without an internal structure, which go beyond the theme of the furniture item produced industrially from the '50s and '60s, to suggest, through the new materials, unusual seating postures and alternative uses.

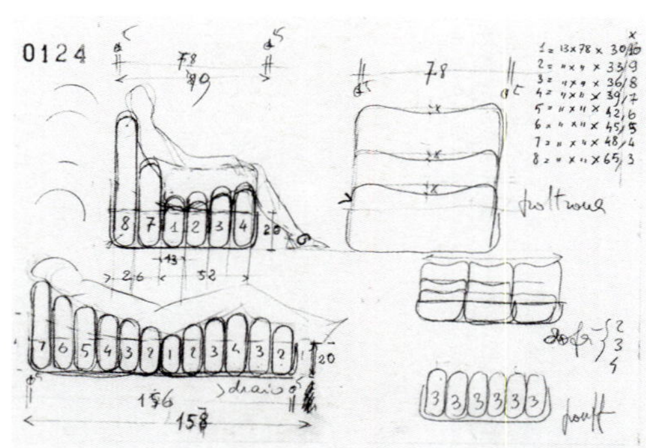

Jonathan De Pas, Donato D'Urbino and Paolo Lomazzi, Blow armchair in an apartment in Milan, produced by Zanotta, 1968.

Inspired on one hand by pneumatic Pop architectures, on the other by the poor technology of inflatable dinghies, Blow was the first Zanotta product to have a mass diffusion. Produced in transparent PVC or in primary colours, it was defined "the armchair to have not only in the home but to take to the countryside and the seaside".

Gio Ponti, Superleggera chair, produced by Cassina, 1957.

"This chair is light, costs little, and is very strong. This chair, made of domestic ash, covered with beautifully coloured, straw-like plastic strips, is a 'chair-chair', made simply to cost little and work well. Yet everyone welcomed it as an extraordinary innovation. As 'THE innovation'." Gio Ponti, in Domus, *no. 268, March 1962.*

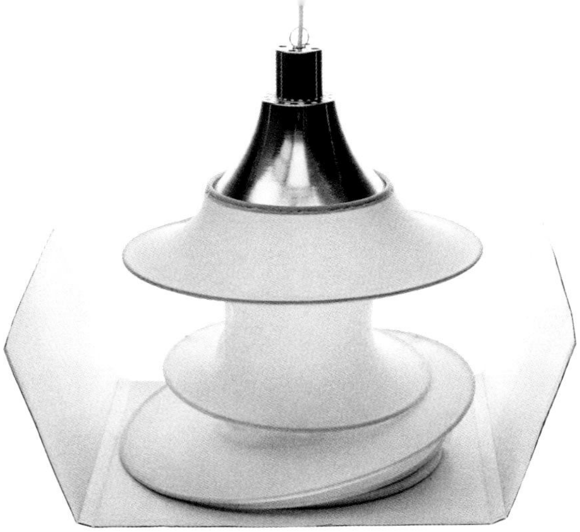

Bruno Munari, Falkland lamp, produced by Danese, 1964.

Bruno Munari created the Falkland lamp for Danese, made of Lycra mesh (polyester thread) that takes on the vibrating qualities of an unlikely Japanese paper: opalescent and light, but also elastic and lasting. A lamp to put away in a small space when you are no longer using it.

of emotional qualities, the humanization of technology.
The Italian path to technology is part of a design attitude that has never wished to limit design action to a formal choice or to the search for a solution to a construction problem, but has always attempted to find a meaning for it. An attitude that continues to teach through its powerful treasury of resonance: Italian industry, which has made this attitude its own and has taken it all over the world. And that today still makes Italian proposals the protagonists of the most advanced design culture. The experience gained with the iMade® project consolidated what some years previously might have appeared to be a personal intuition. The research in recent years into these themes has clearly shown the international observers that the Italian furnishing industry is today a production model of reference that is very much in fashion for all companies aiming to produce design in this sector.

Giving a meaning to technology

The thread that links the projects of Bruno Munari or Enzo Mari to those of Ettore Sottsass or Paolo Rizzatto, that links the experiences of acute irony of the '60s and '70s with the provocative and irreverent ones of the '80s, or sophisticated and discreet ones of the '90s, is this common attitude of the search for an attentive, though not

Marco Zanuso, Lambda chair, produced by Gavina, 1960.

Zanuso designed the Lambda chair (whose name was a clear homage to the first self-supporting car body produced by Lancia with this name in 1921), referring to the traditional working methods of panel-beaters for the construction of custom-built car bodies.

Opposite, clockwise:
Biagio Cisotti and Sandra Laube, detail of the curved plywood of the Millefoglie chair, produced by Plank, 1998.

Only one supporting structure and only one cutting line, to produce a chair that looks lightweight, but that is structurally sturdy and does not lose the handcrafted flavour of the raw material. An assembly system made possible by specifically designed precision working allows for uniting industrially two identical supporting structures moulded in high frequency from plywood, bent from a single mould.

Antonio Citterio, detail of PVC profiles of the Domus wall system, produced by B&B Italia, 1992.

Typologically one of the first examples of a wall system based on single horizontal modular elements rather than vertical ones, which can be joined according to size, depending on different functional and dimensional needs. Productively speaking, one of the first uses of a basic and little-known technology, but structurally interesting: rigid-extruded and expanded PVC, which is characterized by less weight and greater mechanical strength than the rigid one.

Paola Navone and Abet Laminati Research Centre, HPL Diafos decorative laminates, produced by Abet Laminati, 1987.

Riccardo Blumer, detail of the honeycomb and glass plate of the Light Glass table, produced by Alias, 1998.

A thin honeycomb of aluminium between two plates of crystal responds to stress as if it were much heavier and thicker.

Marco Zanini, Union bookcase, produced by Memphis, 1983.

obvious, interpretation of material design themes, in search of a broader meaning of technology. There are many examples that we could cite, and it is no coincidence that they represent objects that have crossed the confines of fashion and geography, long to remain on the international markets.
A not insignificant part of these designs has been oriented over the years to establishing a more direct relationship with technology.
Among others, the experiences of Franco Raggi with Fontana Arte using industrial glass or those of Alberto Meda with Alias using carbon fibres, as well as the lengthy work of Gaetano Pesce with Cassina using polyurethanes belong to this design seam. These experiences are the fullest manifestation of the capacity to use technology, with all its wealth and extraordinariness, not as a means to surprise, but as a filter to look at reality in a different way.
Through this filter, a slender, light chair is revealed to be solid, resistant and practically indestructible, just as a fragile, thin glass becomes a taut sail that delicately diffuses light. Projects that transmit the idea of a discreet and elegant technology: just a simple gesture is needed to activate it and to fully enjoy all its qualities, just like with grandma's old blanket.
From this humanistic vision of technology appeared objects made with very up-to-date techniques and materials, but built to be understood, attended to and loved with extreme simplicity. Objects that have taught us a different way to understand the new and are the best demonstration of the fact that a dialogue between technical and symbolic language is possible or, rather, desirable.
Objects and materials that are innovative, but also always "natural" and close to the dimension of the craftsman used to making things well, according to those historical roots of Italian design founded upon a continuous dialectic between the technical-production world and the world of art and experimentation.
At other times in Italian design, technology has offered the opportunity to reinvent materials that are not at all extraordinary, but rather derived from economical technologies, such as the metal rods with which supermarket trolleys are made, or corrugated board for packaging. Materials that are poor in users' imaginations, to which the project has once again restored a certain dignity, a formal beauty and, last but not least, a cultural weight, by simply using them for what they are. The Sof Sof chair by Enzo Mari from 1972, which was followed soon afterwards by the Delfina – again for Driade – or the Cartoons screen by Luigi Baroli for Baleri Italia, which finds its historical precedent twenty years earlier in a cardboard bookcase by Mari for Danese, and the Spiros clothes-stand by Vico Magistretti for Morphos Acerbis, much later, are just some of the most significant examples of a design attitude that has always considered as "new materials" the inexpensive ones, derived from rather unattractive technologies.
While today, in the midst of a minimalist climate, these products represent understood values, in the years of their birth they were full-blown provocations "through" technology. As was the Lambda chair, designed by Marco Zanuso for Gavina in 1960, obtained from the electric welding of two metal sheets, a construction technique that allowed ultra-thin thickness and a light and elegant design, one that has been taken up often even in recent times.

Giving materials an identity

Beyond the contributions for a poetic and iconoclastic reading of technology inside the home, the Italian path to material innovation has passed through another important experience.
Working on the same terrain as the technicians, in the '70s and '80s a new

iMade® came about in 1999 as a project by Federlegno Arredo, with the intention of opening up a new terrain for reflection around the theme of Italian quality: that of innovation in production.
The first results of this project, implemented with coordination by Clac, contributions by Domus Academy Research Centre and patronage by ADI, were the two exhibitions of the same name at the International Furniture Show in collaboration with Cosmit, in April 2000 and 2001, which for the international public represent one of the most authoritative observatories on themes of industrial research underlying the birth of Italian furnishing products today.
The exhibitions were prepared by Frida Doveil with fitting-out by Franco Origoni.

Philippe Starck, La Marie chair, produced by Kartell, 1998.

Lengthy study of the material and a complex process of technological fine-tuning have led to the construction of a single piece, injection moulded with sharp corners and maximum elastic flexibility, due to an ultra-pure, highly transparent polycarbonate.

Ross Lovegrove, detail of the polycarbonate casing of the Agaricon table lamp, produced by Luceplan, 2000.

A translucent, lightweight material, ribbed according the structure's lines of force, where everything is designed to be as small as possible. It expresses very well the contemporaneity of injection moulding technology when it becomes a means for producing casings that are lightweight and nearly evanescent yet strong and durable as polycarbonate.

Werner Aisslinger, Soft chaise longue with Technogel polyurethane gel "padding", produced by Zanotta, 2000.

An industrial technology, to date only applied to relatively small objects, is used here to produce a thin and lightweight seamless mattress, which works the same way as foam padding and has the visual lightness of a thin net. The mattress of the Soft chaise longue is made of Technogel®, a polyurethane gel, which provides remarkable comfort even when made into a thin seat.

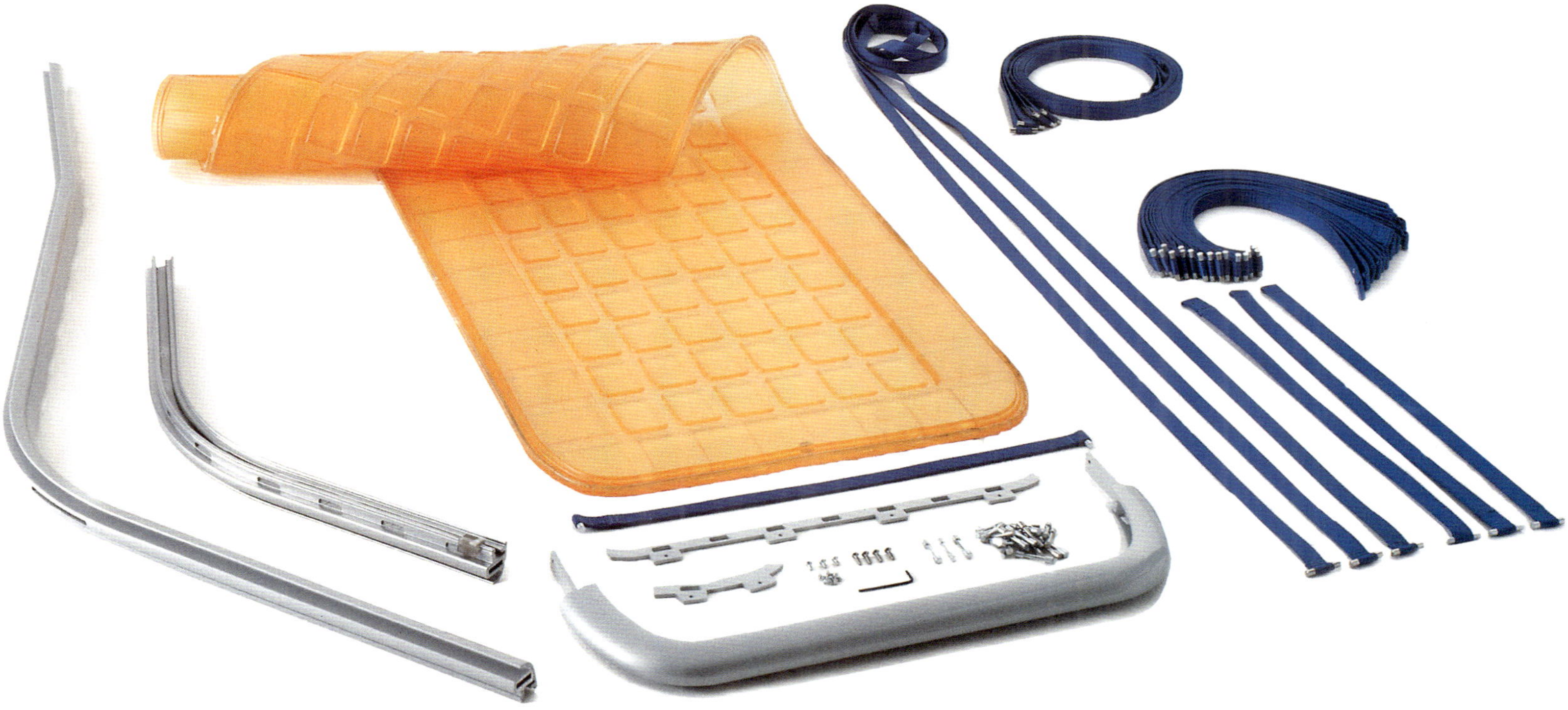

Ross Lovegrove, Air One armchair, produced by Edra, 2000.

Air One and Air Two are two monocoques made of polypropylene foam comfortable, lightweight, stackable and even waterproof, using a rather simple production process, already utilized by both automotive and food packaging industries.

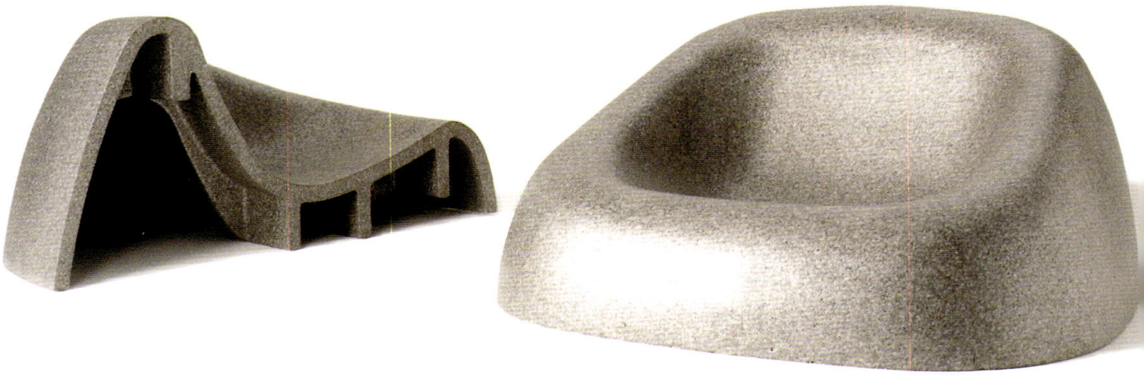

Poltrona Frau Research Centre, detail of Wing chair, produced by Poltrona Frau, 2000.

Detail of the frame in carbon fibre compound and polyurethane foam with which the single material Wing chair has been made. It is normal to produce hi-tech industrial pieces and limited production runs in the aeronautical industry, but not so in the furniture industry, which, after collaborating with these sectors, however, has gained a particular aptitude for building hi-tech objects with almost sartorial attention.

design front opened up in Italy: that of the design of the material, which intervenes where the material is acquiring its supply of chromatic, acoustic, visual and surface properties, to give it a specific, culturally recognizable identity. This attention to the designing of the material has put materials at the centre of a profound reflection on the psychological and emotional relationship of people with the objects that surround them, and has had a certain influence, particularly in the home.

With the proposals in the design of surfaces, starting from the early '70s with the first experiences of Clino Castelli and Andrea Branzi on the decorative laminate, and then continued ideally with the linguistic research into new artificial woods by Ettore Sottsass, Italian design opened up the path to a more deeply felt and participatory relationship with the world of materials; even the newer ones, making them begin to play an active part in the relationship with the home space. Thanks to the cultural tension of those years, materials have taken on a full autonomy with respect to the form of things, and have become part of the design grammar of the habitat with their own role. We need only think of the experiments with colour by Ettore Sottsass and Clino Castelli with Olivetti, when computers still had a neutral colour, or those of Paola Navone with decorative laminates for Abet, at a time when synthetic coverings only seemed to be able to imitate more noble and precious materials. These were the years of the experiences of Memphis and Alchimia on the theme of the decorative surface. These were highly desecrating experiences that on one hand introduced the idea that it was possible to make a "loose and unbiased" use of new materials, and on the other also launched a different relationship with the materials of the figurative domestic tradition. This is what happened, for example, with ceramic tiles, which – also thanks to the evolution of techniques – have completely modified their own grammar, shifting from figurative decoration to structured surfaces and to very particular chromatic effects. Yet those experiences have also opened up the path to a more deeply felt and participatory relationship with the world of artificial materials, one that has led to new and unexpected combinations, to the limit of the possible, between materials.

However, from those Italian experiences a new democracy of material has come about: today, materials old and new, natural and artificial, humble and precious coexist freely, in dialogue with each other to form the new scenarios of aesthetics and use. Those experiences, though perhaps more theoretical than practical, have had the merit of accustoming the industry of production for the home, which then collaborated with Italian designers, to comparison and dialogue between materials that differed considerably from

Riccardo Blumer,
Laleggera range of seats,
produced by Alias, 2000.

A cage in curved solid wood, only 5 mm thick, placed edgeways, resists the pressure loads contrast, closed by sheets of sliced wood, 1 mm thick, curved when hot and bound along the extrados, to resist strain from shearing stress. Apart from the formal aspects, these objects represent one of the most successful expressions of research on the limit of material which nowadays keeps a large part of the most sophisticated exploration in the Italian furniture industry updated.

Ross Lovegrove, Pod Lens system, produced by Luceplan, 1998.

A "pod diffusor" of sensual shape and unusual colour: a pod with sinuous, organic lines and polycarbonate prism lenses borrowed from the retroreflectors incorporated into the latest generation of car headlights.

each other, making it more open to proposals that were unusual and apparently risky for the consolidated domestic tradition.
The major innovation that has come out of Italian production in recent years is precisely the idea of a new "artificial-natural" capable of mixing the abstract languages of plastic with the sincere ones of natural wood; the sensuality of the new polyurethane gels with the malleability of diaphanous and thin or transparent woods, such as Texluce®, conceived by Paolo Nava for Piarottolegno & Binova, in 1998. Today we no longer think in terms of "good" and "bad", natural and artificial materials. The old competition between "different natures" is over, and a different type of comparison has emerged: that between generic materials, without specific qualities, and designed materials, with their own identity. This in the home as well.

The Italian factory of innovation

The objects of recent years, particularly those of the most recent Italian production, are a good testament to the influence of those experiences.
If Italian design played such an important role – in various senses unique – in the construction of the new material universe, this was also made possible thanks to the industry that produced it. Its good fortune lay in the concomitance between a design culture created by the Italian architects of the second half of the century, original and with a long tradition, and an industrial culture of visionary entrepreneurs, good craftsmen and creative technicians, equally unique, also thanks to the support of an extensive network of relationships with spheres of industrial production very different from their own. These different components were able to result in a wide-ranging and highly structured generation of products that affected material day-to-day life in a way that had never occurred elsewhere, in terms of intensity and value. It was the successful meeting between an intuitive technical culture, willing to experiment, a design culture with great expressive liberty and a production culture prepared for industrial risk, but above all also able to proceed with the mentality of the designer. A very unusual mix, made possible by the variety and articulated structure of the Italy System, a very flexible production and transformation system, accustomed to producing for the car as well as for textiles and furnishings, thanks to which the Italian furnishings factory has been able to produce innovation according to much differing degrees of industrialization: from the small-scale handicraft production to the "made-to-measure" industrial product, acting at the same time with the high technology of large-scale industry and the craftsman's ability. Italian production culture, committed on the home front, was not only among the first to invest in design culture, when most of major industry was not yet doing this, but also in its role as the "promoter" of design, the Italian furnishing industry was able to avail itself of this network of production relationships. This enabled it to adopt the researching attitude to the theme of production proper to design culture, increasingly focusing on where it intended to arrive, even when it did not know how to arrive there. This insight put it at the top of innovation, even in a field – such as that of material diversification – that did not see the home as one of the most advanced sectors.

The Italian Home is therefore not only an aesthetic style founded upon design and manufacturing quality. It is also and above all a type of design approach to material innovation, shared by Italian design and industry. An approach that characterises the whole Italy System and today puts the Italian culture of the home at the centre of the new contemporary culture of the home.

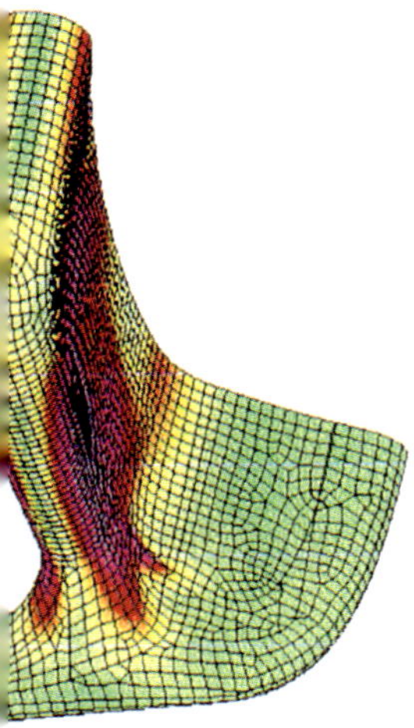

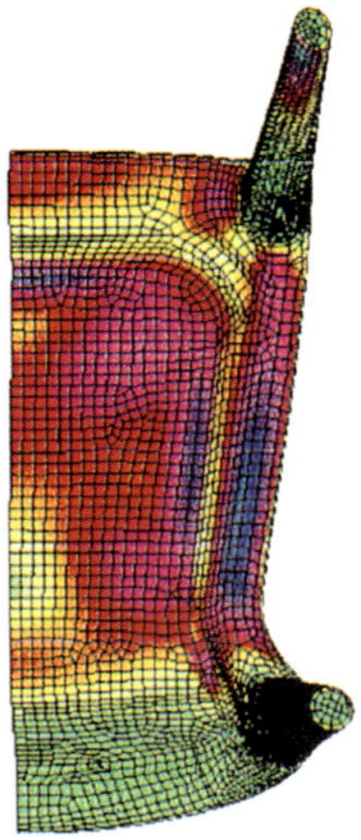

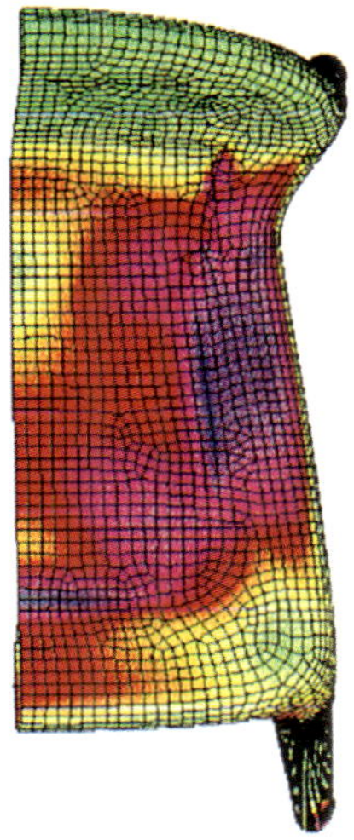

Stefano Giovannoni, Yuyu stool, linear analysis of stress status, produced by Magis, 2000.

The Yuyu stool is a monocoque in mass-coloured and air-moulded fiberglass reinforced polypropylene. A solid but light object to handle freely, that is also stable and shockproof, thanks to the technology and material used.

Antonio Citterio and Oliver Loew, Lastra lamp, produced by Flos, 1998.

Four steel cables support a plate of glass which produces low voltage electricity on which the adjustable projectors rest. An intelligent reinterpretation of the technology in which electric power is used to heat the rear windows of automobiles.

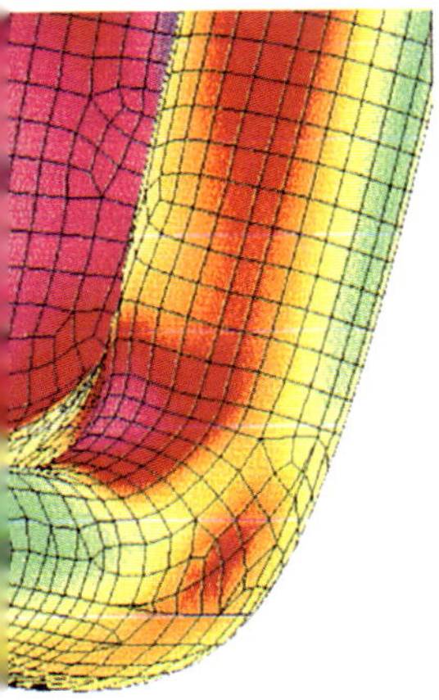

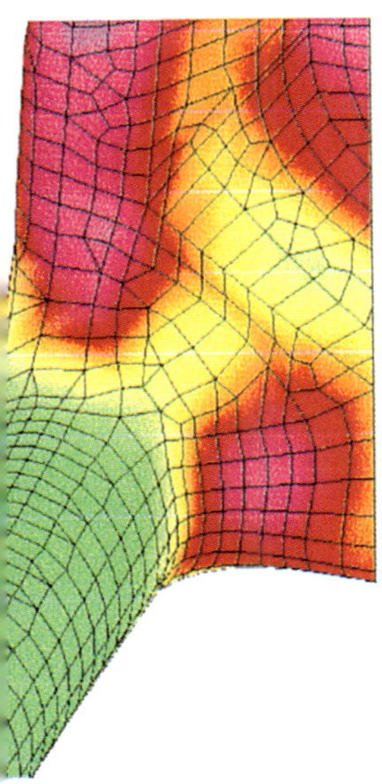

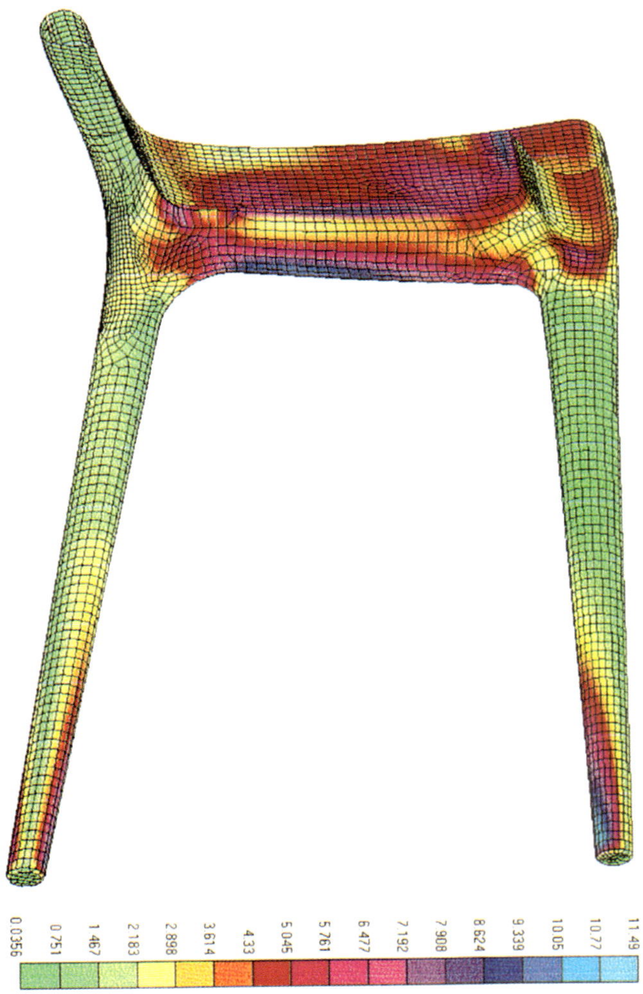

Giampiero Bosoni

Living in Movement

Travel experiences of the Italian domestic model

Mario Bellini with Dario Bellini, Francesco Binfaré and Giorgio Origlia, interior of the Kar-a-Sutra travelling housing cell designed for the exhibition *Italy: the New Domestic Landscape*, New York, 1972.

The idea of living that has evolved in Italy over the past fifty years has also seen a special area of development in the dimension of living in movement.
Italian design, famous throughout the world for the forms and inventions brought into the domestic space, is indeed also prized on account of certain important projects in various transport sectors. Though these may appear distant from the idea of domesticity, they in fact propose a way of living that is also a way of inhabiting. Let us consider the scooter phenomenon that came about soon after the war, the study of habitability reduced to minimal terms for the famous small economical cars of the '50s, the sophisticated style of custom-built cars, the sumptuous interiors of cruise ships, so reminiscent of high-class dwellings, and the original solutions of the compartments of certain high-speed trains. This culminates in the extreme, but very interesting, case in terms of mobility, of clothing (*abito*) – the microhabitation cell in movement *par excellence* – which, in Italian, through a wordplay of linguistic assonance, seems to derive directly from the term for inhabiting (*abitare*): clothing as inhabiting[1]. Here, interwoven under the sign of domesticity, are thus an original culture of habitation as lifestyle, the design of the custom-built car produced in Italy with the taste and practicality of Italian fashion, and the variety and wealth of age-old hand crafting experiences still alive in this country, enhanced by technological innovation and revisited with great creativity and flexibility by small and medium-sized Italian industry.
The historical cases are many and each brings with it many small stories of hand crafting wisdom, original creativity and above all, in the cases of greatest success, a courageous and resourceful entrepreneurial culture.
Let us consider the scooters, Vespa (1946) by Piaggio and Lambretta (1947) by Innocenti, together with the multitude of clones that derived from them. These paved the way for the formation of new rites and lifestyles in Italian cities (in which the exterior public spaces have been designed with the same care as the most refined domestic internal spaces, in continuity with Italian architectural planning, which has historically sought to maintain the relationship between interior and exterior). The scooter was a typological innovation celebrated by such famous films as *Roman Holiday* (1953) with Audrey Hepburn and Gregory Peck, and *La Dolce Vita* (1960) by Federico Fellini, where in a certain sense the scooters (the Vespa in the former film, the Lambretta in the latter) also functioned as original companions that were more suited than ever to rediscovering Rome. Through an irony of fate, in the early '50s the eternal city was in this way relaunched on the great international tourist circuit.
On the occasion of the Holy Year in 1950, there set off, again from Rome, heading in the direction of Milan, the first new generation electric train of the postwar period, the ETR 300, known as Settebello. In terms of form (designer Giulio Minoletti) and technological and typological innovation, this train stood out as one of the most advanced solutions proposed at international level. It launched a research path taken up again in the early '70s with the Pendolino series, which in 1996, with the third generation ETR 460, was to encounter the design of Giugiaro for both interiors and exteriors. The Pendolino model was joined in 1986 by the ETR 500, a direct descendant of the ETR 300 of 1949, for which Pininfarina studio was called upon for the interior and exterior design.
The design of the great cruise ships is a sector in which Italy boasts a noteworthy tradition, confirmed in the '30s by the admirable work of designer Pulitzer

[1] In fact, the term *abito* derives from the Latin *habitus* (demeanour, appearance), whereas *abitare* is from the Latin *habitare* derived from *habere* (to have).

Corradino Di Ascanio, Vespa 98 cc., produced by Piaggio, 1946.

Finali, between 1949 and 1950 we find Gio Ponti, assisted by an ample entourage of artists, committed to giving the form of "an Italian villa on the sea" to the famous steamboat *Andrea Doria*, launched in 1951 and tragically sunk in 1956 off New York, following a ramming incident with the Swedish ship *Stockholm*. This model of Italian style travelling on the seas provided the inspiration for the ships designed in the '80s and '90s by Renzo Piano for P&O and above all by Pierluigi Cerri (with Ivana Porfiri) for Costa Crociere.
For the world of the automobile perhaps just a few renowned names are sufficient, such as those of constructors Ferrari, Maserati, Lamborghini, Lancia, Alfa Romeo, and the car-body designers Pininfarina, Bertone, Zagato, and Ghia. To this first élite list we must also add the models of small economical cars for everybody, known as *utilitarie*, such as the 600 (1953), the 600 Multipla (1957) and the Nuova 500 (1957), all designed by Dante Giacosa and manufactured by Fiat, and some less known vehicles such as the model Isetta (1953) produced by Iso and subsequently also by BMW in Germany for a number of years.
Still in the world of the car, one very special case worthy of a note in its own right is the model of the travelling housing cell on wheels, a kind of roofless mobile home, denominated Kar-a-Sutra, designed by Mario Bellini on the occasion of the exhibition *Italy: the New Domestic Landscape* at the MoMA in New York in 1972.
In this rapid survey of models representative of the Italian style of living in movement, we must again stress

Scooter by Rumi Fonderie Officine. Ornamental patent deposited on 28 July 1954.

the particular link between the culture of Italian living and the style of Italian fashion that has made its mark on the world.
Interestingly, "clothing" – as can be read in a dictionary of etymology – "represents the 'case' of the individual, while the house represents the wrapping of the community. In some languages, house and clothing (shirt) have the same root of 'wrapping'", and we can well understand how interesting it is to extend our look onto the broad and highly structured landscape of the culture of living in Italy.

Cesare Pallavicino and Pierluigi Torre, model B Lambretta, produced by Innocenti, 1947.

Three-wheeled motor vehicle for passengers, produced by Innocenti. Ornamental patent deposited on 31 May 1950.

Piero De Vecchi, aluminium picnic service, produced by Metallarte, 1947. Diploma of Honour at 8th Triennial in Milan.

Dante Giacosa, Fiat 600 utility car, 1955.

Luigi Fabio Rapi, 8V two-seater saloon, produced by Fiat, 1952.

Franco Scaglione, assistant Giorgetto Giugiaro, Giulietta Sprint, Bertone body design, produced by Alfa Romeo, 1954.

Pininfarina, Dino spider, produced by Fiat, 1966.

Pio Manzù, prototype of City Taxi, produced by Fiat, 1968.

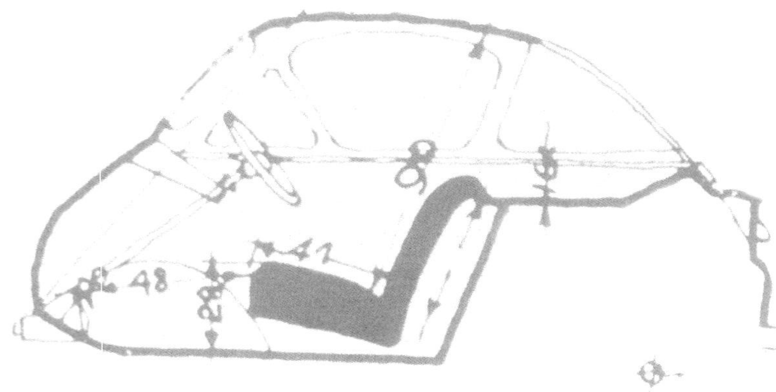

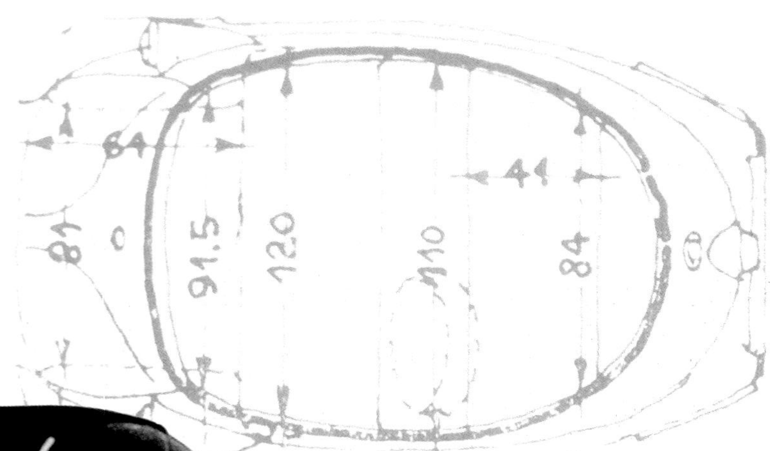

Emilio Preti, exterior views and interior encumbrance of the Isetta mini car, produced by Iso, 1953.

Francesco Tagliabue, interior bed for motorcar, model 600, formed by metal mesh folding net acting as seat and transformable. Utility patent deposited on 23 May 1960.

Dante Giacosa, 600 Multipla single volume car, produced by Fiat, 1955.

Dante Giacosa, 600 Multipla single volume car, vertical section of the interior volume with lowered seats, and illustration of habitability.

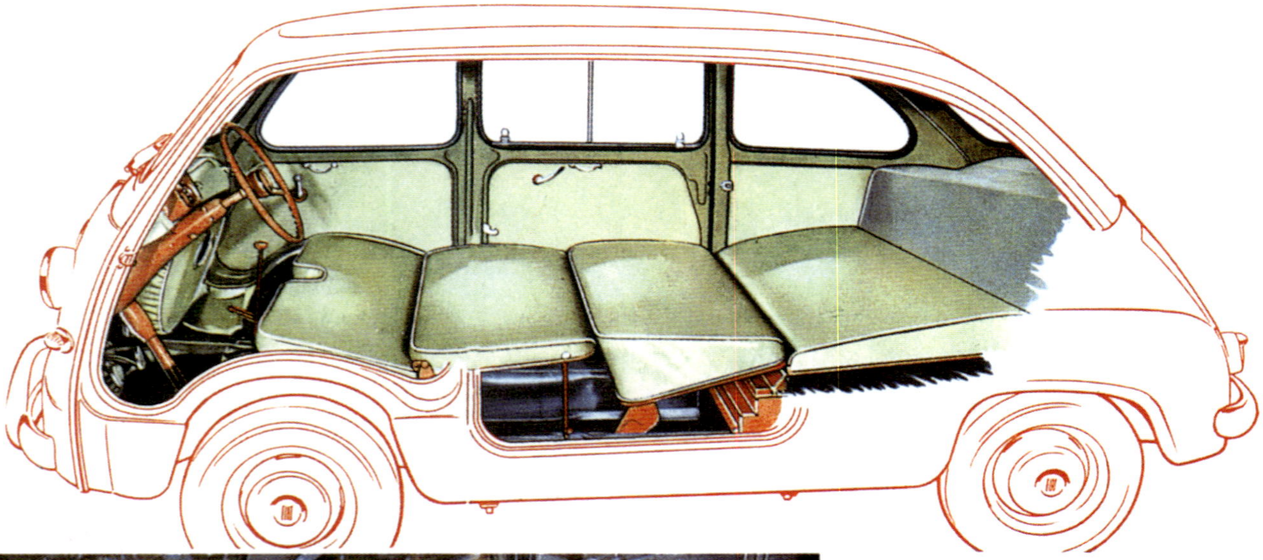

Covers of the magazine
L'Auto Accessorio, '50s.

Possibility of using the
electric razor in the car,
mid-'50s.

Renzo Zavanella,
Belvedere OM railcar,
produced by Officine
Meccaniche, 1948.
Exterior and interior views.

Giulio Minoletti, ETR 300 Settebello electric train, produced by Breda, 1949–50.

Opposite: Giulio Minoletti, interior of the Belvedere panoramic cabin on the Settebello electric train, 1950.

Giulio Minoletti, interior of the particular type of extendable compartment with mobile seats, designed for the carriages of the Settebello electric train, 1950.

Buffet service for carriages with corridor and compartments, mid-'60s.

Ettore Sottsass, "Dressed and undressed, that is, all are dressed", 1972, in *Argomenti e immagini di design*, no. 8, November-December 1972.

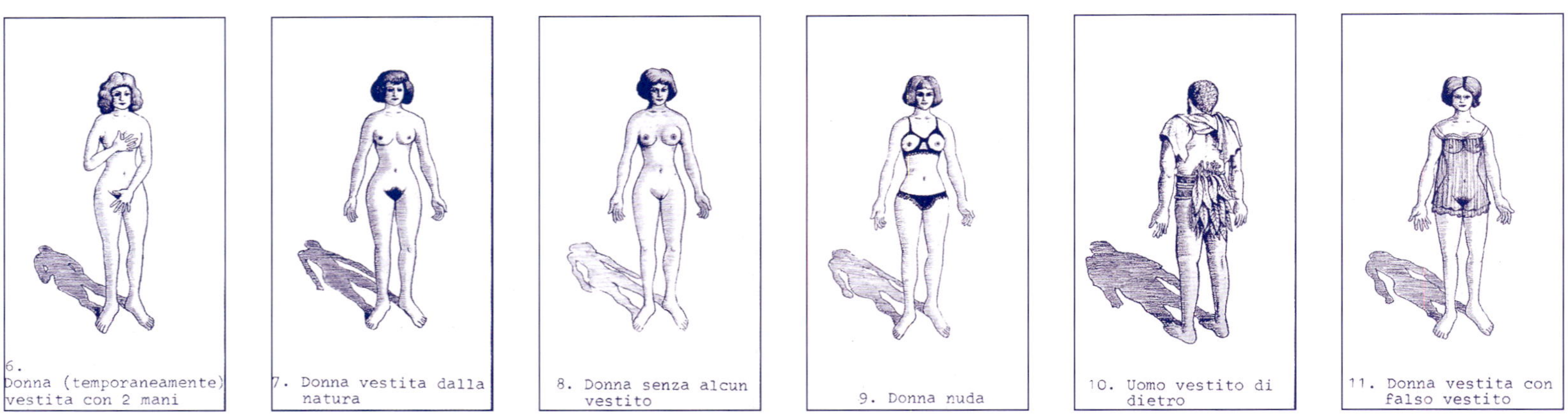

Interior of the restaurant car on the Cisalpino ETR 470 electric train, produced by Fiat Ferroviaria e Consociate.

24. Uomo vestito da utopista

25. Uomo vestito di morte

26. Uomo vestito da ladro

27. Donna vestita per un rito

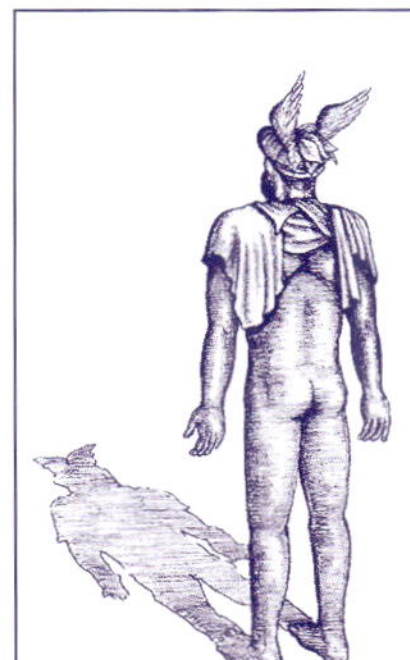

28. Uomo vestito col complesso della legge di gravità

29. Uomo vestito da monumento

Pierluigi Cerri with Ivana Porfiri, interiors of cabins for cruise ships, produced by Costa Crociere, 1989–2000.

Gio Ponti with Piero Fornasetti, interior of first class cabin on the liner *Andrea Doria*, 1950.

Right and below: Ferrari 550 Maranello, exterior and interior views.
Far right: Ferrari F355 Spider.

Mario Bellini with Dario Bellini, Francesco Binfaré and Giorgio Origlia, Kar-a-Sutra travelling housing cell designed for the exhibition *Italy: the New Domestic Landscape*, New York, 1972.

Ten Designers for the Home System

Andrea Branzi

Achille Castiglioni

Jonathan De Pas
Donato D'Urbino
Paolo Lomazzi

Angelo Mangiarotti

Enzo Mari

Alessandro Mendini

Bruno Munari

Gio Ponti

Ettore Sottsass

Marco Zanuso

Italian designers have worked a great deal within and around the so-called Home System, tackling various types of objects and using varying materials. As a result of the whims of chance, but also because of an attitude towards the discovery of new areas of research, some designers more than others have taken their projects into different fields of this system that we may define initially as being environmental, and only subsequently as an industrial system. The selection of designers set out in the following pages does not claim in any way to be comprehensive, nor even classificatory, but wishes simply to offer a point of reference to discover some exemplary systems of objects for the home that emerge from Italian design.

Furnishings
Century sofa,
produced by Memphis, 1982.

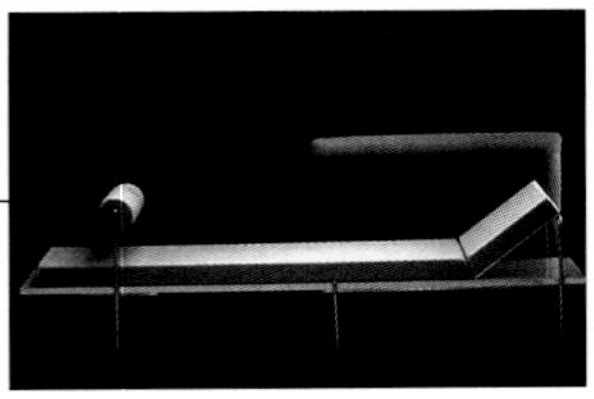

Silverware
Labrador sauce boat,
produced by Memphis, 1982.

Andrea Branzi

Tiling
Enamelled *cottoforte*
and silk-screen printing,
produced by Toscoceramica,
1982.

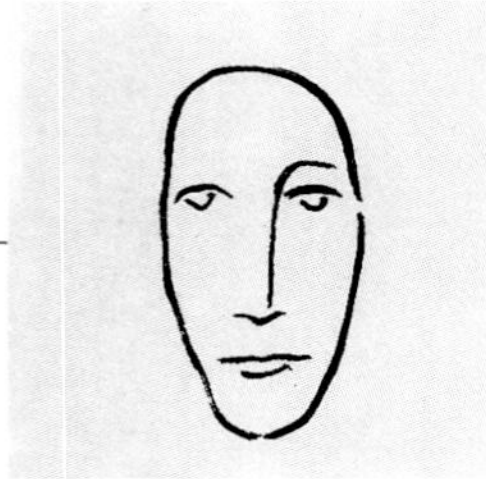

Achille Castiglioni

Furnishings
Primate armchair,
produced by Zanotta, 1970.

Lamp
Taccia table lamp,
produced by Flos, 1962
(with Piergiacomo Castiglioni).

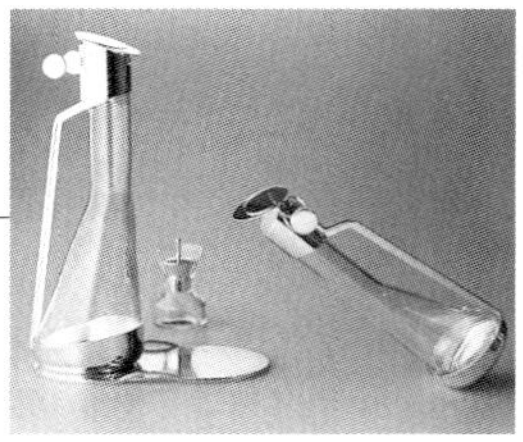

Silverware
Acetoliere oil and vinegar set,
with tops that open as the cruets
are tilted, and salt-cellar,
produced by Alessi, 1984.

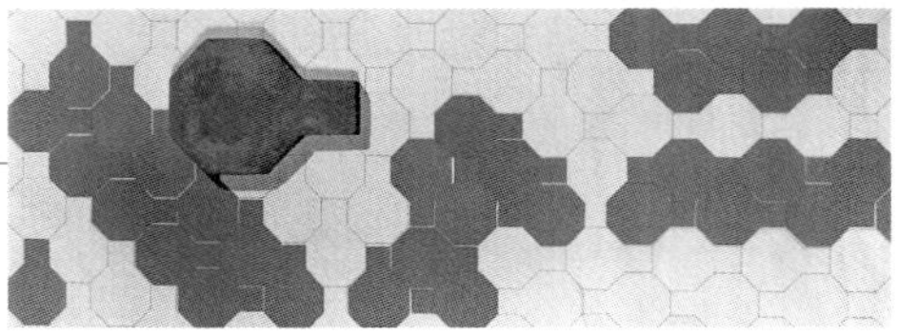

Tiling
Terra-cotta floor with sectional tile,
produced by Ruggeri della Cà Tortona,
1956 (with Piergiacomo Castiglioni).

Furnishings
Joe sofa,
produced by Poltronova, 1970.

Lamp
Sidone ceiling lamp,
produced by Artemide, 1983.

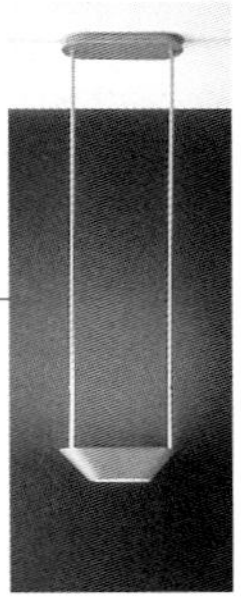

Jonathan De Pas, Donato D'Urbino, Paolo Lomazzi

Silverware
Ceremonial Lights series of Jewish lamps,
designed at the invitation
of the Jerusalem Museum, 1985.

Tiling
Segni tiles with sectional decorations,
produced by Gabbianelli, 1978.

Furnishings
Expanded polystyrene armchair, covered,
with aluminium legs, 1963.

Lamp
Lesbo shaded blown glass lamp,
produced by Artemide, 1966.

Angelo Mangiarotti

Silverware
Silver centrepiece,
preliminary studies 1971,
produced by Cappellini, 2000.

Marble
Eros series of marble tables
with gravity joint,
produced by Skipper, 1971,
then Cappellini, 2000.

Furnishings
Tonietta chair, produced by Zanotta, 1985.

Lamp
Sistema Aggregato lighting equipment, produced by Artemide, 1976 (with Giancarlo Fassina).

Silverware
Alzata silver fruit bowl, produced by Danese, 1982 (made by Gabriele De Vecchi).

Enzo Mari

Marble
Paros D3 table ashtray, produced by Danese, 1964.

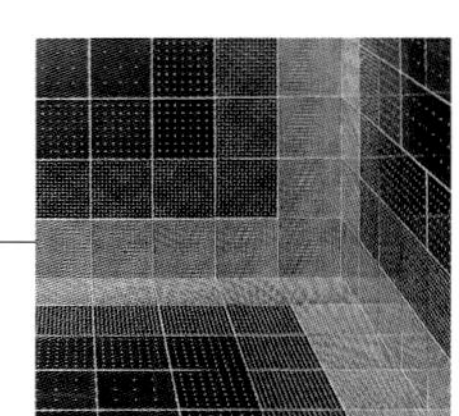

Tiling
Serie Elementare system of graphic decorations and sectional modules for majolica tiles, produced by Gabbianelli, 1968.

Alessandro Mendini

Furnishings
Proust's armchair,
produced by Alchymia, 1978,
today produced by Cappellini.

Lamp
Alioth floor lamp,
produced by Venini, 1993.

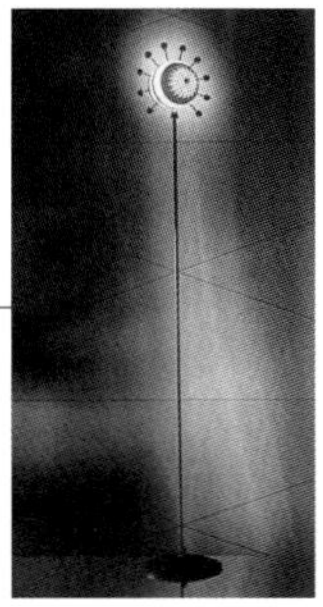

Silverware
Tea & Coffee Piazza silver service,
produced by Alessi, 1983.

Tiling
Enamelled *cottoforte*
and silk-screen printing,
produced by Bastula, 1983.

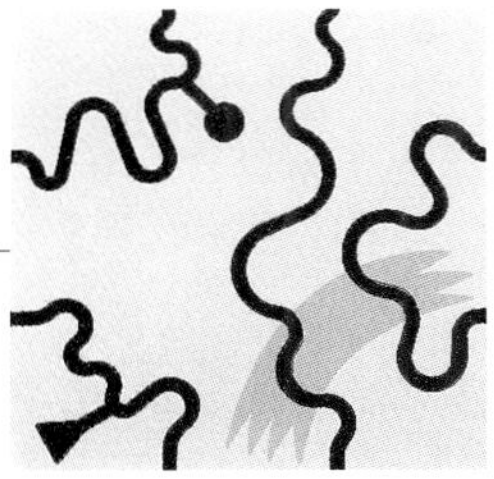

Furnishings
Divanetta sofa for outdoors,
produced by Robots, 1986.

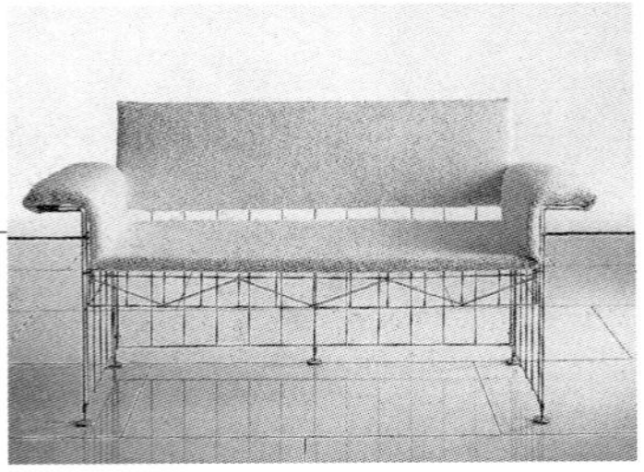

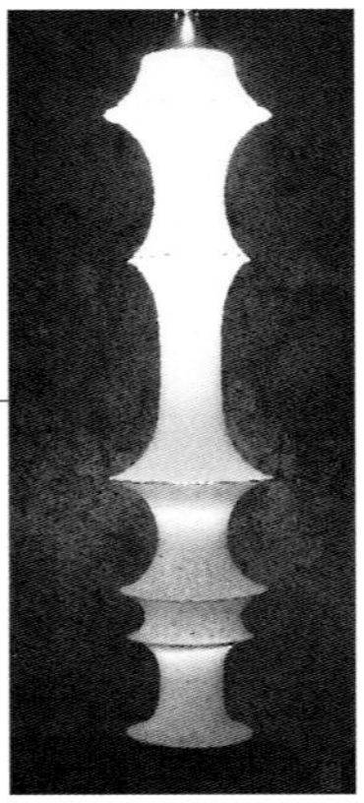

Lamp
Falkland ceiling lamp,
produced by Danese, 1964.

Bruno Munari

Tiling
Enamelled *cottoforte*
and silk-screen printing,
produced by Gabbianelli, 1982.

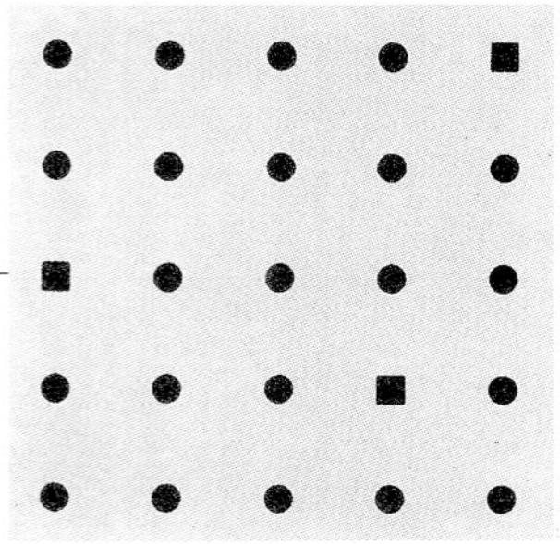

Furnishings
Superleggera chair,
produced by Cassina, 1957.

Lamp
Pirellina table lamp,
produced by FontanaArte, 1967.

Gio Ponti

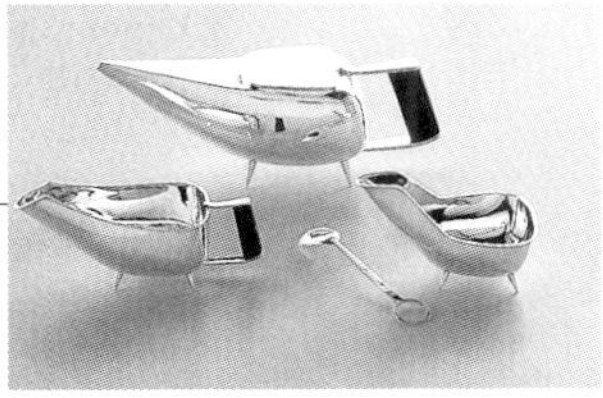

Silverware
Silver tea service, made by Piero
De Vecchi for Calderoni Gioielli, 1956.

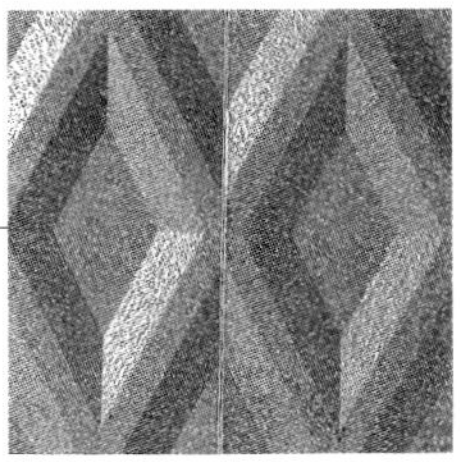

Tiling
Grès tiles in enamelled relief,
produced by Joo Gresite, 1960.

Ettore Sottsass

Furnishings
Carlton laminate furniture,
produced by Memphis, 1981.

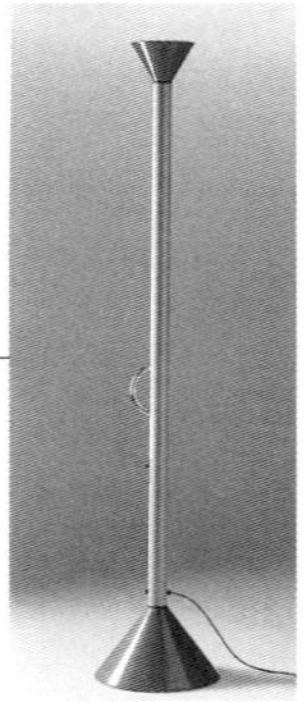

Lamp
Callimaco floor lamp,
produced by Artemide, 1982.

Silverware
Murmansk fruit bowl,
produced by Memphis, 1982.

Tiling
Earthenware and silk-screen printing,
produced by Cedit, 1968.

Marco Zanuso

Furnishings
Antropus armchair, produced by Arflex, 1978, prototype 1949.

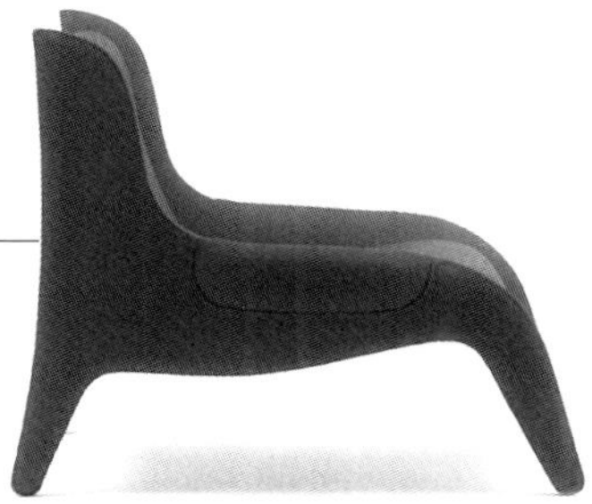

Lamp
275 table lamp, produced by O-Luce, 1965.

Tiling
Alberto Scarzella and Marco Zanuso, enamelled earthenware in a number of colours, produced by Cedit, 1959.

Associations

Assomarmi

Assopiastrelle

ATI

AVR

Federargentieri

Federlegno-Arredo

The Abitare system, with its 54 billion euros of production, 22 billion euros of exports and 541,000 workers, bears witness to the world of the finest synthesis of tradition and innovation, design and creativity. In terms of the quality and quantity of products exported, it is a world leader in the supply of Italian goods to homes and offices in an increasing number of countries.
Furniture, tiles, marble, lighting systems, furnishings, and silver articles are sent from Italy to every part of the world.
A number of industrial and crafts associations represent these sectors at a national level. In particular, six Associations are working for the project addressed to the worldwide markets.

Assomarmi

The association deals with problems nationally for the safeguarding of members at every level: institutional, Community and international. In terms of promotional activities, Assomarmi follows the spread in use of natural stone in all of its many guises, as well as the consolidation of its presence in traditional markets, and helps to promote its greater use in developing markets.
The quantity of stone quarries present in Italy places the country at the top of the list of producer countries.
Marble is a natural, unique and prestigious material, which over the centuries has celebrated the magnificence of many ages and cultures.
In the last twenty years, Italian marble, which is known and appreciated throughout the world, has undergone significant commercial growth.
This has been possible thanks also to technological advances that have reduced the costs of extraction, and to the revolutionary processes that make it possible to work the stone even in extremely thin slabs. The production includes many varieties quarried in different regions of the country.
The Italian marble and stone industry has an overall turnover of about 5 billion euros, 2 billion of which come from exports throughout the world. It employs 73,000 workers.
Many of the Italian stone industries import and process a broad selection of marbles, granites, limestone and onyx from around the world. These stones are worked using the most sophisticated and up-to-date materials.

Assopiastrelle

Ceramic Tiles of Italy is the brand promoted by Assopiastrelle – the national association of producers of ceramic tiles and refractory materials – which represents and promotes the Italian ceramic tiles industry on the international markets. This industry leads the world thanks to a whole range of factors such as tradition, product and process innovation, design, versatility of use and the technical excellence of the product.
An annual production of about 640 million square metres, an overall turnover exceeding Lire 10,000 billion, exports amounting to 70 % of total sales; these are the figures that delineate the world leadership of the Italian industry of ceramic tiles, a leadership that is renewed annually thanks to constant technological innovation and to a continuous development of product types, both in terms of quantity and quality.
Today, Italy's production of ceramic tiles represents almost 20% of world-wide production and 43% of that in the European Union. Italy also holds about 40% of the international trade in ceramic tiles.
Tiles that are made in Italy are sold and appreciated throughout the world and are everywhere the expression of quality, design and style.

ATI

ATI (Associazione Tessile Italiana - Italian Textile Association) represents the collective enterprises working in the Italian textile fiber industry, safeguarding the specific interests of the textile industry in all its forms and segments (textiles for clothing and furnishings, household linens, technical and innovative fabrics).
Promotion represents a fundamental tool for ATI in increasing the competitiveness of its member companies and for disseminating the unique values of Italian-made textiles. ATI's efforts are directed to strengthening and enhancing the Italian textile industry, whose primacy derives from the perfect synthesis of technical research, process automation,

product innovation and creativity, and from the unequalled added value that the Italian operators express on the level of excellence in all the various textile applications.
Furnishing textiles and household linens constitute artistic and commercial assets which exhibit an increasing communicative value. The intrinsic link with the design and the overall concept of "inhabiting" confirms the lines of an evolution that brings the world of furnishings increasingly closer to that of fashion and lifestyle. Italian textiles for the house are a synonym for quality, innovation and warmth, and agree perfectly with all the elements that go into creating, evoking and selling the inimitable Italian style of "living" and "dwelling".

AVR

The bathroom faucets industry, represented by AVR (Associazione Costruttori Valvolame e Rubinetteria - Association of Valve and Faucet Manufacturers), is one of the most important production sectors in the Italian economy. A centennial tradition, constantly expanding production, efficient and technologically advanced plants, and the highest quality products have made the companies in this segment well known and sought after not only in Italy, but also in international markets.
Against increasingly cutthroat competition and an ever more demanding clientele, AVR has supported and strengthened the competitive advantages of Italian manufacturers, concentrating its efforts in the area of quality. Participation in Europe-wide technical committee meetings and the subsequent communication of the outcomes and resulting legislation to its associates has meant the progressive achievement of the most rigorous standards, to which the majority of the associated enterprises now adhere. This quality also includes the materials used, the efficiency of the production processes and the functionality of the products. Innovativeness of the product, depth of range, customer service, brand image and design have become the weapons used by industry players to defend their market share both nationally and internationally.
The job of promoting the association abroad is given a further advantage by the flexibility in developing new products and services which characterizes the Italian companies in adapting to the changing demands and tastes of end users.

Federargentieri

In the history and culture of the home and of the ABITARE system, silver has played a "precious" role in applied art through the centuries and in particular from the Renaissance to the modern day.
Silver enriched and still enriches elegant and beautiful furnishings, blending harmoniously with the style of the architectural decorations and fixtures, the furniture and the objects.
In the late Roman Republican and Imperial era it was silver to attract attention in the wealthiest households. Cicero himself tells how silver, after its use was adopted at banquets, "was laid out on the table so the host could show it off to his guests", as a testament to the wealth and good taste of the master of the house.
Silver plates and trays overflowing with fruit were often painted on the walls of houses and villas in Campania, similar to those possessed by the lord of the house before the eruption of Vesuvius destroyed everything.
In the Renaissance era, the silver pieces for the palaces of lords were designed by the same architects who built the house and were often produced in the workshops of the artists called upon to create sculptures or paintings.

This symbiosis continued in the following centuries, in Italy as well as in France, Spain, Germany and especially in Great Britain following the success of the architects, Robert and James Adam.
Still today, prestigious residences are adorned with silver designed and coordinated by the same interior-designers or interior-decorators who directed the decoration or the construction.

Federlegno-Arredo

Federlegno-Arredo protects and represents the interests of the Italian furniture industry, ranging from the processing of the raw material – timber – to the production of furniture and accessories, including the use of materials other than wood, for the global system comprising Home, Office, City.
The Federation was set up by the companies in the Italian Legno Arredo sector to represent the category's interests with a single, strong voice, and to create projects and services using shared resources that the individual companies would not be able to arrange with equal effectiveness.
Over 2,200 industrial companies are members of Federlegno-Arredo, which is divided into ten category associations: assArredo, Assogiocattoli, assoLegno, assoLuce, assoPannelli, assUfficio, Edilegno, Fedecomlegno, Specialegno, Terziario Legno Arredo.
The size of the sector, according to the figures for the year 2000, is as follows:
– Overall turnover: 38,062 million euros.
– Number of employees: 410,000.
– Exports in 2000: 12.2 billion euros.
– Imports in 2000: 5.3 billion euros.
The Italian furniture industry is:
– A world leader in the quantity of products exported.
– A world-wide point of reference as regards trends in the development of lifestyles in terms of the product, its setting, technology and organization of production.
– The guarantor in Europe of rules that define the quality of production (it is Italy's duty to manage the commissioning of regulations regarding the areas of furniture and padding).

Bibliography

Claudio Demattè
The Secrets of the Italian Supply System

M. J. Priore and C. F. Sabel, *The Second Industrial Divide: Possibilities for Property*, Basic Bales, Inc., New York 1984.
M. E. Porter, *The Competitive Advantage of Nations*, The Free Press, New York, 1990.

Guido Martinotti
The Virtual Desktop within the Writing Desk

Virgino Bettini et al., *Elementi di ecologia urbana*, Einaudi, Turin 1996.
Franco Bianchini and Michael Parkinson (eds.), *Cultural Policy and Urban Regeneration. The West European experience*, Manchester University Press, Manchester 1993.
Giorgio Bocca, *Metropolis. Milano nella tempesta italiana*, Mondadori, Milan 1993.
Anthony Giddens, *The Consequences of Modernity*, Stanford University Press, Stanford 1990.
Vittorio Gregotti, "Lo spazio. La città assediata", in *Equilibri. La rivista per lo sviluppo sostenibile*, no. 1, April 1998, pp. 47–54.
Ian Masser et al., *The Geography of Europe's Futures*, Belhaven Press, London 1992.
William J. Mitchell, *City of Bits. Space, Place, and the Infobahn*, MIT Press, Cambridge 1995.
Peter W. G. Newman and Jeffrey R. Kenworthy, "Transport and Urban Form in Thirty-two of the World's Principal Cities", in William Young (ed.), *Proceedings of International Symposium on Transport, Communication and Urban Form: 2, Analytical Techniques and Case Studies*, Monash University, Victoria 1987.
Denise Pumain and Francis Godard, *Données urbaines*, Anthropos, Paris 1996.
Deyan Sudjic, *The 100-Mile City,* Flamingo, London 1993.
Sherry Turkle, *Life on the Screen. Identity in the Age of the Internet*, Simon and Schuster, New York 1995.

Vittorio Marchis
Machines to Make Home

Corrado Beguinot, "L'architettura è intelligente se è capace di (inter)connettere", in *Telema*, no. 15, winter 1998–99.
Daniel Defoe, *A Tour through the Whole Island of Great Britain* (1724-26), Penguin, London 1971.
Le Corbusier, *Almanach d'architecture moderne*, 1926.
Publication des brévets, Paris 1868, s. II, t. XLI.
Jeffrey T. Schnapp (ed.), *Gaetano Ciocca. Costruttore, inventore, agricoltore, scrittore*, Skira, Geneva-Milan 2000.
Gianni Scudo, *L'ibridazione tra bio-ecologia e tecnologia per costruire in accordo con l'ambiente*, http://www.resident.it/simbiosi.htm.

Raimonda Riccini
The Appliance-Shaped Home

Abitare, 1965–69.
Apparecchi elettrodomestici nella casa moderna, 1970–80.
Casalinghi Stile, 1964–66.
Casa Novità, no. 1, June 1961, then *Abitare*, 1962–70.
Elettrodomestica. La tecnica nella casa moderna, 1952–60.
La cucina italiana, 1980–96.
Emilio Ambasz (ed.), *Italy: the New Domestic Landscape. Achievements and Problems of Italian Design*, exhibition catalogue, Museum of Modern Art, New York 1972.
Mary Annovazzi, *Il libro dell'arredamento*, Mondadori, Milan 1982.
Corrado Barberis, *La società italiana. Esperienze di un secolo*, Franco Angeli, Milan 1995.
Mario Bellini and Georges Teyssot, "Pensate, architetti, alla casa degli uomini", in *Il progetto domestico. La casa dell'uomo:*

archetipi e prototipi. Progetti, 18th Milan Triennial / Electa, Milan 1986.
Eugenio Bettinelli, *La prossima casa. Progetto e tecnologia dell'automazione domestica*, BTicino / Idea Books, Milan 1991.
Massimo Bonfantini and Emilio Renzi, *Oggetti Novecento*, Moretti & Vitali, Bergamo 2001.
Giampiero Bosoni and Andrea Nulli, "Italia: storie parallele tra progetto e consumo", in *Storia del disegno industriale*, vol. 3, *1919–1990. Il dominio del design*, Electa, Milan 1991, pp. 122–148.
Andrea Branzi, *La casa calda. Esperienze del Nuovo Design Italiano*, Idea Books, Milan 1984.
Centro studi investimenti sociali (Censis), *Gli anni del cambiamento. Il rapporto sulla situazione sociale del paese dal 1976 al 1982*, Franco Angeli, Milan 1982.
Centro studi investimenti sociali (Censis), *A metà decennio. Riflessioni e dati sull'Italia dall'80 all'85*, Franco Angeli, Milan 1986.
Centro studi investimenti sociali (Censis), *Consumi in Italia '87. Le cose, i messaggi, i valori*, Franco Angeli, Milan 1987.
Centro studi investimenti sociali (Censis), *Consumi Italia '83. Tradizione e politeismo*, Franco Angeli, Milan 1982.
Centro studi investimenti sociali (Censis), *Gli anni del cambiamento. Il rapporto sulla situazione sociale del paese dal 1976 al 1982*, Franco Angeli, Milan 1982.
Flavio Conti and Maria Rosa Conti (eds.), *La cucina*, Gorlich, Novara 1984.
Cucina e cultura. Dal fornello al computer: un percorso verso il 2000, exhibition catalogue, ed. by Alberto Maria Prina, Filsma, Milan 1984.
Giuseppe De Rita, "L'impresa-famiglia", in Piero Melograni (ed.), *La famiglia italiana dall'Ottocento a oggi*, Laterza, Rome-Bari 1988, pp. 383–416.
Arturo Dell'Acqua, "Pochi pezzi facili", in *La cucina italiana*, no. 5, May 1993, pp. 136–139.
Enciclopedia delle 3B d'oro. Buonamensa Buonacasa Bellacasa, Labor, Milan 1948.
Tersilia Faravelli Giacobone, Paola Guidi and Anty Pansera, *Dalla casa elettrica alla casa elettronica. Storia e significati degli elettrodomestici*, Arcadia, Milan 1989.
Siegfried Giedion, *Mechanization Takes Command*, Oxford University Press, New York 1955.
Paul Ginsborg, *Storia d'Italia dal dopoguerra a oggi. Società e politica 1953–1988*, vol. 2, *Dal "miracolo economico" agli anni '80*, Einaudi, Turin 1989.
I mille consigli di Casa mia, Rizzoli, Milan 1969.
Il progetto domestico. La casa dell'uomo: archetipi e prototipi, 17th Milan Triennial, Electa, Milan 1986, 2 vols.
Silvio Lanaro, *L'Italia nuova. Identità e sviluppo 1861–1988*, Einaudi, Turin 1988.
Giovanna Massobrio and Paolo Portoghesi, *Album degli anni Cinquanta*, Laterza, Bari 1977.
Giorgio Origlia, "Mangiare come progetto", in *Progetto mangiare*, ed. by Mario Bellini, Electa, Milan 1981.
Gianfranco Petrillo, "Il trionfo dell'elettricità nella vita civile", in Valerio Castronuovo (ed.), *Storia dell'industria elettrica in Italia*, vol. 4, *Dal dopoguerra alla nazionalizzazione 1945–1962*, Laterza, Bari 1994, pp. 453–481.
Donald S. Pitkin, *The House that Giacomo Built. History of an Italian Family, 1898–1978*, Cambridge University Press, Cambridge 1985.
Raffaella Poletti, *La cucina elettrica*, Electa, Milan 1994.
Publifoto 1946–66. Immagini di vita italiana dall'archivio di una grande azienda, Fabbri, Milan 1983.
Marco Romanelli, Marta Laudani and Luca Vercelloni, *Gli spazi del cucinare. Appunti per una storia italiana 1928–1957*, Electa, Milan 1990.
Georges Teyssot, "Lo spazio-tempo della casa", in Claudia Donà (ed.), *1961–1991. Mobili italiani. Le varie età dei linguaggi*, Cosmit, Milan 1992.
Antonio Tosi, *Abitanti. Le nuove strategie dell'azione abitativa*, Il Mulino, Bologna 1994.

Giampiero Bosoni
Architecture of Interiors. 1945–2000

R. Banham, "Neoliberty. The Retreat from Modern Architecture", in *The Architectural Review*, no. 747, 1959.
Massimo Martignoni, "Gio Ponti. Gli anni di *Stile*", in *Abitare*, no. 404, March 2001.
Emilia Muselli, *Lo spazio della casa in Italia (1940-1960)*, Guerrini e Associati srl, Milan 1995.
Edoardo Persico, *La casa nuova* (1935), published in Giorgio Ciucci and Francesco Dal Co, *Atlante dell'architettura italiana del Novecento*, Electa, Milan 1991.
Giacomo Polin, "Gli interni di Figini e Pollini come paesaggio artificiale", in *Rassegna*, no. 31, September 1987.
Gio Ponti, "La casa all'italiana", in *Domus*, no. 1, 15 January 1928.
Gio Ponti, "Il fattore italianità nelle nostre arti applicate moderne", in *Domus*, 1930.
Gio Ponti, *Amate l'architettura. L'architettura è un cristallo*, Società Editrice Vitali e Ghianda, Genoa 1957.
Paolo Portoghesi, "Dal neorealismo al neoliberty", in *Comunità*, no. 72, 1959.
Ernesto Nathan Rogers, "Ortodossia dell'eterodossia", in *Casabella*, no. 216, 1957.
Ernesto Nathan Rogers, "Programma Domus: la casa dell'uomo", in *Domus*, no. 295, 1946.
Manfredo Tafuri, *Storia dell'architettura italiana 1944-1985*, Einaudi, Turin 1982.
Guido Canella and Vittorio Gregotti (eds.) "Nuovi disegni per il mobile italiano", in *L'osservatorio delle arti industriali*, March 1960.
Bruno Zevi, "L'andropausa degli architetti moderni", editorial in *L'architettura - Cronache e storia*, no. 46, 1959.
Bruno Zevi, "Torniamo al Liberty", in *L'Espresso*, 24 May 1959.